Seek Ye
Earnestly...

Seek Ye Earnestly...

by
President Joseph Fielding Smith

Compiled and Edited by
Joseph Fielding Smith, Jr.

Published by
DESERET BOOK COMPANY
Salt Lake City, Utah
1972

Library of Congress number 77-136-242

SBN Number 87747-367-6

Copyright 1970

Deseret Book Company

Second Printing 1972

Jacket and Frontispiece photographs

by Merrett Smith

Printed by

DESERET NEWS PRESS

in the United States of America

Seek Ye Earnestly . . . The scriptures are replete with admonition to seek earnestly, diligently, for the best gifts, to seek for knowledge, wisdom, and understanding. "No man can be saved in ignorance." "The glory of God is intelligence." President Joseph Fielding Smith has spent a lifetime pleading with the members of the Church to study, to pray, to gain an understanding of the scriptures and to develop a testimony of the divinity of the mission of Jesus Christ. He has labored tirelessly to disseminate information with a great desire that the members of the Church might become more enlightened as to the principles of the gospel.

"The Lord has promised to reveal unto those who are diligently seeking him, all the mysteries of his kingdom," President Smith has said. "The fact that a person is a member of The Church of Jesus Christ of Latter-day Saints does not insure his salvation. He has to keep himself in touch with these sacred principles and know and live them. . . . The gospel of Jesus Christ is not merely a code of laws, it is more than that. It requires a spirit of humility, of faith, and a prayerful disposition. . . . The fact remains that too many of us take our membership as a matter of course. We do not study. We do not attend to the ordinary duties the Lord requires of us, and therefore we do not have an abiding testimony of the truth."

This compilation of President Smith's sermons and writings represents a companion volume to "Take Heed to Yourselves." It is felt that the two greatest messages of

President Smith's life have been the necessity for repentance
and the need to seek earnestly for knowledge and understanding of the saving principles of the gospel—a living
testimony of the true message of the gospel of Jesus Christ.

Seek ye earnestly. . . .

Joseph Fielding Smith, Jr.

Contents

And I give unto you a commandment that you shall teach one another the doctrine of the kingdom.

Teach ye diligently and my grace shall attend you, that you may be instructed more perfectly in theory, in principle, in doctrine, in the law of the gospel, in all things that pertain unto the kingdom of God, that are expedient for you to understand;

Of things both in heaven and in the earth, and under the earth; things which have been, things which are, things which must shortly come to pass; things which are at home, things which are abroad; the wars and the perplexities of the nations, and the judgments which are on the land and a knowledge also of countries and of kingdoms— (D&C 88:77-79.)

Adam did only what he had to do. He partook of that fruit for one good reason, and that was to open the door to bring you and me and everyone else into this world.

Adam's Role in Bringing Us Mortality

The singing of the choir has called my attention to the fact that there is a divine Redeemer, the Lord Jesus Christ. When Adam was placed in the Garden of Eden, he was in the presence of God our Eternal Father. He talked with the Father and the Father with him. But something happened, and it had to happen: Adam partook of certain fruit. My Bible, the King James version, says in the margin, speaking of Adam's fall, "Man's shameful fall." Well, it wasn't a shameful fall at all.

Adam came here to bring mortality upon the earth, and that resulted in the shutting out from the presence of the Eternal Father of both Adam and Eve and their posterity. The Son of God comes upon the scene from that time henceforth as our Redeemer, as we have just heard in the song this choir has sung. It is the Savior who stands between mankind and our Heavenly Father. We do not pray to God, except through the Son. The Son is the mediator between mankind and the Eternal Father. You seldom hear a prayer that is not offered to our Heavenly Father in the name of his beloved Son, and that is right. Christ came into this world to represent his Father. He came into this world to teach mankind who his Father is, why we should worship him, how we should worship him. He performed the greatest work that was ever performed in this mortal world by the shedding of his blood, which paid a debt that mankind owes to the Eternal Father, and which debt we inherited after the fall of Adam.

Adam did only what he had to do. He partook of that fruit for one good reason, and that was to open the door to bring you and me and everyone else into this world, for Adam and Eve could have remained in the Garden of Eden; they could have been there to this day, if Eve had not done something.

One of these days, if I ever get to where I can speak to Mother Eve, I want to thank her for tempting Adam to partake of the fruit. He accepted the temptation, with the result that children came into this world. And when I kneel in prayer, I feel to thank Mother Eve, for if she had not had that influence over Adam, and if Adam had done according to the commandment first given to him, they would still be in the Garden of Eden and we would not be here at all. We would not have come into this world. So the commentators made a great mistake when they put in the Bible at the top of page 3, as I think it is (it may not be the same page in every Bible), the statement "Man's shameful fall."

Well, that was what the Lord expected Adam to do, because that opened the door to mortality; and we came here into this mortal world to receive a training in mortality that we could not get anywhere else, or in any other way. We came here into this world to partake of all the vicissitudes, to receive the lessons that we receive in mortality from or in a mortal world. And so we become subject to pain, to sickness. We are blessed for keeping the commandments of the Lord with all that he has given us, which, if we will follow and be true and faithful, will bring us back again into the presence of God our Eternal Father, as sons and daughters of God, entitled to the fulness of celestial glory.

We Are in School

That great blessing of celestial glory could never have come to us without a period of time in mortality, and so we came here in this mortal world. We are in school, the mortal school, to gain the experiences, the training, the joys, and the sufferings that we partake of, that we might be educated in all these things and be prepared, if we are faithful and true to the commandments of the Lord, to become sons and daughters of God, joint heirs with Jesus Christ; and in his presence to go on to a fulness and a continuation of the seeds forever, and perhaps through our faithfulness to have the opportunity of building worlds and peopling them.

Brethren and sisters, let us thank the Lord, when we pray, for Adam. If it had not been for Adam, I would not be here; you would not be here; we would be waiting in the heavens as spirits pleading for somebody to do what the scriptures say—a "shameful thing," which it was not—or to pass through a certain condition that brought upon us mortality.

We are in the mortal life to get an experience, a training, that we could not get any other way. And in order to become gods, it is necessary for us to know something about pain, about sickness, and about the other things that we partake of in this school of mortality.

So do not let us, brethren and sisters, complain about Adam and wish he had not done something that he did. I want to thank him. I am glad to have the privilege of being here and going through mortality, and if I will be true and faithful to the covenants and obligations that are upon me as a member of the Church and in the kingdom of God, I may have the privilege of coming back into the presence of the Eternal Father; and that will come to you as it will to me, sons and daughters of God entitled to the fulness of celestial glory.—(*Conference Report*, October, 1967.)

How foolish it is to look upon Adam as a man just beginning to comprehend the blessings of civilization. The Lord chose him and placed him at the head because of superior intelligence. Because of his intelligence and his call to be at the head, he is made a prince over his posterity forever.

The Authority of Adam

Because of the meager account of the life of Adam found in Genesis and the few references to him scattered through the scriptures many false ideas are entertained by Bible teachers, and taught to the people. Without the aid of modern revelation we would not know that the Ancient of Days and Michael, mentioned in the Bible, were titles applied to Adam. Practically all of our knowledge of Adam, outside of the few chapters in Genesis and one or two references by the prophets, has come to us through the restoration of the gospel. It is a reasonable thing, however, for those who accept the Bible as the word of the Lord, to believe that the Lord gave commandments to Adam and that he held divine authority and officiated in ordinances of salvation. It would not be reasonable to believe otherwise. Adam was not left to reason out principles of righteousness, and segregate them from principles of unrighteousness, and organize his own plan of salvation.

In the year 1830, the Lord said to Joseph Smith:

But, behold I say unto you that I, the Lord God, gave unto Adam and unto his seed, that they should not die as to the temporal death, until I, the Lord God, should send forth angels to declare unto them repentance and redemption, through faith on the name of mine Only Begotten Son.

And thus did I, the Lord God, appoint unto man the days of his probation—that by his natural death he might be raised in immortality unto eternal life, even as many as would believe.[1]

Adam and Eve Received Commandments

In the Book of Moses we obtain the information that Adam and Eve received commandments and were instructed that they should worship the Lord, their God, in the name of Jesus Christ. Adam was also taught the law of sacrifice, and after many days, an angel of the Lord appeared to him and asked him why he offered sacrifice. Adam answered:

. . . I know not, save the Lord commanded me.

And then the angel spake, saying: This is a similitude of the sacrifice of the Only Begotten of the Father, which is full of grace and truth.

Wherefore, thou shalt do all that thou doest in the name of the Son, and thou shalt repent and call upon God in the name of the Son forevermore.

And in that day the Holy Ghost fell upon Adam, which beareth record of the Father and the Son, saying: "I am the Only Begotten of the Father from the beginning, henceforth and forever, that as thou hast fallen thou mayest be redeemed, and all mankind, even as many as will.

And in that day Adam blessed God and was filled, and began to prophecy concerning all the families of the earth, saying: Blessed be the name of God, for because of my transgression my eyes are opened, and in this life I shall have joy, and in the flesh I shall see God. . . .

And Adam and Eve blessed the name of God, and they made all things known unto their sons and their daughters.[2]

In this manner the gospel was revealed to Adam and the authority to officiate in all the ordinances given to him. Enoch bore witness of this and informs us that Adam was baptized in water for the remission of his sins. By the power

---

[1]D&C 29:42-43.
[2]Moses 5:6-10, 12.

of the priesthood, also, he blessed his posterity and conferred authority on his descendants that they, too, might officiate in the ordinances of the gospel.

Erroneous Doctrines in the World

This doctrine is not in harmony with the prevailing view in the world, where they have an idea that the gospel of Jesus Christ was first given to man in the days of the Savior's ministry. Those who hold to this view are partly excused because of the lack of clearness in the scriptures, for many of the plain and precious parts have been eliminated since the time when the prophets and scribes of old recorded them. The idea is quite universal that it was some other plan of salvation that held sway over the earth in ancient times, and this is due to the fact that so little is said in the Old Testament of the gospel plan, even of immortality. It is not the fault of the scriptures that this is true, but because of wickedness and unbelief among the people, and the elimination of plain doctrines by writers who did not understand them.

We have evidence in the scriptures that records were written and knowledge of the principles of the gospel imparted in the earliest times. There is also evidence that these records were handed down for thousands of years, even to New Testament times; for instance, Paul speaks of Melchizedek and reveals something of him which is not found elsewhere in the Bible. Jude speaks of Enoch and his prophesying; of Michael contending with the devil over the body of Moses, and the angels who kept not their first estate. Peter also refers to these angels and their punishment. These events are not recorded elsewhere in the Bible. Moreover, there are many books referred to in both the Old Testament and in the New that are lost to the world today.

Some of these scriptures, in part at least, have been revealed through the Prophet Joseph Smith. In June 1830,

Joseph Smith received by revelation the visions of Moses, which the Lord gave to Moses at a time when he was caught up into an exceeding high mountain. These writings are given to us in the first chapter of the Book of Moses in the Pearl of Great Price. The Prophet was commanded by the Lord to revise the scriptures, and by the spirit of revelation he received many of the precious things that had been removed by uninspired scribes and translators and which make clear many passages that were obscure before. The writings of Moses commencing with chapter two of the Book of Moses, are taken from the Prophet's inspired revision of the ancient scriptures. A copy of this revision is preserved in the Historian's Office, Salt Lake City. From these writings we learn that the principles of the gospel as we understand them today were taught to Adam, and that he received the priesthood. The promise was given to him that the same priesthood would be found in the earth in the last days.

The Book of Abraham

The Book of Abraham, also in the Pearl of Great Price, came into the hands of the Prophet in a miraculous manner, as the Lord opened the way. On the third day of July, 1835, Michael H. Chandler came to Kirtland exhibiting four mummies and some rolls of papyrus covered with Egyptian hieroglyphics. Mr. Chandler had been directed to the Prophet as one who could translate the characters. At the request of Mr. Chandler the Prophet made a translation of a few of them, which Mr. Chandler said agreed with statements he had received from learned men who had examined them. After the interview some of the Saints purchased the mummies and the manuscripts, and, with Oliver Cowdery and William W. Phelps as scribes, Joseph Smith translated one of the records. To their great joy they discovered it was written by Abraham. After the translation had been completed it was published in Nauvoo, in March 1843, in the *Times and Seasons*. In the year 1851, Elder Samuel W. Richards republished the Book of Abraham with the Book of Moses and some revelations given to the Prophet Joseph Smith, in pamphlet form and called the publication the "Pearl of Great Price." Later editions have been published, with some of the revelations which are in the Doctrine and Covenants eliminated, and the Pearl of Great Price as we have it today was accepted by the Saints in general conference, October 10, 1880, as a standard work of the Church. These records are of great value to the Church for the additional light they throw upon the dealings of the Lord with the people in ancient times. They make clear that the principles of the gospel, as they are taught today, are eternal, were in the beginning, and have not changed.

Ordinance of Sacrifice

The ordinance of offering sacrifice was instituted in the days of Adam in the similitude of the great sacrifice for the sins of the world by our Redeemer. This, we are informed, was to continue until the coming of Christ. It was by authority of the Holy Priesthood that Adam offered sacrifice as did those who followed after. When Adam was driven out of Eden the Lord placed cherubim and a flaming sword to guard the east of the Garden, the way by which Adam departed, and he journeyed for some distance and built an altar in the place known as Adam-ondi-Ahman, and in that place he dwelt.

The following information concerning Adam and his authority was given to us by the Prophet Joseph Smith:

The Priesthood was first given to Adam; he obtained the First Presidency, and held the keys of it from generation to generation. He obtained it in the Creation, before the world was formed, as in Genesis 1:26, 27, 28. He had dominion given him over every living creature. He is Michael the Archangel, spoken of in the Scriptures. . . . The Priesthood is an everlasting principle, and existed with God from eternity, without beginning of days or end of years. The keys have to be brought from heaven whenever the Gospel is sent. When they are revealed from heaven, it is by Adam's authority.

Daniel in his seventh chapter speaks of the Ancient of Days: he means the oldest man, our Father Adam, Michael; he will call his children together and hold a council with them to prepare them for the coming of the Son of Man. He (Adam) is the father of the human family, and presides over the spirits of all men, and all that have had the keys must stand before him in this grand council. This may take place before some of us leave this stage of action. The Son of Man stands before him, and there is given him glory and dominion. Adam delivers up his stewardship to Christ, that which was delivered to him as holding the keys of the universe, but retains his standing as head of the human family.[3]

At another time the Prophet said:

Commencing with Adam who was the first man, who is spoken of in Daniel as being the "Ancient of Days," or in other words, the first and oldest of all, the great, grand progenitor of whom it is said in another place he is Michael, because he was the first and father of all, not only by progeny, but the first to hold the spiritual blessings, to whom was made known the plan of ordinances for the salvation of his posterity unto the end, and to whom Christ was first revealed, and through whom Christ has been revealed from heaven and will continue to be revealed from henceforth. Adam holds the keys of the dispensations of the fulness of times; i.e., the dispensation of all the times have been and will be revealed through him from the beginning to Christ, and from Christ to the end of all the dispensations that are to be revealed. . . .

The angels are under the direction of Michael, or Adam, who acts under the direction of the Lord. . . .

God will not acknowledge that which he has not called, ordained, and chosen. In the beginning God called Adam by his voice. "And the Lord called unto Adam and said unto him, Where art thou? and he said, I heard thy voice in the garden, and I was afraid because I was naked, and hid myself." Adam received commandments and instructions from God; this was the order from the beginning.

That he received revelations, commandments and ordinances at the beginning is beyond the power of controversy; else how did

---

[3]*DHC* Vol. III:385-386.

they begin to offer sacrifices to God in an acceptable manner? And if they offered sacrifices they must be authorized by ordination. . . .

This then, is the nature of the Priesthood; every man holding the presidency of his dispensation, and one man holding the presidency of them all, even Adam; and Adam receiving this presidency and authority from the Lord, but cannot receive a fulness until Christ shall present the kingdom to the Father, which shall be at the end of the last dispensation. . . . Christ is the Great High Priest, Adam next.[4]

Adam Had Superior Intelligence

How foolish it is to look upon Adam as a man just beginning to comprehend the blessings of civilization. The Lord chose him and placed him at the head because of superior intelligence. Because of his intelligence and his call to be at the head, he is made a prince over his posterity forever. In his hands were committed the keys of salvation under Jesus Christ. This is most natural, since he was worthy of the blessing and chosen before the world to take his place as the progenitor of the race. In a revelation given in March, 1832, the Lord spoke of Adam-ondi-Ahman whose foundations he had established. At that time the location of this place was unknown. The information is also given that the Lord "hath appointed Michael your prince, and established his feet, and set him upon high and given unto him the keys of salvation, under the counsel and direction of the Holy One, who is without beginning of days or end of life."[5]

This place of honor was given to Adam when he was chosen in the pre-mortal state, for at that time his mission was appointed unto him, as missions were appointed to others. It was there in the rebellion caused by Lucifer that Adam was called on to marshal the forces of righteousness, and under the direction of the Holy One to cast Lucifer and

---

[4]*DHC* Vol. IV:207-209.
[5]D&C 78:16.

his followers out of heaven, as John declared in his Revelation:

> And there was war in heaven: Michael and his angels fought against the dragon; and the dragon fought and his angels,
> And prevailed not: neither was their place found any more in heaven.[6]

It will be Michael who shall marshal his forces to contend against that same dragon at the end of the world as it is written in the Doctrine and Covenants:

> . . . and Satan shall be bound, that old serpent, who is called the devil, and shall not be loosed for the space of a thousand years.
> And then he shall be loosed for a little season, that he may gather together his armies.
> And Michael, the seventh angel, even the archangel, shall gather together his armies; even the hosts of heaven.
> And the devil shall gather together his armies; even the hosts of hell, and shall come up to battle against Michael and his armies.
> And then cometh the battle of the great God; and the devil and his armies shall be cast away into their own place, that they shall not have power over the saints any more at all.
> For Michael shall fight their battles, and shall overcome him who seeketh the throne of him who sitteth upon the throne, even the Lamb.[7]

Conflict Began in Heaven

This conflict which began in heaven at the time of the rebellion of Lucifer has been going on ever since; Michael contending for truth and righteousness, and Lucifer contending for falsehood and wickedness. Many times since that beginning have these forces clashed. It was Michael who contended with the devil over the body of Moses, when Lucifer claimed that Moses must die because he had been guilty of shedding blood, referred to by Jude. It was Michael who came to the rescue of Daniel when he was opposed by

---

[6]Revelation 12:7-8.
[7]D&C 88:110-115.

the forces of darkness as recorded in the tenth chapter of that book. Could we have seen behind the veil at the time of the Prophet Joseph's vision we might have seen a similar conflict, and when Joseph Smith received the plates of the Book of Mormon, we might have discovered that it was Michael who was present with his forces, contending against the powers of darkness. Brigham Young and Heber C. Kimball both relate that on the night that the prophet received the plates they saw armies in the heavens going to battle, and unbeknown to mortals there may have been on that occasion a conflict between the power of righteousness and the power of evil.

When the time comes that man shall be called forth from the dead, the Lord has said that "Michael, mine archangel, shall sound his trump and then shall all the dead awake, for their graves shall be opened, and they shall come forth—yea, even all."[8] At that time, clothed with the authority of the resurrection, our progenitor Adam shall sound the trump to call forth the dead to stand before the great judgment when the books shall be opened and men judged according to their works.

Three years before the death of Adam he called Seth, Enos, Cainan, Mahalaleel, Jared, Enoch, and Methuselah together in the valley of Adam-ondi-Ahman and there blessed them. These men were high priests, so we are informed in the revelation.[9] At the time of this gathering the Lord appeared unto them and the sons of Adam rose up and blessed him, and called him Michael, the prince, the archangel.

And the Lord administered comfort unto Adam, and said unto him: I have set thee to be at the head; a multitude of nations shall come of thee, and thou art a prince over them forever.

And Adam stood up in the midst of the congregation; and, notwithstanding he was bowed down with age, being full of the Holy

---

[8]D&C 29:26.
[9]D&C 107:53.

Ghost, predicted whatsoever should befall his posterity unto the latest generation.

These things were all written in the book of Enoch, and are to be testified of in due time.[10]

---
[10]D&C 107:55-57.

Experience has taught man that any kind of government is better than no government at all. Government, law, order, as a means of safety must be recognized even where the guidance of the Almighty has been rejected. Authority among peoples and nations is just as essential as law is anywhere else. Even in hell there is organization, a form of government; someone presides and others recognize authority, even in the carrying out of works of darkness and rebellion against the authority of God.

Authority in Organized Society

After the creation the Lord "saw everything he had made, and, behold, it was very good."[1] He placed man upon the earth and gave him dominion over all things upon its face and commanded him to obey his voice. Laws were given and Adam was guided by revelation and the voice of the Lord in all his temporal affairs as well as in the plan of eternal salvation. When the first government was formed on the earth, the Lord directed it by revelation and gave laws for the guidance of the people. In course of time when men began to multiply they refused to hearken to the voice of revelation and rebelled against the divine mandates that had been given them. They forgot the object of their earth existence and became a law unto themselves feeling fully capable of conducting their governments without the aid of the Eternal Father. In this manner the kingdom of God, as it was established by the Lord and intended by him to continue through all ages, came to an end. In its stead man-made governments were formed and man usurped the authority which rightfully belongs to his Maker.

There have been times when governments have been directed by the Lord, and his will has been followed as it was

---

[1]Genesis 1:31.

made known through divinely appointed prophets. This was the condition in the city of Enoch; in the days of Israel in Palestine, when they were not rebellious; among the Nephites through much of their history, especially during the two hundred years following the crucifixion of Christ. However with these and a few other exceptions, almost from the beginning men have rejected the guidance of the Lord; they have cast out or killed the prophets and have refused to recognize the voice of God in their affairs. The earth is the Lord's and the fulness thereof, but that has not retarded fallen man in his usurpation of governmental authority which does not rightfully belong to him.

Words of Orson Pratt

On this subject Elder Orson Pratt, one of the clearest and most profound thinkers of modern times, said:

The kingdom of God is an order of government established by divine authority. It is the only legal government that can exist in any part of the universe. All other governments are illegal and unauthorized. God having made all beings and worlds, has the supreme right to govern them by his own laws, and by officers of his own appointment. Any people attempting to govern themselves by laws of their own making, and by officers of their own appointment, are in direct rebellion against the kingdom of God. The antediluvians were overthrown by a flood, because they rejected the government of the Almighty, and instituted their own government in its stead. Noah and his family were the only loyal and obedient subjects to the legal power; they alone were saved. The universal desolation and utter abolishment of all unauthorized man-made governments of the world, should have been an everlasting warning to all future generations to avoid the same rebellion, and to establish no governments on the earth of human origin. But alas! the posterity of Noah soon revolted from the only legal, rightful power, and set up for themselves forms of governments of their own inventions. The rebellion soon became so general that all the inhabitants of the earth, except Melchizedek, Abraham, Lot, and a very few others, engaged in their usurped authority, and suffered themselves to be governed by human laws, instead of revealed laws of God. From this time until the present, empires, kingdoms, principalities, republics, and numerous other corrupt, illegal, unauthorized powers, have multiplied themselves in the four quarters of the globe. At various times during the last four thousand years, God has asserted his rights, and endeavored to establish his own authority, his own laws, and his own government among the children of men. But so great was the opposition manifested by those illegal, rebellious powers, that his government while on earth was exceedingly limited in numbers. The vast majority of mankind made war against it—overcame, killed, and destroyed its officers and loyal subjects, until not a vestige of it was left remaining on the earth.[2]

No matter how independent man may desire to become, or how proud and mighty he may feel, he has discovered that it is impossible to dwell in safety among his fellows without some enactment of law, and authority vested in someone to enforce the law in the interest of the whole community. If each family formed its own laws and endeavored to enforce them, it would result in confusion, strife, anarchy, destruction. For this reason wherever a family, a clan, tribe, or nation has existed, someone has been appointed or has assumed the reigns of government. Power vested in him has been accepted by those who were governed. Experience has taught man that any kind of government is better than no government at all. Government, law, order, as a means of safety must be recognized, even where the guidance of the Almighty has been rejected. Authority among peoples and nations is just as essential as law is anywhere else. Even in hell there is organization, a form of government; someone presides and others recognize authority, even in the carrying out of works of darkness and rebellion against the authority of God.

Since the beginning of time there have been various forms of government. The earliest government was patriarchal, and the oldest man of the tribe or family presided. This was the government in the days of Adam and the antediluvian patriarchs, and it continued for some time, and in

---

[2]Orson Pratt, *Kingdom of God,* pp. 1-2.

some sections of the land after the flood. Adam and his successors presided by virtue of the priesthood. They were led by revelation from the Lord. However, many of their children refused to follow them and rebelled against government based on divine guidance. We learn from the Book of Abraham that the government of Egypt was patriarchal. Pharaoh was a righteous man, although he was denied the priesthood, and governed his people wisely imitating the patriarchal form of government "established by the fathers in the first generations, in the days of the first patriarchal reign, even in the reign of Adam, and also of Noah."[3]

President John Taylor Quoted

Speaking of the rightful government, President John Taylor has said:

God never gave man unlimited control of the affairs of this world; but always speaks of man as being under his guidance, inhabiting his territory, and responsible to him for his acts. The world is His Vineyard, and man is the agent. . . .

Again God demanded worship and sacrifices, and when Cain and Abel offered them, he received one and rejected the other; and further, when Cain was wroth on account of his sacrifice not being accepted, the Lord said unto him, "Why art thou wroth? And why is thy countenance fallen? If thou doest well, shalt thou not be accepted? And if thou doest not well, sin lieth at the door."[4] After the destruction of the world, which was in consequence of the people sinning against God, he blessed Noah, and spake to him, and gave him the same dominion which had been given before to Adam.[5]

If the world be the Lord's he certainly has a right to govern it; for we have already stated that man has no authority, except that which is delegated to him. He possesses a moral power to govern his actions, subject at all times to the law of God; but never is authorized to rule on the earth without the call and direction of the Lord; therefore, any rule or dominion over the earth, which is not given by the Lord, is surreptitiously obtained, and never will be sanctioned by

---

[3]Abraham 1:26.
[4]Genesis 4:7.
[5]President John Taylor, The Government of God, p. 49.

him. . . . The prophet Hosea complains, that "they have set up kings, but not by me; they have made princes, and I knew it not."[6]

After the flood when men again began to spread over the face of the earth, they rebelled against divine authority vested in Noah and his sons. As the people began to increase they gathered together usually in small communities, and kings were appointed to rule over them. In the days of Abraham there were many of these petty nations scattered over the land. Abraham maintained the patriarchal form of government, and so did Isaac and Jacob after him. Abraham was as powerful as the kings among whom he resided. These ancient rulers exercised absolute authority over their subjects. It was the recognized right of all rulers, whether in kingdoms, tribes, or families, to exercise absolute authority over all who were subject to them. As time went on and the ambitions of men were exercised, the smaller peoples succumbed to the more powerful and were swallowed up by them. In this way great kingdoms were established such as Egypt, Babylon, Persia, Greece and Rome.

Problems of Absolute Authority

When absolute authority has been maintained usually the people have been subject to despotic rulers with little regard for the sacred rights and lives of their subjects. Because of this and kindred evils, the Lord endeavored to give to his chosen people, Israel, rulers who held the priesthood and who could direct them by divine revelation. But even Israel rebelled against the authority of God and demanded that they be given a king that they might be like other nations. This was very displeasing in the sight of the Lord, and Samuel his prophet, remonstrated with them and pointed out the evils that would come upon them if they had a king. They still demanded a king. The Lord told his prophet to grant them their request, saying that they

---
[6]*Ibid.*, p. 58.

had rejected the Lord who had nourished and protected
them through all their former history. However, the Lord
was not ready to relinquish all authority over his people at
that time. Their long and painful history of bondage and
suffering under their kings fulfilled the predictions of Samuel
their prophet. Since they were the chosen people of the
Lord, when they fully turned from him, killed his prophets
and refused to be governed by the law of the Lord, but
began to worship other gods, the Lord removed them from
the land of their inheritance.

With the exception of Greece and some few other peoples, the nations of the earth until quite recent times were
governed by despotic monarchs with assumed and delegated
authority which was absolute. In medieval times the Lord
prevailed upon the people to break the yoke of their bondage.
The despotic power of kings and princes began to wane.
The granting of the Magna Charta to the British peoples
was the dawning of political freedom. Little by little since
that time, the people of all countries have demanded more
liberty and more voice in the affairs of government, until
today their right to a voice in the affairs of government is
almost universally recognized. This political freedom has
come to pass through the will of the Lord, who prepared the
world for the restoration of the gospel in the dispensation
of the fulness of times.

Established by Righteous Men

The American government was established by righteous
men. Under the guiding hand of the Lord its constitution
and basic laws were formed, but in that day there was no one
to speak by authority in the name of the Lord for the Church
of Jesus Christ had not been established. His hand is over
this nation, and under his control it shall prosper and assist
in the fulfilling of his purposes as long as men fear God and
worship him. When they turn away and give a deaf ear to

the teachings of Jesus Christ, the anger of the Lord shall be kindled against them. They shall perish as other peoples have perished from the face of this land which is choice above all other lands.

While it has been the tendency of peoples to break away from the power and government of the Lord and to organize themselves according to their own worldly desires, yet it is impossible for them to get entirely free from the control and direction of the Lord. He has never acknowledged that man's power is superior to his, or that man's right to rule is greater than his. Thus he has turned them to fulfil his purposes, and has destroyed them when their cup of iniquity has been full. No nation that ever existed has been able to take a course contrary to the will of the Lord and maintain it for any length of time. The wreck of nations all down the ages is proof of this. We may truthfully say that no nation has perished from the face of the earth while in a condition of righteousness; when they have had just rulers and have been lovers of virtue and truth. The history of every nation of the past will show that they were in a state of wickedness when destruction came upon them, for the anger of the Lord was kindled against them for their wickedness and he permitted their destruction.

Nations Accountable before God

The Lord has from time to time, unbeknown to them, used man-made governments to punish other governments and to work out his purposes in the earth. Nations stand in a similar position as do individuals in relation to their accountability before God. The individual will have to answer for his deeds. If he has rebelled against the Almighty, he will have to pay the price, although he has the exercise of free will. Nations also hold their power and dominion through the sufferance of the Lord, and although they may reject him, and do not acknowledge his hand over them in all their affairs, yet they are in his hand and judgment will be meted out to them according to their works.

No sane person would be likely to say that idolatrous Babylon was a nation in favor with the Lord, receiving divine approval, and their kings reigning by divine appointment; yet the Lord called Nebuchadnezzar his "servant" because he appointed him to punish the rebellious kingdom of Judah. When the king of Babylon came upon the Jews and carried them away captive where they remained for seventy years for their wickedness, he did not realize that he was carrying into effect the mandates of the Lord. So far as he was concerned he was on a war of aggression, seeking more dominion and power, and coveting greater wealth. Nevertheless he and his successors were made to understand that the hand of the Lord had been in their conquest. Later, it was the turn of Babylon to be punished for her sins. The Lord called Cyrus his "anointed" and said he had chosen him to restore his people and to build his temple at Jerusalem. This was said more than one hundred years before Cyrus was born, and more than forty before the captivity of the Jews. Yet the nation of the Medes was not a nation with recognized divine authority. It in turn was punished and lost its place when overcome by another power. The Lord used these nations to bring to pass his purposes as he has done from the beginning of time.

Hand of the Lord Controls Destinies of Nations

In the great world war the hand of the Lord is seen controlling the destinies of the nations. Men may plot and plan, but if the Lord is not in the thing they do it shall not prosper. Nations are pawns in the hands of the Almighty when they rebel against him, and he overrules the acts of men and turns the thoughts of kings and rulers to serve him even wherein they contemplate evil. It would be well for the nations of the earth to learn this great lesson. The experiences of the past teach it very plainly, yet men will continue to defy the power of God and endeavor to accomplish their own strange acts in opposition to his will.

The time will come when the Lord will make an end of all man-made nations, and in their stead the government of Jesus Christ shall be established to hold rule to the end of time and for ever. When that time comes we will have a theocratic government. A government of God, Jesus Christ being the King, and the people being governed by their own common consent, for the Lord will recognize the agency of man then, even as he has recognized it since before the foundation of the world. When that time comes, however, man will have learned to be obedient to the principles of righteousness and to obey the law of God and Jesus Christ his Son, whose right it is to reign. This will be the one perfect form of government, and it shall for this reason abide forever.

The attitude of the Latter-day Saints towards governments of the earth and their established laws is clearly set forth in the revelations of the Lord. The twelfth Article of Faith reads as follows: "We believe in being subject to kings, presidents, rulers and magistrates, in obeying, honoring and sustaining the law." Again the Lord commanded the Saints in the hour of their great distress and suffering: "Wherefore, be subject to the powers that be, until he reigns whose right it is to reign, and subdues all enemies under his feet."[7]

Comprehensive Declaration

Section 134 of the Doctrine and Covenants is a comprehensive declaration of our belief in relation to laws and governments and it is unnecessary to repeat it. I give but one paragraph:

We believe that all men are bound to sustain and uphold the respective governments in which they reside, while protected in their

---

[7]D&C 58:22.

inherent and inalienable rights by the laws of such governments; and that sedition and rebellion are unbecoming every citizen thus protected, and should be punished accordingly; and that all governments have a right to enact such laws as in their own judgment are best calculated to secure the public interest, at the same time, however, holding sacred the freedom of conscience.[8]

This is in harmony with the admonition given by Peter to the Former-day Saints:

Submit yourselves to every ordinance of man for the Lord's sake; whether it be to the king as supreme;

Or unto governors, as unto them that are sent by him for the punishment of evil doers, and for the praise of them that do well.

For so is the will of God, that with well doing ye may put to silence the ignorance of foolish men:

As free, and not using your liberty for a cloak of maliciousness, but as the servants of God.

Honor all men. Love the brotherhood. Fear God. Honor the king.[9]

---

[8]D&C 134:5.
[9]I Peter 2:13-17

If we look with the eye of faith and in the spirit of humility we will see, beyond the power of the microscope, the Mastercraftsman of the universe at work, just as he has said, giving to each particle of matter, each compound great and small, the law by which it is governed.

Authority as a Universal Principle

The heavens declare the glory of God; and the firmament sheweth his handywork.

Day unto day uttereth speech, and night unto night sheweth knowledge.

There is no speech nor language, where their voice is not heard.[1]

Authority is an eternal principle operative throughout the universe. To the "utmost bounds" of space all things are governed by law emanating from the Lord our God. On Kolob and other giant governing stars and in the tiny electron infinitismally small, and of which all things are composed, divine authority is manifest in the form of immutable law. All space is filled with matter and that matter is controlled and directed by the all wise and omniscient Creator who "comprehendeth all things, and all things are before him, and all things are round about him; and he is above all things, and in all things, and is through all things, and is round about all things, and all things are by him, and of him, even God, forever and ever. And again, verily I say unto you, he hath given a law unto all things, by which they move in their times and their seasons."[2]

---

[1]Psalm 19:1-3.
[2]D&C 88:41-42.

To Moses the Lord said:

And worlds without number have I created; and I also created them for mine own purpose; and by the Son I created them, which is mine Only Begotten. . . .

But only on account of this earth and the inhabitants thereof, give I unto you. For, behold, there are many worlds that have passed away by the word of my power. And there are many that now stand, and innumerable are they unto man; but all things are numbered unto me, for they are mine and I know them. . . .

And as one earth shall pass away, and the heavens thereof even so shall another come; and there is no end to my works, neither to my words.[3]

Abraham Saw the Stars

The Lord showed the stars to Abraham through the aid of the Urim and Thummim, and Abraham wrote of them:

And I saw the stars, that they were very great, and that one of them was nearest unto the throne of God; and there were many great ones which were near unto it;

And the Lord said unto me: These are the governing ones; . . .[4]

From these scriptural references we learn that the controlling authority in the universe is vested in God; that his authority is manifest in all things both great and small. In a revelation to Joseph Smith the Lord said:

All kingdoms have a law given;

And there are many kingdoms; for there is no space in the which

---

[3]Moses 1:33, 35, 38. Professor Harlow Shaples of the Harvard Observatory, writing on the subject of astronomy in an article said that the stars of our universe "are numbered by the thousands of millions," and that the extent of the universe "is measured in hundreds of thousands of light years, and the probable past duration in time is inexpressible in its immensity." *Literary Digest,* June 13, 1925. It was not so long ago that all the known stars could be numbered in thousands; but the telescope, with its modern attachments, has revealed stars innumerable existing in space measured in terms that are incomprehensible to man. And the question arises, what is still beyond? Yet the Lord says he knows them all and to him they are numbered; they obey his command and fill the measure of their creation according to the edicts that have gone forth from the throne of the Eternal Father.

[4]Abraham 3:2-3.

there is no kingdom; and there is no kingdom in which there is no space, either a greater or a lesser kingdom.[5]

The significance of this expression we could not understand before the very recent discoveries in the field of science pertaining to atoms, electrons, protons, and the ether of the universe. The probabilities are that we do not understand it now except in small degree, and that future revelation will add to the lustre of this wonderful truth in relation to the composition of the universe and the controlling laws by which it is governed.

On this very point one of the world's greatest scientists has said:

The vast interplanetary and interstellar regions will no longer be regarded as waste places in the universe. . . . We shall find them to be already full of this wonderful medium (ether); so full that no human power can remove it from the smallest portion of space, or produce the slightest flaw in its infinite continuity.—Clerk Maxwell.[6]

Sir Oliver Lodge Quoted

Sir Oliver Lodge, in his valuable little work, *Ether and Reality,* speaking of the composition of matter says:

. . . That is one of the first things to realize about matter: there are great gaps between its particles. You may say, That all is very well for the sky and the stars and planets; but what about the earth? What about a piece of rock, or furniture, or any solid subject? Do you mean to say that the particles of a body like that are widely separated, with great spaces between them in proportion to their size, and that a straight line might penetrate them deeply without encountering a particle? Yes I do: that is what I mean by the discontinuity of matter. It is discontinuous on a small scale as well as on a large scale. It does not appear so, but that is only because our senses are not fine enough to tell us about things on a small scale; we can only see things on a big scale. . . . No microscope, however powerful, can show us an atom, still less can it show us how an atom is composed and how far apart its ultimate particles are: we know this

---

[5]D&C 88:36-37.
[6]Sir Oliver Lodge, *Ether and Reality,* p. 25.

otherwise and indirectly. It is however common knowledge, now, that matter is built up of minute electric charges, both negative and positive, which are called electrons and protons. It is also known that these electric units are so extremely minute that they are separated from one another like the planets in the solar system: the greater part of the atom is empty space, just like the sky on a small scale. Or, more clearly, if we could take a solid body and magnify it sufficiently (which is impossible) we should see it something like the night sky.[7]

I quote these sayings merely to point out the fact that the scientist today is confirming what the Lord said to Joseph Smith by revelation in relation to the universe—"All kingdoms have a law given; and there are many kingdoms; for there is no space in which there is no kingdom; and there is no kingdom in which there is no space, either a greater or a lesser kingdom." How wonderfully this is confirmed by the astronomer who studies and charts the stars of the universe; and how equally wonderful it is confirmed by the scientist who divides and examines the substance of the atom. All is subject to the direction and control of the Eternal Father.

The Structure of a Living Creature

What is there more wonderful than the structure of a living creature, whether it be a gnat or a mighty mastodon? Think of the wonderfully constructed human body, the highest of all creation! Contemplate how delicately and wonderfully it is fitted together and how our Father has given it the means of development, when quickened by the spirit, from a tiny cell to the perfect man endowed with intelligence. Each organ performs the special function given it. The blood flows with life preserving power through the arteries and carries the building material to take the place of that which has served its purpose, and then through the veins the blood returns to be purified in the lungs and to be

---

[7]Ibid., pp. 36-37.

pumped by the heart again and again on its continuous round during the whole of mortal life.

What makes the heart beat? How does the blood obtain its power to fight disease by marshalling its warriors to the attack? How are they created? In what manner does the food we eat become digested and assimilated? By what power do the nerves receive and forward their messages to the brain and control the muscles and organs of the body? From whence comes a thought, and how is it created? Where is the seat of life and from whence did it come? Who can answer these and a million other questions that could be asked, except the Divine Creator? Men have searched; they have studied; they have formed their opinions and built their theories, but before the structure even of the body of a butterfly, much less to speak of man, they stand completely baffled.

But this we know: not only is man governed by law, but so are the minutest particles of his body. This is also true of every other creature. The reason for the law may be understood, but how it comes and why it works, no man knows. These secrets have not been given to man, but are jealously and sacredly held by the Author of life and the light of men.

Unto Every Law There Are Certain Bounds

Where can you turn in the entire field of research and find chaos, disorder, and confusion, reigning supreme independent of the controlling influence of divine power? It is perfectly true, as the Lord revealed to the Prophet Joseph Smith, that "unto every kingdom is given a law; and unto every law there are certain bounds also and conditions. All beings who abide not in those conditions are not justified."[8] Moreover, that which "seeketh to become a law unto itself, and willeth to abide in sin, and altogether abideth in sin, cannot be sanctified by law, neither by mercy, justice, nor

---
[8]D&C 88:38-39.

judgment. Therefore, they must remain filthy still."[9] Even
in the violation of law, the violator is subject to law. There
are laws that govern even in the case of broken law, so, no
matter where we turn we come face to face with the divine
mandates from our Eternal Father. Nothing has been overlooked, nothing forgotten.

How true the words of the Psalmist:

O Lord, thou hast searched me, and known me.
Thou knowest my downsitting and mine uprising, thou under-
standest my thoughts afar off.
Thou compassest my path and my lying down, and art acquainted
with all my ways.
For there is not a word in my tongue, but, lo, O Lord, thou
knowest it altogether.
Thou hast beset me behind and before, and laid thine hand
upon me.
Such knowledge is too wonderful for me; it is high, I cannot
attain unto it.
Whither shall I go from thy spirit? or whither shall I flee from
thy presence?
If I ascend up into heaven, thou art there: if I make my bed in
hell, behold, thou art there.
If I take the wings of the morning, and dwell in the uttermost
parts of the sea;
Even there shall thy hand lead me, and thy right hand shall
hold me.
If I say surely the darkness shall cover me; even the night shall
be light about me.
Yea, the darkness hideth not from thee; but the night shineth as
the day: the darkness and the light are both alike to thee.[10]

Man Foremost of Every Creature

It is reasonable to suppose that all things, whether man,
beast, or element, that violates law, must remain "filthy
still," for under such conditions there can be no sanctification. Man should, however, because of his superior intelli-

---

[9]D&C 88:35.
[10]Psalm 139:1-12.

gence and power to act, be the foremost of every creature in the service of the Lord in regard to the obedience to law. Man has been endowed with superior intelligence because he is the offspring of God, and within him is the spark of divinity. He has been given dominion over all things upon the face of the earth, and the fulness of it is his:

> ... the beasts of the field and the fowls of the air, and that which climbeth upon the trees and walketh upon the earth;
> Yea, and the herb, and the good things which come of the earth, whether for food or for raiment, or for houses, or for barns, or for orchards, or for gardens, or for vineyards;
> Yea, all things which come of the earth, in the season thereof, are made for the benefit and the use of man, both to please the eye and to gladden the heart;
> Yea, for food and for raiment, for taste and for smell, to strengthen the body and to enliven the soul.[11]

With all these blessings man should be able to improve his time, to increase in knowledge, to show greater humility and gratitude to his Eternal Father than any other creature. Moreover, to him the promise is made that through his obedience to divine law he may come back into the presence of the Father and the Son to receive a fulness of joy as a son and heir.

Man was placed on the earth that he might have joy, and all the blessings enumerated and many thousands more, are his, and all our Father has asked of him is that he obey his law. "And in nothing doth man offend God, or against none is his wrath kindled, save those who confess not his hand in all things, and obey not his commandments."[12] But notwithstanding the many blessings he receives, and the abundant mercy that is shown him by a kind loving Father, man is the only creature that shows ingratitude and manifests rebellion to a marked degree.

---

[11]D&C 59:16-19.
[12]D&C 59:21.

The Wonders of Snow

Several years ago I cut out of a newspaper an article on the wonders of snow, an excerpt is given here:

Snow crystals obey an immutable law of six. They are six-sided jewels, or six-pointed stars. They never answer to the law of four or five. Snow is crystalized water, and water always crystalizes in six-sided forms. Why? No one knows; no one ever will know. There is no more apparent reason for the sixness of crystalized water than for the monoclynic prisms of sugar crystals. Water and sugar and the complex minerals which make the granite rocks all follow laws which are utterly unchangeable, but which are, as far as we can see, without any special reason. It is as profitable to speculate why the chlorophyl of vegetation is green and why the blood of animals is red. . . .

No one should accept the snow too much as a matter of course. A pocket magnifier will disclose gems of wonderful brilliancy to whomsoever will look. When the next lazy snowfall comes, when the flakes are not hardened and beaten by the tempest, study the designs of infinite variety that are built by the master craftsmanship of nature on the rigid plan of six. It will give the snow a new and finer meaning.

What is here said of snow, the sugar cube, the granite rock and chlorophyl of vegetation, is also true of every other particle of matter and combination of matter wherever they are found; but we must look beyond the fact that these are "laws of nature" and cannot be understood. The laws of nature are God's laws as much as is the law: "Thou shalt not steal,"[13] or "Thou shalt love the Lord thy God with all thy heart, and with all thy soul, and with all thy mind."[14] If we will look with the eye of faith and in the spirit of humility, we will see, beyond the power of the microscope, the Mastercraftsman of the universe at work, just as he has said, giving to each particle of matter, each compound great and small, the law by which it is governed. Moreover, we will

---

[13]Exodus 20:15.
[14]Matthew 22:37.

likely discover by careful investigation that everywhere matter, animate and inanimate, is inclined to obey the voice of the Great Creator and show some gratitude for its existence, except man.

The fact that snow crystals and every other substance throughout the immensity of space obey law that is "utterly unchangeable" is conclusive evidence that nothing has come by chance. The most foolish and inconsistent thought ever expressed is that there is no controlling and governing Power directing all things in the universe. Neither has organized matter been created to be destroyed. The Eternal Father and Creator has not made anything to come to an end, but knowing all things, the end from the beginning, he builds for eternity. While man and other creatures must pass through the temporal life, and eventually death will claim them for a season, that is not the end. There shall come a regeneration, a renewal, an eternal awakening.

Said the Lord:

For all old things shall pass away, and all things shall become new, even the heaven and the earth, and all the fulness thereof, both men and beasts, the fowls of the air, and the fishes of the sea;

And not one hair, neither mote, shall be lost, for it is the workmanship of mine hand.[15]

All things, therefore, are owned and controlled by the Lord and enjoy their existence due to the mercies and power of the Divine Creator, the Lord our God.

A Great and Glorious Truth

Most, if not all, remarkable and fundamental facts coming to the knowledge of man have been made known through direct revelation. This is true of the knowledge we have received of the light of Christ. This great and glorious truth was made known to ancient prophets. John the Reve-

---

[15]D&C 29:24-25.

lator has mentioned it in the introduction to his account of the ministry of Jesus Christ; but the world lost this precious gem, and it remained hidden until restored by revelation to Joseph Smith. John said:

> In the beginning was the Word, and the Word was with God, and the Word was God.
> The same was in the beginning with God.
> All things were made by him; and without him was not any thing made that was made.
> In him was life; and the life was the light of men.[16]

In the Pearl of Great Price this same truth is found, and we are informed that it was through the Son that worlds are and have been created. More wonderful still is the revelation in the Doctrine and Covenants, Section 88, of the "light of Christ." Perhaps it is best to quote the doctrine just as it appears:

> He that ascended up on high, as also he descended below all things, in that he might be in all and through all things, the light of truth;
> Which truth shineth. This is the light of Christ. As also he is in the sun, and the light of the sun, and the power thereof by which it was made.
> As also he is in the moon, and is the light of the moon, and the power thereof by which it was made;
> As also the light of the stars, and the power thereof by which they were made;
> And the earth also, and the power thereof, even the earth upon which you stand.
> And the light which shineth, which giveth you light, is through him who enlighteneth your eyes, which is the same light that quickeneth your understandings;
> Which light proceedeth forth from the presence of God to fill the immensity of space—
> The light which is in all things, which giveth life to all things, which is the law by which all things are governed, even the power

---
[16]John 1:1-4.

of God who sitteth upon his throne, who is in the bosom of eternity, who is in the midst of all things.[17]

In another revelation further knowledge is imparted of this great power:

For you shall live by every word that proceedeth forth from the mouth of God.

For the word of the Lord is truth, and whatsoever is truth is light, and whatsoever is light is Spirit, even the Spirit of Jesus Christ.

And the Spirit giveth light to every man that cometh into the world; and the Spirit enlighteneth every man through the world, that hearkeneth to the voice of the Spirit.[18]

Again it is recorded:

And that I am the true light that enlighteneth every man that cometh into the world; . . .

The Spirit of truth is of God. I am the Spirit of truth, and John bore record of me, saying: He received a fulness of truth, yea, even of all truth; . . .

The elements are the tabernacle of God; yea, man is the tabernacle of God, even temples; and whatsoever temple is defiled, God shall destroy that temple.

The glory of God is intelligence, or, in other words, light and truth.

Light and truth forsake that evil one.[19]

Governing Force in the Universe

There is a world of meaning in these revelations. It is impossible to comprehend them fully, yet we learn the great and fundamental truth that the light of Christ, or the spirit of truth, is the governing power and the controlling force in the universe. It is from this source of power which radiates from God, that all kingdoms are made and governed. The light of Christ is the power, not only by which worlds

---

[17]D&C 88:6-13.
[18]D&C 84:44-46.
[19]D&C 93:2, 26, 35-37.

are made, but is the power by which they are preserved.
This great power is made manifest in various ways. It is
the life-giving, or quickening power of all things, worlds,
the animal kingdom, the vegetable kingdom, and man. It is
the power that quickens the intellect, or intelligence of man.
Every man is born with this quickening power and if he will
hearken to its teachings he will be eventually led to the
fulness of truth, the gospel of Jesus Christ.

Man, therefore, is not left to blindly feel his way, but
has been given the quickening power by which truth is discerned and error detected. From God this power goes forth
to fill the immensity of space and through it he quickens all
things. Without this gift all things in the universe would
die, for there would be withdrawn from them the life-giving
and preserving power. The spirit of truth is in no way associated with wickedness, but forsaketh the evil one. Therefore, Satan, and those who follow him are without this
quickening power.

We did not come into this world just to have the privilege of keeping the commandments of the Lord. We came to be tried. Did you ever stop to think that one of the first things that happened in this world when man was placed upon it was that the devil was sent here? What for? To try us.

Opposition Essential to Progress

My dear brothers and sisters, I will be very happy to give you my blessings. It is a great privilege which is given to us to come together as we are now and be instructed in things pertaining to our eternal welfare. I am going to be very brief in what I am saying to you, but I want to say something that is extremely important.

Mortal life, which we are now in, is perhaps the most important period of our existence. Why? Because we are here on probation. We are here face to face with everything that is evil. Let me put it this way: The devil was put here and he came into this world to test us and try us to see if we would keep the commandments of the Lord or if he could destroy us.

Did you ever watch a group of pigeons fly in the sky? What keeps them up? Without opposition they could not fly. Because of opposition the weight of the wings in the air keeps them going. We did not come into this world just to have the privilege of keeping the commandments of the Lord. We came here to be tried. Did you ever stop to think that one of the first things that happened in this world when man was placed upon it was that the devil was sent here? What for? To try us. Do you know the birds could not fly if they did not have opposition and did not have to face opposition; therefore, the pressure—the wings upon the air keep them going. You remove the privilege of having that opposition and a bird could not fly. It would fall to the earth.

Opposing Evil Is Essential

It is not opposition that is so dreadful. The dreadful thing is yielding to it; but the opposition to righteousness helps to make us strong. Every time you resist temptation you are building up your strength. When the Lord sent man into this world, what else did he do? He let Satan come here Did you think of that? Satan came with the determination on his part of destroying the sons and daughters of God, to lead them away to everlasting destruction. So we have to resist him. That is what makes us strong.

I had an unfortunate thing happen to me one time when I fell and broke a leg. That was not my fault. My brother and I were coming in with a load of hay. It was the last load, and we did not want to go back again. We built up what was really two loads. When we went in with what was to be pay-our-tithing load, I was swept off the top because there was a bar across the gate, and I fell and broke a leg. Well, that was my carelessness. I only mention that because of this purpose—to impress upon us that opposition is just as essential as anything else to bring to pass salvation in the kingdom of God. If a bird never attempted to use its wings, it could not fly.

Why does a boxer spend so much time in practice before he goes into a fight? He does not want to get licked, but it is to gain the strength that he can overcome. And we are here in this life faced with opposition. I have had people say to me, "If I had been running this world, I never would have permitted Satan to come here." Would you? The Lord did permit him; he let him come here. He came here to try us, to see if we would keep the commandments of God under his opposition. He came here to destroy us.

In the Book of Mormon it states that there needs be opposition in all things. That is true. If there were no opposition, salvation could not amount to very much, because we are taught to overcome the provocation, not to give way to it.

So I repeat, the Lord says there must needs be opposition in all things. We would not accomplish anything if we did not have opposition, and that is what makes us strong and gives us power to overcome.—Ward Conference, Eighteenth Ward, Ensign Stake, January 18, 1970.)

It is my judgment that there are many members of this Church who have been baptized for the remission of their sins, who have had hands laid upon their heads for the gift of the Holy Ghost, who have never received that gift, that is, the manifestations of it. Why? Because they have never put themselves in order to receive these manifestations. They have never humbled themselves. They have never taken the steps that would prepare them for the companionship of the Holy Ghost.

"Seek Ye Earnestly..."

This morning we listened to a wonderful discourse addressed to friends and businessmen, prominent individuals outside of the Church, which I think was most timely, but I wish to address my remarks to the members of the Church, and more especially to those who are wayward and indifferent, and who do not seem to realize the value of their membership. I would like to read to you a covenant which is taken by each individual who enters the waters of baptism.

And again, by way of commandment to the church concerning the manner of baptism—All those who humble themselves before God, and desire to be baptized, and come forth with broken hearts and contrite spirits, and witness before the church that they have truly repented of all their sins, and are willing to take upon them the name of Jesus Christ, having a determination to serve him to the end, and truly manifest by their works that they have received of the Spirit of Christ unto the remission of their sins, shall be received by baptism into his church.[1]

Baptism into the Church Is Not Enough

Baptism into the Church is not enough to save us. It is for the remission of sins, that is true, but there is another

---
[1]D&C 20:37.

baptism which is just as essential, and that is the baptism of
the spirit, or the bestowal of the gift of the Holy Ghost.
After we are baptized, we are confirmed. What is that confirmation for? To make us companions with the Holy
Ghost; to have the privilege of the guidance of the third
member of the Godhead—companionship, that our minds
might be enlightened, that we might be quickened by the
Holy Spirit to seek for knowledge and understanding concerning all that pertains to our exaltation in the kingdom of
God.

In this same revelation from which I read, the Lord has
also said:

And we know that justification through the grace of our Lord
and Savior Jesus Christ is just and true;
And we know also, that sanctification through the grace of our
Lord and Savior Jesus Christ is just and true, to all those who love
and serve God with all their mights, minds, and strength.
But there is a possibility that man may fall from grace and
depart from the living God;
Therefore let the church take heed and pray always, lest they
fall into temptation;
Yea, and even let those who are sanctified take heed also.[2]

Baptism and confirmation into the Church do not
necessarily insure our exaltation in the kingdom of God.
They do, provided we are true and faithful to every covenant
and obligation required of us in the commandments of our
Eternal Father. It is he who endures to the end that will
be saved, and there is a danger that confronts us through
the temptations of the adversary if we yield to those temptations that we may lose it all. The greatest punishment that
can come to any individual in this world is punishment that
will come to those who have received the light and truth of
the gospel of Jesus Christ, who have passed through the
waters of baptism, who have hands laid upon their heads

---

[2]D&C 20:30-34.

for the gift of the Holy Ghost, and then turn away from the truth, for the Lord will not hold them guiltless.

Sons of Perdition

I think I am safe in saying that no man can become a Son of Perdition until he has known the light. Those who have never received the light are not to become Sons of Perdition. They will be punished if they rebel against God. They will have to pay the price of their sinning, but it is only those who have the light through the priesthood and through the power of God and through their membership in the Church who will be banished forever from his influence into outer darkness to dwell with the devil and his angels. That is a punishment that will not come to those who have never known the truth. Bad as they may suffer, and awful as their punishment may be, they are not among that group which is to suffer the eternal death and banishment from all influence concerning the power of God.

Now, I say I want to talk to those who are indifferent and a little wayward sometimes, those who do not appreciate the privileges and the opportunities that are given unto them to serve God and keep his commandments. If they are not here, I hope they are listening to what is going on in this building today. They do not come to the conferences— at least, not very many of them. But after receiving the light and the knowledge and the information which the Spirit of the Lord can give, it is an awful thing to turn away.

However, it is my judgment that there are many members of this Church who have been baptized for the remission of their sins, who have had hands laid upon their heads for the gift of the Holy Ghost, who have never received that gift, that is, the manifestations of it. Why? Because they have never put themselves in order to receive these manifestations. They have never humbled themselves. They have never taken the steps that would prepare them for the companionship of the Holy Ghost. Therefore they go through life without that knowledge, and they have not the understanding. Therefore when those cunning and crafty in their deceit come to them, they disturb them in their faith, if they have faith left. They criticize the Authorities of the Church. They criticize the doctrines of the Church, and these weak members do not have understanding enough, information enough, and enough of the guidance of the Spirit of the Lord to resist the false doctrines and teachings of those who come to them, the wolves in sheep's clothing, and they listen to them, and think that perhaps after all they have made a mistake, and first thing you know they find their way out of the Church, because they do not have understanding.

Letters from Disturbed People

I get letters frequently from people, members of this Church, who have been disturbed principally by two organizations which seem to have dedicated their lives to the destruction of The Church of Jesus Christ of Latter-day Saints. These people go into the homes of our weak members, disturb them in their faith, get them all riled up, and they do not know whether they did the right thing when they were baptized or whether they did not; but if they had lived as they should and had received the guidance of the Holy Spirit, they would not be moved. They would not be influenced by the false teachings and false statements regarding our doctrines that these people present to them.

The gospel is simple. There is nothing difficult about it. There are mysteries, no doubt. We do not need to bother about the mysteries, but the simple things pertaining to our salvation and exaltation we can understand.

Now let me refer to another passage of scripture.

But ye are commanded in all things to ask of God, who giveth liberally; and that which the Spirit testifies unto you even so I would that ye should do in all holiness of heart, walking uprightly before me, considering the end of your salvation, doing all things with prayer and thanksgiving, that ye may not be seduced by evil spirits, or doctrines of devils, or the commandments of men; for some are of men, and others of devils.[3]

Lord Has Given Us Warning

So the Lord has given us a warning.

Wherefore, beware lest ye are deceived; and that ye may not be deceived seek ye earnestly the best gifts, always remembering for what they are given;

For verily I say unto you, they are given for the benefit of those who love me and keep all my commandments, and him that seeketh so to do; that all may be benefited that seek or that ask of me, that ask and not for a sign that they may consume it upon their lusts.

And again, verily I say unto you, I would that ye should always remember, and always retain in your minds what those gifts are, that are given unto the church.[4]

Now the Lord would give us gifts. He will quicken our minds. He will give us knowledge that will clear up all difficulties, and put us in harmony with the commandments that he has given us, and with a knowledge that will be so deeply rooted in our souls that the knowledge can never be rooted out, if we will just seek for the light and the truth and the understanding which is promised to us, and which we can receive if we will only be true and faithful to every covenant and obligation pertaining to the gospel of Jesus Christ.—(Conference Report, October, 1958.)

---

[3]D&C 46:7.
[4]D&C 46:8-10.

Who among us wants to be satisfied by merely entering the celestial kingdom? The Lord did not say that baptism would exalt us. Are we going to be satisfied with merely entrance? Evidently there are many members of the Church who are going to be so satisfied, because they will not prepare themselves, or do not prepare to receive exaltation.

Exaltation Requires More Than Baptism

My brethren and sisters, I do not expect to tell you anything new. I endorse all that has been said during these sessions as pertaining to the temple work and salvation of the dead, but in the few minutes that I stand here I would like to present a few thoughts in just a little different way, nothing new but a different point of view.

From the days of Adam until the days of Jesus Christ there was no work done in any temple or outside of any temple for the dead. You read in the parable of the story of Lazarus that there was a gulf that could not be crossed. Christ went into the spirit world and after his resurrection the salvation for the dead was introduced. I call your attention to this for this purpose, to impress upon us the great importance of the responsibilities which are ours. We have been commanded to seek after our dead, and as far as we can trace them from generation to generation we should obtain that information and then perform the labor in the house of the Lord.

Now, I am talking about the great work that devolves upon us for our dead. We have also work to perform for ourselves if we want salvation in the celestial kingdom of God.

Astonished at Questions

I have been asked quite a number of times by members of the Church if baptism would permit a person to enter the celestial kingdom. Each time I have been astonished that any member of the Church would ask that question after all that has been written and the words of the Savior himself. When he sent his disciples out after his resurrection he said, they who would repent and believe and are baptized should be saved, and they who would not repent and would not be baptized should not be saved. That is the doctrine the Lord has given to the Church in our day.

Who among us wants to be satisfied by merely entering the celestial kingdom? The Lord did not say that baptism would exalt us. Are we going to be satisfied with merely an entrance? Evidently there are many members of the Church who are going to be so satisfied, because they will not prepare themselves, or do not prepare to receive the exaltation. What will happen to those who are baptized, who are satisfied thus far? They will enter into that kingdom to be servants, to wait upon those who are worthy of a far more and exceeding weight of glory. The Lord says they will be angels, ministering servants, but they will not be Gods, and that will be their destiny, for he says it will endure worlds without end. So we cannot be satisfied merely with baptism. The Lord expects us to be worthy to go on and receive the fulness of his kingdom, to be clothed with the power of perfection and become like him. That can only be done by observing the ordinances and receiving the covenants in the house of the Lord, each of us individually and for our dead. We must perform these like services for them.

Marriage for Eternity

Much has been said about marriage for eternity. That is the crowning blessing which will bring that exaltation.

The Lord speaks in another of the revelations of the Church of the Firstborn. What is the difference, if there is a difference between the Church of the Firstborn and The Church of Jesus Christ of Latter-day Saints, or of any day saints? Well, the members of the Church of the Firstborn are members of the Church of Jesus Christ, but not all those who are members of the Church of Jesus Christ become members of the Church of the Firstborn, for they are they unto whom the Lord has given all things. They are priests and kings. They are they who have received the exaltation, they who are made equal in power, and in might, and in dominion, who attain to the fulness and become the sons, and for the sisters, the daughters of God.

One more thought, the Lord also speaks of those who receive the eternal deaths. Who are they? Everyone will receive a resurrection, not one soul shall fail and so they will receive back their bodies, spirit and body being reunited again, and that will endure eternally. So when the Lord says something of eternal deaths, he has reference to those who remain separately and singly, who have not been willing to accept and hence have not obtained the fulness of his kingdom, those who are not married for time and all eternity.[1] Eternal death means that they remain separately and singly and they have no increase. Therefore, the Lord says, they come to an end and remain separate and single in their saved condition. Then he speaks of eternal lives. By obedience to the laws of the gospel, I can get eternal life, that is, live forever, and be in the celestial kingdom. But only through the eternity of the marriage covenant, do we obtain eternal lives, which means eternal increase, and they who are willing to abide in all the laws and receive all the ordinances and covenants that our Father in heaven has offered us, receive the power of eternal increase; husbands and

---

[1]See Marriage in Eternity, *Answers to Gospel Questions* Vol. II, published by Deseret Book Company, Salt Lake City, Utah, 1958, pages 34-35.

wives, receiving in the eternities an increase of posterity, for there shall be no end. Brethren and sisters, we cannot be satisfied with just membership in this Church. We should live to be worthy of and pray for the fulness of the blessings of our Father's kingdom. That we may do so, I humbly pray.—(Dedicatory services, Los Angeles Temple, March 13, 1956.)

The more nearly perfect our lives are here, the more nearly perfect they will be there. If we have practiced principles of perfection, and sought the will of the Father here, then we will find it less difficult to continue on the same paths when we pass beyond this mundane sphere.

"Seek Ye First the Kingdom"

I have enjoyed the conference. The theme, "MIA Prepares the Way," is something to be remembered, and if we walk in paths of righteousness for his name's sake, we will always be blessed. Your theme taken from Section 130:18, in the Doctrine and Covenants is true, and President McKay has pointed out to the young people five of the most common things in which the unrighteous indulge. The theme is printed on the programs and you should read it and memorize it, and it will help you on your road to gain eternal life which we are striving for.

Be Ye Therefore Perfect

The words of the Savior in his sermon on the Mount, "Be ye therefore perfect, even as your Father which is in heaven is perfect," have served as a text for many a sermon. We have been informed that his meaning is that we, in this life, should try to perform every duty and keep every law and thus endeavor to be perfect in our sphere, as the Father is in his.

This is all good and true, but does it go far enough? Was our Lord confining his remarks to our present everyday actions?

Paul, for instance, in addressing the Ephesian Saints informs them that the Savior has placed in the Church apostles, prophets, evangelists, pastors, and teachers, "for the perfecting of the saints, for the work of the ministry, for the edifying of the body of Christ; till we all come in the unity of the faith, and of the knowledge of the Son of God, unto a perfect man, unto the measure of the stature of the fulness of Christ."[1]

But shall we limit the meaning of these words spoken to the disciples of our Lord to this life? I like to think of them in relationship to another remark from the same sermon, for it seems to me they are closely connected:

But seek ye first the kingdom of God, and his righteousness, and all these things shall be added unto you.[2]

Majority Seek Things of This Life

The majority of mankind are seeking the things of this life rather than the kingdom of God and his righteousness, but as members of the Church it is our duty to prepare ourselves for eternity.

The more nearly perfect our lives are here, the more nearly perfect they will be there. If we have practiced principles of perfection, and sought the will of the Father here, then we will find it less difficult to continue on the same paths when we pass beyond this mundane sphere. Now what is the full duty of man? The Preacher says:

Fear (love) God and keep his commandments; for this is the whole duty of man.
For God shall bring every work into judgment, with every secret thing, whether it be good, or whether it be evil.[3]

Shall we not continue on to perfection after the resurrection? Is not the promise given that we shall, if faithful

---

[1]Ephesians 4:11-13.
[2]Matthew 6:33.
[3]Ecclesiastes 12:13-14.

in all things, become like Jesus Christ and the Father? And then pass through the resurrection we go on, as we read in Hebrews, unto perfection through continued faithfulness.

Latter-day Saints believe in this progression in eternity until, eventually, we become worthy through knowledge, wisdom, humility, and obedience, to be like God, and then to have the privilege of being made equal in power, might and dominion,[4] and to possess all that the Father hath.

If such mighty blessings are promised to those who are willing to keep the whole law unto the end, are they not to continue on in the road of perfection after the resurrection until the fulness is reached and they shall be like our Eternal Father?

Slothful Servants

President Brigham Young declared that, "Every man and woman who has talent and hides it will be called a slothful servant. Improve day by day upon the capital you have. In proportion as we are capacitated to receive, so it is our duty to do." He also said, "I shall not cease learning while I live, nor when I arrive in the spirit world, but shall there learn with greater facility; and when I again receive my body, I shall learn a thousand times more in a thousand times less time; and then I do not mean to cease learning."[5]

Add to all this unlimited possibility the fact that our former knowledge, which was taken away, shall be returned, as taught by President Joseph F. Smith. This being so, and there is no reasonable thought to oppose it, then we shall have a wonderful fund of information on which to build, for who knows how long we were learning in the eternity already past when we walked with God our Father?

---

[4]D&C 76:95.
[5]*Discourses of Brigham Young* (Salt Lake City, Deseret Book Company) p. 382.

A wise man will hear, and will increase learning; and a man of understanding shall attain unto wise counsels. . . .

The fear (love) of the Lord is the beginning of knowledge; but fools despise wisdom and instruction.[6]

All of this instruction is given to help us to become perfect, and the Saints were further instructed to cease from all light speeches, loud boisterous laughter, lustful desires, pride, and wicked doings. They were to keep themselves clean morally, spiritually, and physically, by a proper observance of the laws given them. Thus they would become sanctified so that they might dwell in the presence of the Lord.

If we are able to do all this, surely we could be considered perfect in our sphere, and have that much the start towards perfection in the celestial kingdom. The Lord has promised to reveal unto those who are diligently seeking him, all the mysteries of his kingdom.

Promise Through Obedience

So here we have the promise that we shall, through obedience and faith, obtain a fulness of all truth and become like Christ, to share with him, as joint-heirs, "all that the Father hath." We shall become as sons and daughters of God, enjoying the fulness of glory in the abundant, or perfect life, which Jesus Christ came into the world to give us, and *only by keeping in the strait way shall we find the fulness of joy and the life which is perfect.* This is the goal which all who truly love the Lord are seeking, and through diligent and faithful service and endurance to the end, they shall find it. —(MIA June Conference, July 1, 1962.)

---

[6]Proverbs 1:5, 7.

We have members of the Church who set aside the commandments the Lord has given us, who fail strictly to observe them. That is not your right. It is just your privilege, the privilege the Lord has given you to act for yourself. You are agents with the power within you to obey or to disobey. If it were not so, no one could be tried for disobedience.

"He That Hath My Commandments and Keepeth Them"

For a theme I thought I would take the words of Jesus: John 14:21—"He that hath my commandments, and keepeth them, he it is that loveth me; and he that loveth me shall be loved of my father. . . ."

One week from tomorrow we will be celebrating the day quite universally accepted as the birthday of our Savior Jesus Christ. Therefore, throughout the entire country today I think people are listening to discourses, or have listened to them, in regard to our Lord and Savior Jesus Christ. But many of those discourses will be by men who do not know him, by some who do not receive him as the Son of God. But throughout The Church of Jesus Christ of Latter-day Saints, in all the discourses that have been and will be delivered, mention will be made of the fact that he is in very deed our Redeemer, the literal begotten Son of God, our Eternal Father. Of course I would be entirely out of place if I do not speak of him and his mission.

Moreover, since this is the anniversary of the birth of the Prophet Joseph Smith, I feel inclined to say a word about him, about his mission. As one of the greatest of the

prophets, he presides over the last dispensation and no
prophet has been given a greater mission, save perhaps it
could have been Adam; and no prophet in the past has done
more for the salvation of the human family, in my judgment,
than did Joseph Smith, the Prophet. As the Lord revealed
to Lehi, in the record that was kept by Joseph who was sold
into Egypt, the Prophet Joseph Smith was named, his mission was pointed out by that great ancestor of most of us,
who became the ruler in Egypt and one of the great prophets,
too, of God. Joseph Smith came into this world to perform
a work in the greatest of all the dispensations since the world
began, to bring salvation again to a fallen world, a world
that had gone astray, a world that in large measure professed
to worship the Son of God but that knew not how to worship him—because they had been taught so many traditions,
had received so many terms regarding the Christ and regarding the gospel which he brought to mankind—that the world
has been in constant error throughout the ages of time.

Joseph Smith Sent to Restore

Joseph Smith was sent to the world to restore what had
been taken away, that which men had rejected because, as
our Savior says, we loved darkness rather than light. So
I had to mention the Prophet tonight. Much can be said
about him and his mission that would be very profitable,
but I must forego that and speak of the mission of our Savior
Jesus Christ.

I am going to read to you a few words of Paul the
Apostle who spoke to the Corinthian Saints. The people
out in the world have a strange idea about these epistles of
Paul and of the men who have written the epistles we have
and the Bible. They read these epistles and apply them
unto themselves and they look upon them as being declared
as messages to all the world. But that is not so. Definitely,
each of these epistles was written to members of the Church

—not to denominations—but to those who heard the words of the apostles of old, had received them and had been baptized and confirmed members of the Church of Jesus Christ in that dispensation.

Therefore, we should have the understanding when we read these scriptures that the things said by the apostles are not things that apply to those who have not made covenants through the gospel of Jesus Christ and did not in that day. I am going to read a most definite statement, an emphatic statement to members of the Church, some of them who had been drifting a little—like we do today —some who were not fully converted, some who had forgotten the messages that the brethren taught to them and which they received when they came into the Church— just like members of the Church are today.

Paul's Instructions to the Corinthian Saints

So Paul instructing these members of the Church calls attention to certain conditions which are peculiar to those who have made covenants with Jesus Christ. And Paul is not speaking to this generation. He is speaking of the generation in which he lived. And so to these Corinthian members he said:

Now if any man build upon this foundation gold, silver, precious stone, wood, hay, stubble;
Every man's work shall be made manifest: for the day shall declare it, because it shall be revealed by fire; and the fire shall try every man's work of what sort it is.
If any man's work abide which he hath built thereupon, he shall receive a reward.
If any man's work shall be burned, he shall suffer loss: but he himself shall be saved; yet so as by fire.
Know ye not that ye are the temple of God, and that the Spirit of God dwelleth in you?[1]

---

[1]Corinthians 3:12-16.

Paul could not say that to those who had not been baptized and confirmed, for the Lord has said definitely that those who are not members of the Church can not receive the Holy Ghost, and so Paul has said.

If any man defile the temple of God, him shall God destroy; for the temple of God is holy, which temple ye are.

Let no man deceive himself. If any among you seemeth to be wise in this world, let him become a fool, that he may be wise.

For the wisdom of this world is foolishness with God. For it is written. He taketh the wise in their own craftiness.[2]

We should take notice of this. We can not build on any other foundation. I think that there are members of the Church who have pride, who have placed gold, silver, precious things — because the world considers these — as their great goal. And they have neglected their duties and responsibilities which their membership in the Church requires of them.

We Are Bought with a Price

Now, let me read another passage spoken to these same members of the Church, many of whom had sadly departed from the true teachings that they had received from Paul and others who had been sent to teach them:

What? Know ye not that your body is the temple of the Holy Ghost which is in you, which ye have of God, and ye are not your own?

For ye are bought with a price: therefore glorify God in your body, and in your spirit, which are God's.[3]

Paul could not say that to those who had not made covenants. He could have told anybody anywhere that he was bought with a price, but he could not tell them that the Holy Ghost had been given to them, because it was not

---

[2]I Corinthians 3:17-19.
[3]I Corinthians 6:19-20.

given except to members of the Church. But the fact remains that every soul upon the face of the earth was bought
with a price—Jew and Gentile, the heathen, the atheist.
No matter where a man lives or what he believes or the
circumstances under which he lives, he was bought and
paid for with a price, a price that was paid by our Lord
and Savior Jesus Christ, and he was the only one who
could pay it. No one else was ever born into this world
who could pay this price.

And from what were we bought? Before I answer that
question, I want to say something else. I have heard people
say, and members of the Church, "I have a right to do as
I please." No, you do not. You have not any right at all to
do as you please. There is only one right that you have,
and that is to do just what I read to you. Keep the commandments of Jesus Christ. He has a perfect right to tell
us so. We have no right to refuse. I do not care who the
man is. I do not care where he lives, do not care what he is;
when the gospel of Jesus Christ is presented to him, he has
no right to refuse to receive it. He has the privilege. He
was not compelled to receive it, because our Father in heav-
en has given to everyone of us in the Church and out, the
gift of free agency. That free agency gives us the privilege
to accept and be loyal to our Lord's commandments, but it
has never given us the right to reject them. Every man who
rejects the commandments of our Father in heaven is rebellious.

Of course I realize, that there are thousands of people
who have never heard the gospel. They are not going to
be punished for that. We can not expect a person to observe
a commandment he never heard. But all those who never
had the privilege of hearing it, at some time will have that
privilege. If it is not in this life, it will be in the spirit world.
And every soul will have the opportunity to accept the
mission of our Savior Jesus Christ or to reject it. When

the Lord commands us, if we love him we will keep the commandments. This is the law to members of the Church, this little paragraph: "He that hath my commandments and keepeth them, he it is that loveth me." Again, the Savior said, "If ye love me, keep my commandments."

You Are Agents with the Power

We have members of the Church who set aside the commandments the Lord has given us, who fail strictly to observe them. That is not your right. It is just your privilege, the privilege the Lord has given you to act for yourself. You are agents with the power within you to obey or to disobey. If it were not so, no one could be tried for disobedience. We read in the scriptures that every man will be tried according to his works. Well, if we are not under obligation, who can try us? Did you ever think of that? If there was no obligation for me to keep the commandments of the Lord, if I broke them, I could not be punished.

We do not punish men for doing something that is not contrary to the laws do we? But the Lord has given us these laws, the gospel of Jesus Christ, not because it is pleasing to him, not because he is going to get anything out of it. He has given us these laws that we might get something out of them. And of course every person who keeps his commandments adds that much to his glory. There is no question about that—because when we sustain him and are true and faithful to him, he is the benefactor. But are we not benefited and are not the benefits greater to us by far than they would be to him? Our Lord never gave a commandment in this world to any man that was not intended to be to his eternal benefit. I think sometimes we overlook that.

I hope the Lord will help me to keep his commandments. As I said, his commandments are not hard to keep. He said that himself. Some people say that his commandments are hard to keep. That is an admission, is it not, that we are not keeping them?

Now let us talk about the mission of Jesus Christ. He bought us. Let us go back to that now. He bought us with a price. No one else could pay the price. He has told us in the Doctrine and Covenants, Section 19, verses 16-20, how he suffered for us and finished his work, and how he asked the Father to take it away from him, but he said, nevertheless, glory be to the Father, and I partook and finished my preparations unto the children of men. Wherefore, I command you again to repent.

We Do Not Fully Realize the Price

We do not fully realize the price. I do not. I am quite sure you do not. I do not think anybody does. All I know is that it was done. I am fully convinced of that. His great suffering was done before he ever went to the cross.

Let me ask you a question. Is there anybody here who has not committed some sin? If so, please raise your hand. I do not see any hands up. I can not raise mine. Well, you have done something wrong then. You admit it. Did you ever, after you had committed some wrong, feel sorry and get the spirit of repentance and wish you had not done it? If you have not felt that way, you had better see your bishop.

I have done things I should not have done and I have felt sorry. I know how I have felt. I never committed murder; I have kept my body clean; I have not been stealing from people. When I was a kid I may have taken something that did not belong to me like the neighbor's apples. But when I have done some wrong, I have been troubled.

The Savior never committed any sin nor carried any troubled conscience. He had not been under the necessity of repenting as you and I have; but in some way that I

cannot understand, he carried the weight of my transgressions and yours and the transgressions of every soul
who comes into this Church from the days of Adam to our
present time. He came and offered himself as a sacrifice
to pay the debt for the things I have done that are wrong
and that each of you individually have done that are wrong,
and each other person who has been willing to repent of
his sins and return to Jesus Christ and keep his commandments. He paid the price. Think of it if you can.

The Savior carried that burden in some way beyond
our comprehension. But he carried it. I know that because
I accept his word. The torment was so great that he pleaded
with his Father that if it were possible he may not drink
the bitter cup and shrink—"but nevertheless, thy will be
done." The answer he got from his Father was, "You
have to drink it."

This Is Such a Little Thing

Can I help loving him? No, I can not. Do you love
him? Then keep his commandments. If you do not, you
will have to answer for them yourselves. "If ye love me,
keep my commandments."

How often we think, "Oh, this is such a little thing.
Surely the Lord will forgive us. We will only do it this
one, just this once." When we do it once, it is rather easy
to do it again. When we do it the second time, it is easy
to do it the third time, and so it goes.

When Adam and Eve were placed in the Garden of
Eden, they did not have to die. They could be there today.
They could have continued on for countless ages. There
was not death then. But it would have been a terrific calam-
ity if they had not broken the law under which they lived.

If they had stayed in the Garden of Eden, we would not
be here; nobody would be here, only Adam and Eve. So

the breaking of that commandment was not a sin. I do not like to hear it spoken of as a sin. It was part of the great plan, but it brought death upon Adam.

Eating of that forbidden fruit subdued the power of the spirit and created blood in his body. No blood was in his body before the fall. The blood became the life thereof. And the blood was not only the life thereof, but it had in it the seeds of death. And so we grow old and we die. But that would have been a dreadful thing if Adam and his posterity had been forced because of the fall to die and remain dead; and there would have been no redemption.

Adam and Eve Became Mortal

That is what Satan wanted, so he worked on them. I think he had the idea, "Now, I have destroyed the Lord's plan. I have caused Adam and Eve to become mortal and they are going to die, and everyone will have to die, and they will become subject to me." And he laughed about it.

There was only one way of redemption, one way in which reparation could be made and the body restored again to the spirit and that was by an infinite atonement, and it had to be made by an infinite Being—someone not subject to death and yet had the power to die.

And so, our Father in heaven sent us his Son, Jesus Christ, into the world with life in himself. And yet, because he had a mother who had blood in her veins, he had the power to die. He could yield up his body to death and then take it again. Let me read his own words:

> Therefore doth my Father love me, because I lay down my life, that I might take it again.
> No man taketh it from me, but I lay it down myself. I have power to lay it down, and I have power to take it again. This commandment have I received of my Father.[4]

---

[4]John 10:17-18.

So he had power to lay down his life, and on the cross he paid the price for our sins, and at the same time for Adam's transgression.

So his infinite atonement resulted in two things, (1) restoration of the body to the spirit, and (2) the redemption of those who accept the gospel of Jesus Christ and who will be loyal in the keeping of his commandments—freedom from their own sins.

What are we going to do? One week from Sunday is the day we celebrate his birthday. Are we going to love him? Are we going to realize the great work he did for us and are we going to be grateful, or are we going to violate his commandments? I am thinking right now of what we are doing in the world.

Many People Show Their Contempt

Sister Smith and I last year passed the liquor store. It was night. The lights were on inside and we could see through the windows, here in our community; and it was so crowded inside that it would be hard for someone else to get in. They were buying liquor so they could celebrate Christmas. What were they doing? They were showing their contempt for their Lord and Master whose day was to be celebrated.

Is that a crime? Yes. Is it not a crime to show contempt for the Son of God? And throughout the world today there will be millions of people carousing, drinking, doing all manner of evil, and to them it is not what it should be to us—a holy day. I would like to read something by Sydney J. Harris entitled, "Would We Believe and Follow?"

If there should be, on Christmas Eve, a second coming—would there not be soon a second crucifixion? And this time, not by the Romans or the Jews, but by those who proudly call themselves Christians?

I wonder. I wonder how we today would regard and treat this man with his strange and frightening and "impractical" doctrines of human behavior and relationships. Would we believe and follow, any more than the masses of people in his day believed and followed?

Would not the militarists among us assail him as a cowardly pacifist because he urges us not to resist evil?

Would not the nationalists among us attack him as a dangerous internationalist because he tells us we are all of one flesh?

Would not the wealthy among us castigate him as a troublemaking radical because he bars the rich from entering the kingdom of heaven?

Would not the liberals among us dismiss him as a dreamy vagabond because he advises us to take no thought for the morrow, to lay up no treasures on earth?

Would not the ecclesiastics among us denounce him as a ranting heretic because he cuts through the core of ritual and commands us only to love God and our neighbors?

Would not the sentimentalists among us deride him as a cynic because he warns us that the way to salvation is narrow and difficult?

Would not the Puritans among us despise and reject him because he eats and drinks with publicans and sinners, prefering the company of winebibbers and harlots to that of "respectable" church members?

Would not the sensual among us scorn him because he fasts for 40 days in the desert, neglecting the needs of the body?

Would not the proud and important among us laugh at him when he instructs the twelve disciples that he who would be "first" should be the one to take the role of the least and serve all?

Would not the worldly-wise and educated among us be aghast to hear that we cannot be saved except we become as children, and that a little child shall lead us?

Would not each of us—in his own way—find some part of this man's sayings and doings to be so threatening to our ways of life, so much at odds with our rooted beliefs, that we could not tolerate him for long?

I wonder.[5]

On Our Knees and Thank the Lord

When we go home tonight let us get on our knees and thank the Lord for his many blessings and our Lord Jesus

[5]*Deseret News* Editorial.

Christ for his mercy and his greatness and goodness for making it possible for us through the keeping of his commandments to go back into the presence of God our Father and dwell with him.—("Know Your Religion Series" sponsored by Brigham Young University, delivered in Seventeenth Ward Chapel, Salt Lake City, Dec. 17, 1966.)

One of the greatest responsibilities that is ever entrusted to any human being is that of building his own personality. The chief business of our lives is to build a house that will bear the weight of eternal life. God has instructed us to use only the finest materials. He cannot look upon sin with the least degree of allowance, because he knows its terrible destructiveness in people's lives.

The Demand for Personal Purity

I am very happy to be here with you today. I hope and pray that I may be able to give you something that will be for your good and the up-building of the kingdom of God.

The demand for personal purity is made by the Church upon both men and women equally. There is no double standard of judgment. "If purity of life is neglected," President Joseph F. Smith once said, "all other dangers set in upon us like the rivers of water when the flood gates are opened."

President Brigham Young was also very emphatic in his denunciation of this evil, and we cannot be too emphatic in denouncing it. It is very prevalent and an almost universal evil. The world is fast coming to its destruction because of it. "Learn the will of God," said President Young, "keep his commandments and do his will, and you will be a virtuous person." How wonderful is the peace and joy which fills the soul of the virtuous person! How terrible are the torments of the unvirtuous! They shall have no place in the first resurrection. When the final judgment comes they are they who remain "filthy still." They cannot enter the Holy City, they are the "dogs, and sorcerers, and whoremongers, and murderers, and idolators, and whosoever loveth and maketh a lie," who are cast out.

Follow the Ways of the Lord

I am sure that if we follow the ways of the Lord our pathways will lead us to doing the right thing. You know the Lord said,

> Know ye not that ye are the temple of God, and that the spirit of God dwelleth in you? If any man defile the temple of God, him shall God destroy; for the temple of God is holy which temple ye are.[1]

And in that same chapter the Apostle Paul said to them, ". . . ye are God's building . . . but, let every man take heed how he buildeth. . . ."[2] One of the greatest responsibilities that is ever entrusted to any human being is that of building his own personality. The chief business of our lives is to build a house that will bear the weight of eternal life. God has instructed us to use only the finest materials. He cannot look upon sin with the least degree of allowance, because he knows its terrible destructiveness in people's lives. God has provided that every man should carry within himself the very things that he seeks, faith, courage and love and we can develop that with which we have already been endowed. We should develop the ability to do "the right thing" instead of allowing ourselves endlessly to do as we please.

He has given us these bodies and told us to keep them clean so that they may be returned to him in purity, then we will receive all that our Father in heaven has to offer us. You remember the story of the prodigal son. He had noble parents, but he was impatient and asked his father to give him the portion of goods that belonged to him. He left his home thinking he could do better, but he wasted

---

[1] I Corinthians 3:16-17.
[2] I Corinthians 3:9-10.

his substance with riotous living. You remember the story how he returned and they gave a feast for him, and the older brother was upset, but the wise father said to the older son: "Son thou art ever with me, and ALL that I have is thine."[3] Is not that a glorious promise? That is what the Lord has promised us if we live as he has commanded us to do. He said we would become heirs of the celestial kingdom and become his sons and daughters.

We learn that there is rejoicing in heaven over every sinner who repents; but those who are faithful and transgress not any of the commandments, shall inherit ALL that our Father hath,"[4] while those who might be sons and daughters but through their riotous living waste their inheritance, may come back through their repentance to salvation to be servants, not to inherit exaltation as sons and daughters of God. Some people think that wealth of worldly goods is all that they need, others want power and position among their fellow men, but there is one inheritance which is worth more than all, it is the inheritance of eternal exaltation.

Joint Heirs with Jesus Christ

The scriptures say that eternal life is the greatest gift of God, and only those shall receive it who are cleansed from all sin. We find that in Section 76 of the Doctrine and Covenants. Is it not wonderful to know that if we keep the commandments of the Lord we will be joint-heirs with Jesus Christ, possessing "all that the Father hath"? I am sure we all want to live so that we may receive these blessings. You know that the record does not tell us about the later life of the prodigal son, if he really learned his lesson. We all excuse our actions during trouble or a crisis. Yet the crisis does not cause the trouble, it only reveals it. Sins,

---

[3]Luke 15:11-32.
[4]D&C 84:38.

like everything else, have offspring. Sins usually do not come singly. Weaknesses and sins feed upon themselves. Each repetition makes the path of least resistance easier to follow. All around us we can see good and evil side by side, and the Lord went to great pains to provide us with opposites. I would like to quote from the *New Dictionary of Thoughts*. "WOMAN—A beautiful and chaste woman is the perfect workmanship of God, the true glory of angels, the rare miracle of earth, and the sole wonder of the world." —Hermes.

When the millennium is ushered in, the earth is to pass through a cleansing. This will not be the final cleansing when the earth shall be consumed and pass away to be renewed again a celestial globe, but it will be the end of unrighteousness. All who have lived the telestial law, will be swept off the face of the earth. All of these will be cast down to hell where they will remain until Christ shall subdue all enemies under his feet and shall have perfected his work. During the thousand years, all of these persons will be in this torment of mind, having ample time to reflect on their misdeeds and receive training in obedience to law, so that they may be prepared to come forth in the resurrection at the end of the world.

Conditions during the Millennium

It will be impossible for the people of this class to remain on the earth during the millennium, for they would be as much out of their element as a fish out of water. The changed condition of the earth, which will be a terrestrial order during this thousand years, will be suited to the capacity of those of the terrestrial world as well as those who have kept the celestial law; and they will have part in the first resurrection.

But with those of the telestial order, this will not be so. These are they who are as stubble, who will be consumed when Christ comes. They will know that Christ has come and that on the earth he reigns in peace and righteousness. They will know that they have lost all of this because of their wickedness; and during the thousand years they will be in torment with their sins, looking forward to the final judgment with fear and trembling.

Yet their punishment will be for their good. The Lord will not punish them merely because he is angry and delights in their suffering. Their suffering must be met, for they will have denied the mercies of Jesus Christ and therefore must suffer, even as he suffered for the sins of the world, for his suffering will not cleanse them. It will be a punishment of cleansing; and when they have paid the price—and it will be a most dreadful, painful ordeal—then will they be prepared to receive such blessings as the Lord, in his great mercy, is prepared to give to them. That is, they must learn to serve him and be obedient to his laws, such as they are worthy to receive. Those who receive punishment in this manner will constitute a countless multitude. And they shall be servants of the Most High; but where God and Christ dwell they cannot come, worlds without end, for they shall be judged according to their works, and every man shall receive according to his own works, his own dominion in the mansions which are prepared.[5]

Now I have my own idea, and I am sure that it is right, because the Lord told us that our secret acts would be heralded from the housetops—I have in mind that we will be judged according to our works, and that it will be shown as on a screen, just as we watch television, and our acts will appear to us just as they were in life. We will not be able to say, "No, I did not do that," because it will be portrayed right before us; and we will, I am sure agree with the Lord. We will see that he is just. You will remember that the Lord said that we would be judged out of what was

_____
[5]D&C 76:111-112.

written in the books. I take that to mean the standard works of the Church. Then he said there would be another book that would be opened, and that would be the Book of Life, and we would be judged out of what was written in that book.

I am here to tell you, that if you follow the teachings of your parents and pray to our Father in heaven, I can promise you that you will not do anything that will keep you out of the kingdom of God. Be true and faithful, and as I have said before do not forget to pray and remember what our Father in heaven has said, "I, the Lord, am bound when ye do what I say; but when ye do not what I say, ye have no promise."[6]—(Talk given to the Mia Maids from Rexburg, Idaho, October 19, 1968.)

---

[6]D&C 82:10.

*I wonder how pleased we are that we are
members of The Church of Jesus Christ of
Latter-day Saints. If we have the right understanding, this is the greatest gift so far as mortality is concerned that can be given to us—
membership in the kingdom of God, his divinely appointed Church.*

Be Worthy of the Guidance of the Holy Spirit

My good brethren and sisters, I wonder how pleased we are to know that we are members of The Church of Jesus Christ of Latter-day Saints. If we have the right understanding, this is the greatest gift so far as mortality is concerned that can be given to us—membership in the kingdom of God, his divinely appointed Church.

There are a great many people—I am told—a number of people scattered throughout the world who are devout, sincere, who are doing the best they know, and they think they are following the commandments of our Lord and Redeemer, but they are following the teachings, the philosophy that has come down for hundreds of years—the doctrine of men. And they do not have the gift of the Holy Ghost and therefore they lack discernment.

I am fearful that a great many members of The Church of Jesus Christ of Latter-day Saints are in that same category. They do not know. They have been taught from their infancy that this is the kingdom of God, but they have not lived in accord with its principles sufficiently to have the guidance of the Holy Spirit. They have been baptized for the remission of sins and had hands laid upon their heads for the receiving of the Holy Ghost, but unfortunately they have never received a manifestation except that following their baptism and confirmation, the reason being because they do not study. They do not think. These are things of the kingdom of God and their minds are set too much on the things of this world.

The fact that a person is a member of The Church of Jesus Christ of Latter-day Saints does not insure his salvation. He has to keep himself in touch with these sacred principles and know them and live them. In my travels from state to state as I have done for these many years in all parts of the world, I find members of the Church who are indifferent, careless, and who can not say definitely with any true knowledge of any such manifestation that this is the kingdom of God. They have not lived for it.

Not Merely a Code of Laws

The gospel of Jesus Christ is not merely a code of laws. it has more than that. It requires a spirit of humility, of faith, and a prayerful disposition. I could make a guess, and I do not think I would be too far out if I did say that one-half of the members of the Church have not read the Book of Mormon. I mean those who are old enough to read, and one-half of them have never read the Book of Mormon. I would like someone to challenge me on that if he can prove I am wrong. But the fact remains that too many of us take our membership as a matter of course. We do not study. We do not attend to the ordinary duties the Lord requires of us, and therefore we do not have an abiding testimony of the truth.

Now each of you can ask yourself a question: whether you have received the gift of the Holy Ghost of the knowledge of the truth of this revealed plan of salvation. I am

going to read a few passages from the 13th chapter of
Matthew:

> Again, the kingdom of heaven is like unto treasure hid in a field;
> the which when a man hath found, he hideth, and for joy thereof
> goeth and selleth all that he hath, and buyeth that field.[1]

How many of us think enough of the gospel of Jesus
Christ if we were faced with that situation would give all
we have, as far as this world is concerned, for the kingdom
of God? We have a great many people who would. There
are those who would sacrifice everything they have. There
are some who would lay down their lives willingly if need be,
but we could be far more devout than we are.

My good brethren are going around throughout the
stakes right now and appointing men and sending them out
to do home teaching. Why is it necessary to send anybody
out to do home teaching? The Lord gave us a plan for
home teaching; but the fact remains that the responsibility
for teaching a family is the father's in the home. How
many fathers, Latter-day Saint fathers, periodically and
frequently, are holding a little family meeting — getting
their children together, sitting down with them, having a
prayer, a blessing, and there discussing the beauties and
the blessings of the gospel of Jesus Christ?

The Lord Gave Us a Perfect Plan

Now we are appointing men and taking them away
from the position of stake president because we feel it so
necessary for them to go through the stakes of Zion to train
brethren to go into the homes and teach people—members
of the Church what their responsibilities are. The Lord gave
us a perfect plan if we follow it.

When I interviewed missionaries—we don't interview
them any more—but when I did, I used to ask them some

---

[1]Matthew 13:44.

questions about their home life. (We leave it all now to the presidents of stakes and bishops of wards.) I used to ask them something about family matters—if they had family meetings; if they had family prayer night and morning. Sometimes these missionaries would say, yes, we have prayer in the morning. We do not have any prayer at night because we get scattered and cannot come together at night. But many of them say no, we never have family prayer. I went to the home of a stake president. I should not tell you this. It was not here. If it were here, I would not say it. It was some distance from here. In the morning when I was ready to leave, the table was set and all chairs were at the table. They were turned with their backs to the table, and one little fellow gave it away. He said, "Dad, what have you got all the chairs turned that way for?" There was silence outside of heaven.

Let me read these other verses to you:

> Again, the kingdom of heaven is like unto a merchant man seeking goodly pearls:
> Who, when he had found one pearl of great price, went and sold all that he had, and bought it.
> Again, the kingdom of heaven is like unto a net, that was cast into the sea, and gathered of every kind:
> Which, when it was full, they drew to shore, and sat down, and gathered the good into vessels, but cast the bad away.[2]

That reminds me of the day that is coming called the day of judgment. Let me read that once more.

> Again the kingdom of heaven is like unto a net, which was cast into the sea, and gathered of every kind:
> Which, when it was full, they drew to shore, and sat down, and gathered the good into vessels, but cast the bad away.

We do not cast the bad away. They go away of their own accord, many of them. Of course we do cast them away because we have to excommunicate them eventually.

---

[2]Matthew 13:45-48.

Parables of the Savior

Now these are parables of the Savior in regard to the Church of Jesus Christ. We have in the Church all kinds. Most of them, I think I can say, are true and loyal, and I feel, who would die for the Church, who if called upon would give everything they had. We have some in the Church who are not of that character. If we love the truth as we ought to love it, we would attend to our meetings, especially the sacrament meeting where we come to renew our covenants by a simple little act of enormous consequence. The person who absents himself from a sacrament meeting week after week and month after month, and nothing prevents him from coming, is not loyal to the truth. He does not love it. If he did, he would be present to partake of these emblems—just a little piece of bread, a little cup of water. He would want to do that to show his love for the truth and his loyal service to the Son of God. This is just a little, simple thing, is it not? I hope that when we hear the priests at the table blessing these emblems, we have a full understanding of the significance of the blessing upon the bread and blessing upon the water.

Why do we partake of it? Anciently they drank wine. They did that here for a time, and I think the Lord was wise when he said that wine was not necessary. We had a better attendance at meetings when we had wine; and I have been informed that where it was done, not only a better attendance, but it took more wine than it does water. But the Lord said we could use water. Why not? Pure water to represent the blood of the Son of God.

I wonder if we ever stop to think of the anguish of soul that came to our Eternal Father when, of necessity, his Son had to go through a terrific torment, suffering, anguish of soul, then hang nailed to a cross until he died in order that we might receive salvation in the kingdom of God. I have tried to think of that dreadful day, with our Father in heaven sitting there knowing all that was going on and knowing the anguish of soul and the torment—physical torment as well as the mental torment—under which his Son was going and yet do nothing about it.

I want to read to you a few of the Savior's words:

But, behold, I say unto you that I, the Lord God, gave unto Adam and unto his seed, that they should not die as to the temporal death, until I, the Lord God, should send forth angels to declare unto them repentance and redemption, through faith on the name of mine Only Begotten Son.

And thus did I, the Lord God, appoint unto man the days of his probation—that by his natural death he might be raised in immortality unto eternal life even as many as would believe.[3]

In other words, the Son of God was sent down here to go through his mission for the salvation of man, to go through all that anguish of soul and torment in order that we might live and have eternal life and come back into the presence of our Eternal Father.

Well, the Savior came. He performed his mission. He went through that terrific torment that we might have eternal life. How much do we appreciate what he did?

Christ Wast Tested to the Finish

I sit down at various times and open my scriptures and begin to read in the New Testament the accounts written by Matthew, by Mark, and Luke about those dreadful days when the Savior was taken and when he went through terrible anguish of soul, and his Father withdrew from him and left him entirely alone. He had to be tested to the finish. What for? That you and I might receive salvation in the kingdom of God and be crowned with crowns and become kings and queens, priests and priestesses in the kingdom of God.

---

[3]D&C 29:42-43.

If we love the Lord as we say we do, as we think maybe we do, then we ought to be willing to abide by every word that he has given us by way of commandment. We ought to be grateful for that which he did.

What he did for us no one else could have done. It required a sacrifice by the shedding of blood of a Son of God. And in the shedding of his blood, he gave back what was given to Adam in the Garden of Eden when be became mortal. He gave back his blood. Blood is the mortal element of the human body. That is, it is the life-giving fluid. It is a wonderful thing, but it is mortal. There will be no blood in the body in the resurrection. We leave our blood here. We do not take it with us; and since Adam received it through the fall, the Savior gave it back through his crucifixion. He paid the debt.

Brethren and sisters, when I stop to think of the Savior, the Son of God, shedding his blood in a manner that was cruel as anything I can imagine—and I don't think anything was more cruel than to die by being nailed to a cross, and yet it was necessary for him to go through all of that. Why? Because, as we sing, he so loved the world, our Father so loved the world, that he gave his only begotten Son to be a sacrifice. There are some things we do not fully understand. But the scriptures tell us definitely—the Book of Mormon, as well as the Bible—that it was essential that one who was without sin and not subject to mortality should die by the shedding of blood to bring redemption to all creation—not just to man. But when Adam and Eve became mortal it was not a sin. They had to—but when that happened, this whole earth was changed and everything upon it from the condition in which it was without death, and death came into this world on every living thing and upon the earth itself. And even this earth has to die. The scriptures tell us that. We read that every living thing will die, but they are all going to live again because the Savior redeemed them. Redeemed the earth? Yes. He redeemed this earth and it is going to receive a resurrection. It will become a glorious place, and our Lord and Savior will dwell here.

Now just another word. We are getting nearer to the resurrection than anybody thinks. I do not know when it is coming. No man knows it. The Lord is not going to tell me nor you nor a single soul. Not one. He is going to catch us when we are all napping or doing something else. He is going to take us by surprise. This is what I think when he is going to come—on a beautiful Sunday afternoon in the summer time when the people—the members of the Church and everybody else—are picnicking in the canyons, and to the lake, or some other resort; on vacation and having a wonderful time doing everything but what the Lord commanded us to do. It may be in a picture show. It will be a Sunday afternoon and then the cry will sound, "Go ye out to meet him," and oh, what scurrying and what confusion there will be.

Now do you not think that is about how it is going to be? He is going to take us by surprise when we are not thinking. What could be better than in the summer time, a beautiful day — Sunday — instead of being in meeting where we ought to be, the people will be in the canyons and resorts, on picnics, and in picture shows—everywhere but where they ought to be. Then the cry will come, "Go ye out to meet him." A very few will be ready. And I can just see in my mind's eye the confusion, the scampering, the hurrying that will come upon people when the angel of the Lord announces the coming of the Son of God.

Brethren and sisters, let us live in accord with his word today and tomorrow and the next day—not with any feeling of fear that we might be caught, but because we love to do the things he has commanded us.

Now I can say truthfully and definitely that there is not anything in this world that can bring the joy and the peace and the satisfaction that comes through obedience to the gospel of Jesus Christ.—(Remarks in the Salt Lake Eighteenth Ward, December 22, 1963.)

Brethren and sisters—parents in Zion—it is your solemn duty to be in attendance regularly at the sacrament service of the Church, and the obligation is also upon you to see that your children who are given into your charge by their Heavenly Father are also there.

Importance of Sacrament Meetings
in the Church

On the night that our Lord observed the feast of the Passover with his Apostles, and immediately preceding his betrayal, he instituted the ordinance of the sacrament. Luke gives the account of this in the following words:

> And he took bread, and gave thanks, and brake it, and gave unto them, saying, This is my body which is given for you: this do in remembrance of me.
>
> Likewise also the cup after supper, saying, This cup is the new testament in my blood, which is shed for you.[1]

Paul, admonishing the Corinthian Saints to be faithful in the observance of this ordinance and rebuking them for their unfaithfulness, has also said:

> That the Lord Jesus the same night in which he was betrayed took bread:
>
> And when he had given thanks, he brake it, and said, Take, eat; This is my body, which is broken for you: this do in remembrance of me.
>
> After the same manner also he took the cup, when he had supped, saying, This cup is the new testament in my blood; this do ye, as oft as ye drink it, in remembrance of me.

[1]Luke 22:19-20.

For as often as ye eat this bread, and drink this cup, ye do shew the Lord's death till he come.

Wherefore, whosoever shall eat this bread, and drink this cup of the Lord, unworthily, shall be guilty of the body and blood of the Lord.

But let a man examine himself, and so let him eat of that bread, and drink of that cup.

For he that eateth and drinketh unworthily, eateth and drinketh damnation to himself, not discerning the Lord's body.[2]

Expedient to Meet Together Often

In the present dispensation, at the time of the organization of the Church, the Lord said: "It is expedient that the church meet together often to partake of bread and wine in the remembrance of the Lord Jesus."[3] Then follows the exact words which are to be used in blessing the bread and the wine, or water, which by revelation has been substituted for wine. To meet together often for this purpose is a requirement made of members of the Church which is just as binding upon them in its observance as the requirement in relation to any other principle or ordinance of the gospel. No member of the Church, who refuses to observe this sacred ordinance, can retain the inspiration and guidance of the Holy Ghost. It is as true today as it was in the days of Paul, that many members of the Church are weak and sickly, in spirit and body, and many sleep, because they have failed to show their love for, and obedience to, the Lord Jesus Christ in the keeping of this commandment.

Ingratitude is the most prevalent of all sins; it is also one of the greatest. Jesus Christ came into the world, not to do the will of man, but to do the will of his Father, and he said, "For God so loved the world, that he gave his only begotten Son, that whosoever believeth in him should not perish, but have everlasting life."[4] The love of our Savior

---

[2]I Corinthians 11:23-29.
[3]D&C 20:75.
[4]John 3:16.

was equally as great, and because of it he was willing to suffer and die, that he might bring to all men the resurrection, and eternal life to those who were willing to believe and obey his gospel.

In remembrance of this great act of infinite love, which has been the means of redeeming a fallen world, those who profess his name show their gratitude and likewise "the Lord's death until he come," by observing this holy ordinance. But the ordinance means more than this. When we eat the bread and drink the water we covenant that we will eat and drink in remembrance of the sacrifice which he made for us in the breaking of his body and the shedding of his blood; that we are willing to take upon us the name of the Son; that we will always remember him; that we will always keep his commandments which he has given us. In this act we witness to the Father by solemn covenant in the name of the Son, that we will do all of these things. Through our faithfulness to these covenants, we are promised that we will always have the Spirit of the Lord to be with us to guide us in all truth and righteousness.

Words of President George Q. Cannon

How can a man who refuses to meet often with his fellow worshipers to keep this commandment have a claim upon the guidance and the blessings of the Lord? Yet strange to say, there are those who seemingly have this false understanding. President George Q. Cannon, many years ago, declared:

The Lord has commanded his people to meet together oft and eat and drink in remembrance of him, of his sufferings and death, and to witness unto the Father that they are willing to keep his commandments which he has given them. . . . Yet there are members of the Church who seem to attach no particular importance to these meetings. They will allow weeks, yes and months, to pass without having the least anxiety or desire to avail themselves of the privilege of partaking of the Lord's Supper. Can there be any wonder at such people being barren, spiritless and indifferent about the work of the Lord: They neglect the means which the Lord has provided for the nourishing of their spiritual natures, and they are in a state of spiritual starvation—a starvation which is as fatal in its effects upon the spirit as the continued refusal to eat food has upon the natural body. No Latter-day Saint who places proper value upon his standing before the Lord will be guilty of this neglect.[5]

President Anthon H. Lund, at the General Conference of the Church, April 4, 1920, which was eleven months before his death, also said:

Now, brethren and sisters, we cannot develop in godliness without going to the meetings. We should be present to hear the servants of God and to partake of the sacrament of the Lord, and renew our covenants with him, showing that we are willing to take upon us his name and keep his commandments. It gives us strength to do so; but by staying away from sacrament meetings, we gradually grow careless, and we think that we cannot be edified by attending them. Do not go to meeting just because a good speaker is going to talk, but go to the meeting as the Lord has commanded that on the Sabbath day we should go to the house of prayer and offer our oblations to the Almighty. Do not let us be lacking in this nor in other duties.

Requirement Made of All Members

This requirement is made of all members of the Church. None are exempt or excused, except it be on account of disability due to sickness or disease. Neither is there any age limit. Many years ago the privilege of administering the sacrament in the Sunday School was granted as it was thought that here the children would be taught reverence for this sacred ordinance. This innovation, however, does not excuse or exempt, and was never intended so to do, any members of the Church from attendance at the regularly appointed sacramental service. This commandment is for all members of the Church, both old and young, the halt, the blind, the deaf and all who are physically able to attend.

---

[5]*Juvenile Instructor*, Vol. 28:89.

The fact that this ordinance has been granted to the Sunday Schools has caused the feeling to grow up among some members of the Church that the children are excused from the regular sacrament service, but this is not the case. "Remember now thy Creator," we read in the scriptures, "in the days of thy youth, while the evil days come not, nor the years draw nigh, when thou shalt say, I have no pleasure in them."[6] And Malachi declares: "Then they that feared the Lord spake often one to another; and the Lord hearkened, and heard it, and a book of remembrance was written before him for them that feared the Lord, and that thought upon his name."[7] So it shall be today, a book of remembrance shall be kept for all those who honor the Lord in the covenants required of us in the ordinance of the sacrament.

Among the Nephites, at the time when their souls had been fully charged with faith due to the personal visit of the Lord, it is written that they found pleasure in walking after the commandments which they had received, and "continued in fasting and prayer, and in meeting together oft both to pray and to hear the word of the Lord."[8] Moreover, their small children were blessed with remarkable manifestations. The Lord has set the age of accountability at eight years. At this age children are to be baptized and thus become entitled to all blessings as members of the Church. A child who has become a member of the Church through baptism is under the same commandment—for it is to all members of the Church—to attend the regularly established sacramental meetings.

Duty of Parents in Zion

Any man who thinks himself to be devout and who is faithful in his own personal attendance at these meetings, but who neglects this duty in behalf of his children, permit-

---

[6]Ecclesiastes 12:1.
[7]Malachi 3:16.
[8]4 Nephi, verse 12.

ting them to run the streets, or otherwise occupy their time
contrary to the way the Lord has commanded, is guilty of
a transgression.   Has not the Lord emphatically declared
that it is the duty of parents in Zion or any of her stakes
to teach their children the doctrines of the kingdom, and if
they neglect this important duty the sin shall be upon the
heads of the parents?

In what better way can parents teach their children
than by example?   Where can the children be instructed
in the ways of the Lord any better than in their attendance
at these sacred meetings?   Yet it is too frequently the case
that the younger members of the Church are absent from
the sacramental meetings.   We are not justified in thinking
that if the children attend the Sunday School, and there
partake of the bread and water in remembrance of the body
and blood of our Redeemer, that they have fulfilled their
duty.   The Lord has required them—as members of the
Church—to be in attendance at the constituted meeting
which he has himself ordained and appointed for the benefit and salvation of all members of his Church.

There is nothing complicated in the plan of salvation
that little children cannot understand.   Some churches have
clouded their doctrines with mysteries and symbolic ceremonies which even adults cannot comprehend, but this is
all foreign to the gospel of Jesus Christ.   Otherwise our
Savior would have placed the year of accountability at the
age of twenty-one or some other period when the mind is
mature and not at eight years of age.   Brethren and sisters
—parents in Zion—it is your solemn duty to be in attendance regularly at the sacramental service of the Church,
and the obligation is also upon you to see that your children who are given into your charge by their Heavenly
Father are also there.

I appeal to you good members who teach our young people in Primary, Mutual, and Sunday School: Let us try to get them to realize the need of serving the Lord, to feel when they go into these meetinghouses that the Savior is really there. I think reverence is a duty which devolves upon us as members of the Church.

How Do We Teach Reverence?

Of all the people on the face of the earth, the Latter-day Saints ought to be the most reverent. We know more; we have far better understanding of salvation and of the mission of Jesus Christ. Yet we are not reverent the way we ought to be. I think that we have faith; we believe the gospel of Jesus Christ; we are convinced of the great mission which he performed. But we certainly have fallen down when it comes to being reverent.

We go into the world and make converts and bring them to our meetings where they find that we are very disorderly. That disorderliness is misunderstood, because we do have faith in our hearts. We believe in the mission of Jesus Christ. But we come into our meetings helter-skelter, particularly our youngsters in Primary, Mutual, and Sunday School.

Now, I do not go to churches in the world very often, but I have been in some of them. The people come in quietly and take their seats. They do not have the gospel, but they have been trained, when they come to a place of worship, to treat it like a place of worship. We bubble over with a fulness of spirits, that is the natural spirit which is within us; and so we come in disorderly.

A Wonderful Responsibility

Our sisters who teach our children in Primary have a wonderful responsibility. Of course, primarily, reverence begins in the home; that is where it should begin. The conduct of fathers and mothers should be such that the children would show that sort of spirit and be taught by their parents the sacredness of holy places, of places of worship, and the greatness and the holiness of the gospel of Jesus Christ and its ordinances. We cannot begin too young to teach these things to our children. If they are taught properly in the home, they are more likely to behave themselves properly when they come into a place of worship.

Meetinghouses Dedicated to the Lord

We dedicate our meetinghouses as places of worship. We dedicate them to the Lord. We have solemn services when we dedicate a meetinghouse. We bless that house for every good and holy purpose, that it might be a place of worship, a place where we can come to bear witness of the truth, to be instructed and guided, a place where we can receive knowledge of the saving principles of the gospel of Jesus Christ. Then should we not come into these buildings with a little more of the spirit of prayer in our hearts? If we refrained from shouting, greeted our friends —kindly of course, and respectfully—and quietly took our seats, do you not think that our influence would be far greater? Do you not think the Lord himself would be more pleased if we would do it that way, rather than doing it the way we do it nearly everywhere throughout the Church?

We do treat our temples with proper respect, reverently. When people go into the temples of the Lord, so far as I know—and I think I know a good deal about it—they go into the temples quietly. There is no laughter, no cracking of jokes, no shouting. We go in, and if we see our friends we may shake hands with them. Then we sit down quietly, and there we do a little reflecting. And where is there a better place to sit and reflect upon the mission of Jesus Christ, on our own salvation and how it can be obtained, on the glorious principles of the gospel? To be thinking things of this kind while the people are getting ready before the bishop is ready to get up and open the meeting with a few words of kindly greeting, we have, I think, quite a long way to go.

Now, we have more faith than the people in the world, because we have the guidance of the Holy Ghost to teach us, and they do not. But down through the ages, they have been taught to be reverent in their churches. They come in reverently, no matter what is in their hearts. It may be just a form; the sermon may mean nothing to them. At the same time they do these things in an orderly fashion, that is, in most of these places they do.

Reverence Is a Sacred Principle

Reverence is a sacred principle. It is a principle of the gospel. We show reverence to our Father in Heaven, to the Lord Jesus Christ. We would not be boisterous in his presence. If he happened to be in this meeting, I am sure we would all go in quietly and take our places. Why cannot we think, when we enter the place of worship, that he is there? He is there by his spirit, and we should feel, "The Spirit of the Lord is here." When we dedicate a meetinghouse we pray that the Spirit of the Lord may dwell in the building so that all who come may feel his presence. But we do not always carry that out in our actions.

I appeal to you good members who teach our young people in Primary, Mutual, and Sunday School: Let us try to get them to realize the need of serving the Lord, to feel when they go into these meetinghouses that the Savior is really there. I think reverence is a duty which devolves upon us as members of the Church.

Let me call attention to a few things that might help us, if they are impressed upon our minds. First of all, we should enter the buildings in a spirit of prayer. This is the house of the Lord. Why am I coming here? To be taught. Taught what? Things pertaining to salvation, things that will help me to live in accordance with the principles of eternal salvation. So we enter the building in a spirit of prayer. Tell your kiddies, your Primary children, to come into the meetings, into Primary classes, in that spirit. Tell it to your young men and women in Mutual, and see if they can not come into a building more reverently.

Duty to Teach the Mission of Christ

Another thing, the greater our knowledge concerning the kingdom of God, the mission of Jesus Christ, the plan of salvation that we have, the more likely we are to be humble and prayerful in our worship. So it is our duty to teach the mission of Jesus Christ. Why did he come? What did he do for us? How are we benefited? What did it cost him to do it? Why it cost his life, yes, more than his life! What did he do besides being nailed on the cross? Why was he nailed there? He was nailed there that his blood might be shed to redeem us from this most terrible penalty that could ever come, banishment from the presence of God. He died on the cross to bring us back again, to have our bodies and spirits reunited. He gave us that privilege. If we will only believe in him and keep his commandments, he died for us that we might receive a remission of our sins and not be called upon to pay penalty. He paid the price.

If we can impress all these things as we ought to upon the minds of the children, they will grow up with a more reverent spirit. Instill gratitude into their souls by teaching them the mission of Christ and his love for us. How grateful we ought to be for the mission of Jesus Christ! How we ought to love him above everything in the world, because he came and died, voluntarily, the most excruciating, the most terrible of deaths because he loved us, and because he wanted to save us from that awful condition of eternal death and bring us back into the presence of God our Father to receive the blessings of his kingdom. All that, he volunteered to do. If we could impress these things upon the minds of both young and old and teach them that it is their duty to have gratitude in their hearts for Jesus Christ, for our Father in Heaven, perhaps we could teach them that we should be extremely humble in our hearts which should be filled with everlasting love for him; and reverence would result.

Our Father in Heaven has a perfect right to tell us, as our first commandment, to love him, and to serve him. If we love him, we are going to love Jesus Christ, for no man could do what he did for us. He did not have to die, he could have refused. He did it voluntarily. He did it because it was a commandment from his Father. He knew what the suffering was going to be; and yet, because of his love for us, he was willing to do it. Can not we think of things like this when we enter our churches.

The Least Part of Savior's Suffering

The driving of the nails into his hands and into the Savior's feet was the least part of his suffering. We get into the habit, I think, of feeling, or thinking that his great suffering was being nailed to the cross and left to hang there. Well, that was a period in the world's history when thousands of men suffered that way. So his suffering, so far as that is concerned, was not any more than the suffering of other men who have been so crucified. What, then, was his great suffering? I wish that we could impress this fact upon the minds of every member of this Church: His great suffering occurred before he ever went to the cross.   It was in the Garden of Gethsemane, so the scriptures tell us, that blood oozed from every pore of his body; and in the extreme agony of his soul, he cried to his Father.   It was not the nails driven into his hands and feet.   Now do not ask me how that was done because I do not know. Nobody knows. All we know is that in some way he took upon himself that extreme penalty.   He took upon him our transgressions, and paid a price, a price of torment.

Think of the Savior carrying the united burden of every individual—torment—in some way which I say, I cannot understand; I just accept—which caused him to suffer an agony of pain, compared to which the driving of nails in his hands and feet was very little.   He cried, in his anguish, to his Father, "If it be possible, let this cup pass!" and it could not pass.   Let me read you just a word or two here of what the Lord says in regard to that:

> For behold, I, God, have suffered these things for all, that they might not suffer if they would repent;
> But if they would not repent they must suffer even as I;
> Which suffering caused myself, even God, the greatest of all, to tremble because of the pain, and to bleed at every pore, and to suffer both body and spirit—and would that I might not drink the bitter cup, and shrink—
> Nevertheless, glory be to the Father, and I partook and finished my preparations unto the children of men.[1]

When I read that it humbles me.   His love for humanity, for the world, was so great that he was willing to carry a burden that no mortal man could carry, and pay an awful price that no other person ever could have paid, that we might escape.   If we could just get our people to understand that, do you not think they are going to love the Lord Jesus Christ?   And if they love him, do you not

---

[1]D&C 19:16-19.

think they are going to be more reverent, and more humble, more willing to abide in his commandments, and walk more humbly? It seems to me so.

Sad to say, there are many members in the Church who do not understand this. They have never visualized as much as it is in our power to visualize the great torment and suffering that the Savior passed through. Of course, we never will understand it, because we are not passing through it. I have seen big strong men, who were not afraid of anything outdoors, cry and tremble and plead for forgiveness of sins that they had committed. Seeing them in the anguish of their souls would just wring your heart; and, yet, that is only one, just one individual. Think of the burden of all that was forced on the Savior Jesus Christ. These are the things that we overlook. If we could keep such things in our minds all the time, I think we would be more reverent.

A Thought on Obedience

One more thought, and that is on obedience. I have heard our Primary, Mutual, and Sunday School teachers ask the young people if they would be more quiet. We ought not to have to ask them. We do not use any drastic measures. We would not if we could, would we? We have to do the whole thing in the spirit of love, and with reason. We have to reason with them, make them understand the sacredness of our buildings, the sacredness of our own lives —that we should keep them clean—the greatness of the mission of Jesus Christ. If we could just get them to feel that his Spirit is there with us when we come together into our meetings, there would not be any boisterous conduct.

I would not like to see our people come into a meetinghouse as if they were going to a funeral. I want them to come into the house smiling, happy. I want them to be able to greet their neighbors, but to do it quietly, in a proper spirit, not by shouting across a number of rows of seats or something of that kind. I want them to come in quietly. We have the habit of assembling in the foyer, if we have one, before the meeting is called; and there we engage in pretty loud conduct and conversation, so that if one wanted to say something to his neighbor he would almost have to shout to tell him. Why can we not come in quietly, hang up our wraps and take our places?" Yes, greet those who are there; but do it quietly and in the spirit of reverence.

Of all places and times in the world when we ought to be reverent, it is when we partake of the sacrament. I have been on the stand looking down over a congregation when members were partaking of the sacrament and have seen people take gum out of their mouths, while they took the piece of bread, and then put the gum back into their mouths. And when the water comes they never stop to take the gum out at all. Do you think that shows a reverent spirit? I do not think it shows a reverent spirit to bring gum and chew it in a sacrament meeting at anytime, or in any other meeting. But I have seen it done.

I have seen two members of the Church sitting together, enter into a conversation, stop long enough for the blessing to be asked on the water or on the bread, then start again on their conversation. Sometimes they even enter into conversation, laughing and talking to each other, while somebody is speaking from the stand. That is shocking to me, and I am sure it is to the Lord. These are the things we have to overcome, and you teachers can do a wonderful work in this regard.

Oh, if we could only understand that by the shedding of his blood, he bought us. We belong to him. He has a right to tell us what to do and what not to do, and to command us to keep his commandments; however, we have our agency, and we act for ourselves.

The Sin of Ingratitude

On one occasion, we read in the scriptures, a young lawyer came to the Savior with a question tempting him and saying:

Master, which is the great commandment in the law?
Jesus said unto him, Thou shalt love the Lord thy God with all thy heart, and with all thy soul, and with all thy mind.
This is the first and great commandment.
And the second is like unto it, Thou shalt love thy neighbour as thyself.
On these two commandments hang all the law and the prophets.[1]

If we will observe this first law, the second naturally will follow, and in fact, as the Savior has pointed it out, we will not be guilty of a breech of the law and the prophets in anything else.

Eternal Life

Jesus Christ came into this world with a definite mission as the Savior of men and the Redeemer of the world. When Nicodemus came to the Savior, making inquiry, and he came by night because he was afraid of the Jews, but

---

[1]Matthew 22:36-40.

believing in Jesus Christ, he asked him some questions. The Savior gave him some definite instruction in regard to baptism by water and by the spirit, and in the course of the remarks, the Savior said this:

And as Moses lifted up the serpent in the wilderness, even so must the Son of man be lifted up:

That whosoever believeth in him should not perish, but have eternal life.

For God so loved the world, that he gave his only begotten Son, that whosoever believeth in him should not perish, but have everlasting life.

For God sent not his Son into the world to condemn the world; but that the world through him might be saved.

He that believeth on him is not condemned: but he that believeth not is condemned already, because he hath not believed in the name of the only begotten Son of God.

And this is the condemnation, that light is come into the world, and men loved darkness rather than light, because their deeds were evil.

For every one that doeth evil hateth the light, neither cometh to the light, lest his deeds should be reproved.

But he that doeth truth cometh to the light, that his deeds may be made manifest, that they are wrought in God.[2]

Then the Savior adds:

He that believeth on the Son hath everlasting life: and he that believeth not the Son shall not see life; but the wrath of God abideth on him.[3]

Atonement of Christ

Now, may I spend a few minutes presenting before us what we all know to be the truth, that Jesus Christ came into this world to die. That was his mission. By that death upon the cross and through the shedding of his blood, to bring redemption, twofold, first, to redeem man from Adam's transgression, to restore them again to life, to

---

[2]John 3:14-21.
[3]John 3:36.

destroy death, gain the victory, which apparently Satan had won through the transgression of Adam. In some manner which I cannot fully explain and which you cannot fully explain, there was a necessity for an infinite atonement, and God dying for a fallen world. That had to be by the shedding of blood, and his blood only could be shed to restore again that life which had been taken away, and bring back again to men the power to live forever. And through his death there comes to us universally, to every living creature, a resurrection of the dead. The Lord does not ask us whether we want to be redeemed from death or not. We were not responsible for it, and therefore, it is not held against us; it is not to our charge. As Paul has said:

For as in Adam all die, even so in Christ shall all be made alive.[4]

That is the free gift of God the Eternal Father, through Jesus Christ, his Son, to every living soul, men, women, children, from the fall of Adam to the end of time.

Now that is a wonderful gift. It comes without our asking. It comes to the wicked as well as to the righteous. In the fifth chapter of John the Lord speaks to the people of the time coming, and he says it was already here, when the dead should hear the voice of the Son of God and they who heard should live. Yes, not only those who heard it, that is, received his truth, for he added this, when they marveled at what he had to say:

Marvel not at this: for the hour is coming, in the which all that are in the graves shall hear his voice,
And shall come forth; they that have done good, unto the resurrection of life; and they that have done evil, unto the resurrection of damnation.[5]

Here is the word of the Lord himself that he was going to carry the message to the dead; they would all hear; they

---

[4]I Corinthians 15:22.
[5]John 5:28-29.

who were willing to receive that message of truth and abide
in it should have everlasting life, but they who would not
receive it or who were not worthy to receive it should come
forth just the same in the resurrection to receive condemnation, but the resurrection was to come to all universally.

Then again, the Savior died for all men upon the face
of the earth, all creatures, that is, human creatures, who
were willing to repent of their sins and keep his commandments. He has not redeemed any of us from our sins except
it be through repentance and faithful adherence to the principles of the gospel and our endurance to the end.

When he stood before his disciples upon this continent,
he said to them:

> . . . no unclean thing can enter into his kingdom; therefore
> nothing entereth into his rest save it be those who have washed their
> garments in my blood, because of their faith, and the repentance of
> all their sins, and their faithfulness unto the end.[6]

This Is Definite

So, he redeemed mankind from death universally. He
has redeemed men from their own sins on conditions of
their repentance, and they will not be redeemed from their
sins unless they do repent and accept him and wash their
garments white in his blood and endure in faith to the end.
It is upon these terms that salvation comes.

Now, stop to think that the Son of God created this
world. All things, the scriptures say, were made by him,
and when we think that he came to this world with that
mission which he accepted before he was born in Bethle-
hem, and by the shedding of his blood gave us life that we
might rise in the resurrection to live forever; and when he,
by the shedding of his blood has offered unto us the remission of our sins and eternal life, through obedience to

---

[6]3 Nephi 27:19.

the gospel—do we not think that we owe him something in return? We owe him everything.

Paul said: "We were bought with a price." That price was the blood of Jesus Christ, and we are not our own. Oh, if we could only understand that by the shedding of his blood, he bought us. We belong to him. He has a right to tell us what to do and what not to do, and to command us to keep his commandments; however, we have our agency, and we act for ourselves.

We cannot comprehend the great suffering that the Lord had to take upon himself to bring to pass this redemption from death and from sin. He spent a few years upon the earth, and during that short sojourn he suffered the abuse of men. They stoned him; they spat upon him; they cursed him; they ridiculed him; they accused him of almost every crime they could think of, and finally they took him and crucified him upon a cross.

Suffering of the Savior

We get into the habit of thinking, I suppose, that his great suffering was when he was nailed to the cross by his hands and his feet and was left there to suffer until he died. As excruciating as that pain was, that was not the greatest suffering that he had to undergo, for in some way which I cannot understand, but which I accept on faith, and which you must accept on faith, he carried on his back the burden of the sins of the whole world. It is hard enough for me to carry my own sins. How is it with you? And yet he had to carry the sins of the whole world, as our Savior and the Redeemer of a fallen world, and so great was his suffering before he ever went to the cross, we are informed that blood oozed from the pores of his body, and he prayed to his Father that the cup might pass if it were possible, but not being possible he was willing to drink.

And here is what he has said to the Church:

For behold, I, God, have suffered these things for all, that they might not suffer if they would repent;

But if they would not repent they must suffer even as I;

Which suffering caused myself, even God, the greatest of all, to tremble because of pain, and to bleed at every pore, and to suffer both body and spirit—and would that I might not drink the bitter cup, and shrink—

Nevertheless, glory be to the Father, and I partook and finished my preparations unto the children of men.[7]

Now, when he said that if we do not repent we will have to suffer even as he did, he had no reference to being nailed to a cross, but it was the torment of mind, of spirit, that he had reference to, before he ever got to the cross, and if man will not repent, they will have to suffer even as he suffered.

Now brethren, briefly, he did all this for us, the Son of God, and he did it because his Father commanded him and because his Father so loved the world that he wanted to save the world from its sins.

Transgressor Shows Ingratitude

Now, he has asked us to keep his commandments. He says they are not grievous, and there are so many of us who are not willing to do it. I am speaking now generally of the people of the earth. We are not willing to do it. That certainly is ingratitude. We are ungrateful. Every member of this Church that violates the Sabbath day, that is not honest in the paying of his tithing, that will not keep the Word of Wisdom, that wilfully violates any of the other commandments the Lord has given us, is ungrateful to the Son of God and when ungrateful to the Son of God is ungrateful to the Father who sent him. If our Savior would do so much for us, how in the world is it that we are not willing to abide by his commandments

[7]D&C 19:16-19.

which are not grievous, which do not cause us any suffering if we will only keep them? And yet, people break the Word of Wisdom; they refuse to attend to their duties as officers and members in the Church; many of them stay away from meetings the Lord has called upon them to support. They follow their own desires if they are in conflict with the commandments of the Lord.

If we understood our position and we loved the Lord our God with all our heart, with all our soul, and with all our mind, or, as he has put it in the revelation given to us in these days:

Wherefore, I give unto them a commandment, saying thus: Thou shalt love the Lord thy God with all thy heart, with all thy might, mind, and strength; and in the name of Jesus Christ thou shalt serve him.

Thou shalt love thy neighbor as thyself. . . .[8]

then we would keep his commandments; when we will not do this, I tell you, my brethren and sisters, we show ingratitude to Jesus Christ.—(*Conference Report*, pp. 144-149, October 5, 1947.)

---

[8]D&C 59:5-6.

Never betray a trust honestly made. . . . Never compromise your convictions of the truth with sin, nor be ashamed of your calling.

Honesty

The thirteenth Article of Faith declares that the Latter-day Saint believes in being honest. Without this virtue there is no salvation in the kingdom of God, for those who enter there must be cleansed from all iniquity. The Church of Jesus Christ of Latter-day Saints, the Lord has said, is "the only true and living Church upon the face of the whole earth, with which I, the Lord, am well pleased, speaking unto the church collectively and not individually.

It would have been a glorious thing if the Lord could have said when this revelation was given that he was pleased with the Church *individually.* He could not say it at that early day; he cannot say it now. Today it must be said that while the Lord may be pleased with the Church collectively, he certainly is not pleased with many of its members, for there are many who have professed his name who do not walk in ways of righteousness. Therefore we may declare today with earnest proclamation the words of Isaiah spoken to ancient Israel:

The sinners in Zion are afraid; fearfulness hath surprised the hypocrites. Who among us shall dwell with the devouring fire? who among us shall dwell with everlasting burnings?

He that walketh righteously, and speaketh uprightly; he that despiseth the gain of oppressions, that shaketh his hands from holding

of bribes, that stoppeth his ears from hearing of blood, and shutteth
his eyes from seeing evil;

    He shall dwell on high: his place of defense shall be the muni-
tions of rocks: bread shall be given him; his waters shall be sure.[1]

Bitterness and Hate

    Today the whole world is in the slough of wickedness.
Bitterness and hate have entered the hearts of the mighty;
their hearts are failing them and fear has overtaken them.
Surely the word of the Lord is true: "the whole world
groaneth under sin and darkness even now."[2]   In our own
fair land, said by the Lord to be choice above all other lands,
dissatisfaction, distress and turmoil reign.   Strikes have for
many months crippled industry.   Capital and labor are at
cross purposes.   Property is being wantonly and maliciously
destroyed.   Force is being used to accomplish selfish ends.
Legislation is advocated to help to reach such ends.   Dis-
content and hatred are born of such conditions and no man
knows where the end will be.

    In the midst of all this turmoil and destruction the
Latter-day Saints should dwell in peace and safety.   This
they may do if they will be honest with themselves, with
their fellowmen and with their God.   Theodore Roosevelt
once said; "On behalf of our people, on behalf no less of the
honest man of means than of the honest man who earns
each day's livelihood by that day's sweat of his brow, it is
necessary to insist upon honesty in business and politics
alike, in all walks of life, in big things and in little things;
upon just and fair dealings as between man and man."

Peace Has Been Taken from the Earth

    Peace has been taken from the earth, and it will not
return until Christ comes to bring it.   When that day ar-
rives he has promised to "send forth his angels, and they

---

[1]Isaiah 33:14-16.
[2]D&C 84:53.

shall gather out of his kingdom all things that offend, and them which do iniquity," but when that day comes he further says, "shall the righteous shine forth as the sun in the kingdom of their Father."

In the presence of complaining friends, Job stoutly maintained his integrity and answering their charges said:

My lips shall not speak wickedness, nor my tongue utter deceit.
God forbid that I should justify you: till I die I will not remove mine integrity from me.
My righteousness I hold fast, and will not let it go: my heart shall not reproach me so long as I live.
Let mine enemy be as the wicked, and he that riseth up against me as the unrighteous.
For what is the hope of the hypocrite, though he hath gained, when God taketh away his soul?[3]

Job knew that he was free from dishonesty. His conscience was clear and in his righteousness he maintained his defense. Would that it could be said by all men: "My lips shall not speak wickedness, nor my tongue utter deceit!" How much better this world would be! If this could be said there would be no turmoil; no envyings; no strife; but men would live righteously under the guiding influence of the Spirit of Truth.

The Lord said to Israel:

Ye shall do no unrighteousness in judgment, in meteyard, in weight, or in measure.
Just balances, just weights, a just ephah, and a just hin, shall ye have: I am the Lord your God, which brought you out of the land of Egypt.[4]

And then in Proverbs we read:

Lying lips are abomination to the Lord: but they that deal truly are his delight.[5]

---

[3]Job 27:4-8.
[4]Leviticus 19:35-36.
[5]Proverbs 12:22.

Are You Honest with the Lord?

You men who have been honored with the power of
divine authority in the Church of Jesus Christ, are you
honest with the Lord? Have you been true to your priesthood, and the covenant you took upon you when you were
ordained? Has your meteyard of service been honest among
your fellowmen? Have you weighed full measure and
running over in your loyalty to the principles of the gospel? to the requirements made upon you by the Church?
Has your ephah been just in the paying of your tithes and
likewise your hin in prayer and fasting?

"Woe to those who profess to be Saints and are not honest," says
President Brigham Young. "Only be honest with yourselves, and you
will be honest to the brethren. . . . Men must be honest, they must
live faithfully before their God, and honor their calling and being
on the earth. You ask if that is possible? Yes; the doctrine which we
have embraced takes away the stony heart. . . . We need to learn,
practice, study, know and understand how angels live with each
other. When this community comes to the point to be perfectly
honest and upright, you will never find a poor person; none will lack,
all will have sufficient. Every man, woman, and child will have all
they need just as soon as they all become honest. When the majority
of the community are dishonest, it maketh the honest portion poor,
for the dishonest serve and enrich themselves at their expense."[6]

Never betray a trust honestly made. It is the duty of
every member of the Church who obtains substance to
pay an honest tithe. The Lord has required it of him. It
is an ancient law again renewed to lead us to a higher law.
Those who are not honest in the payment of their tithes
will not be found worthy to enter into the law of consecration when it is established. They will find themselves
among those who "offend" and hence are to be gathered
out of the kingdom. The man who will not pay an honest
tithe shall not have the privilege of entering into the higher law when the Lord comes to establish it. This will be

---

[6]*Discourses of Brigham Young,* p. 358.

true also of those who offend in any other principle, for those who remain are to be those who are just and true who have overcome by faith, and hence are worthy to stand in the presence of the Lord.

Never Compromise Your Convictions

Never compromise your convictions of the truth with sin, nor be ashamed of your people or your calling. President Joseph F. Smith has said:

Young men should be scrupulously honest and cultivate the strongest possible convictions of what is right and what is wrong and then live by their convictions of right. A young man who compromises his convictions in the hour of temptation demonstrates to himself how unworthy to be trusted he is. The greatest battles of life go on within ourselves. We may not show the white flag today to the world when we have surrendered our honest convictions; but after all, we will not stand so erect in the presence of others as we have been wont to stand; and in the end the repetitions of our surrenders will become open and notorious.

Sometimes men seem to thrive on dishonest methods, but in the end the great majority come to financial grief. If a few go on to the end of the chapter holding on to their ill-gotten gains, it does not argue in favor of the exception; for the great mass come within the universal law that, "honesty is the best policy." The few exceptions of the apparent advantages of dishonest methods are but temptations that try us and test our ability to withstand them.[7]

"Blessed is the man," says James, "that endureth temptation: for when he is tried, he shall receive the crown of life, which the Lord hath promised to them that love him."[8]

We see occasionally the wrecks of men and women who have failed in their honesty and integrity to principles of truth. Their minds are darkened; their hearts have become bitter towards the truth. Such persons are objects of pity among their fellowmen.

---

[7]*Juvenile Instructor,* Vol. 50, 1905, p. 658.
[8]James 1:12.

Procrastination, as it may be applied to gospel principles, is the thief of eternal life—which is life in the presence of the Father and the Son. There are many among us, even members of the Church, who feel that there is no need for haste in the observance of gospel principles and the keeping of the commandments.

Procrastination

Procrastination, as it may be applied to gospel principles, is the thief of eternal life—which is life in the presence of the Father and the Son.   There are many among us, even members of the Church, who feel that there is no need for haste in the observance of gospel principles and the keeping of the commandments.

Nephi wrote of the people of the last days:

> Yea, and there shall be many which shall say: Eat, drink, and be merry, for tomorrow we die; and it shall be well with us.
>
> And there shall also be many which shall say: Eat, drink, and be merry; nevertheless, fear God—he will justify in committing a little sin; yea, lie a little, take the advantage of one because of his words, dig a pit for thy neighbor; there is no harm in this; and do all these things, for tomorrow we die; and if it so be that we are guilty, God will beat us with a few stripes, and at last we shall be saved in the kingdom of God.[1]

Do not think that this was said of the world, or even the "stranger within our gates."   It is said of members of the Church.   Moreover, Nephi warns us that in the last days there will be many who will follow Satan.

---

[1] 2 Nephi 28:7-8. Read also verses 20-29.

We Are Living in the Last Days

We are living in the last days. Have we not heard individuals talk as Nephi said they would? Are there not many who excuse themselves and lull themselves to sleep in "carnal security," thinking that the Lord will overlook their little sins? Are there not those among us who are denying the power of the devil, and who deny that there is a devil? Do they not "spiritualize" the torments of hell, and say there is no hell? Have you not heard these things taught? In this manner Satan is raging in the hearts of the people and members of the Church do not entirely escape his cunning sophistries!

Bad habits are easily formed but not so easily broken. Are we yielding to our evil habits, thinking they are only trifles after all, and we will get rid of them in the grave? Do we expect that our bodies will be cleansed in the grave and we shall come forth with perfect and sanctified bodies in the resurrection? There are some among us who teach such things, and excuse themselves for their practices, saying that they will be cleansed in the grave.

Alma taught a very different doctrine. He said to Corianton:

> Do not suppose, because it has been spoken concerning restoration, that ye shall be restored from sin to happiness. Behold, I say unto you, wickedness never was happiness. . . .
>
> For that which ye do send out shall return unto you again, and be restored; therefore, the word restoration more fully condemneth the sinner, and justifieth him not at all.[2]

The Savior also said, "With what measure ye mete, it shall be measured to you again."[3] Some think that a little punishment will not be so bad, and they are willing to take a chance and suffer for their offenses rather than

---

[2]Alma 41:10, 15.
[3]Matthew 7:2.

keep the commandments of the Lord as we are instructed. If they are able to escape with a "few stripes" they may consider themselves fortunate. But let us remember that sin must be atoned for. *Restitution must be made;* we will have to pay the price if we refuse to repent and to receive the blessings of the gospel. Punishment is not easy to bear, especially when the conscience is troubled. Who could be happy in suffering, and all the while be thinking that the suffering had come because of a wilful, or persistent, breaking of the commandments of God when knowledge had been given and counsel to walk in righteousness? What will the sinner think in that day when he has learned repentance for wilful rebellion, and realizes that the great suffering of our Lord in love, made it *unnecessary* for him to so suffer if he had accepted Christ and his work?

Kingdoms Have Been Prepared

Our Eternal Father has prepared three great kingdoms into which the souls of men will go. It is not the purpose here to discuss these kingdoms. In passing it is only necessary to say that in the telestial will go all those who have not been true; those who have professed and who have not performed;[4] the liars, sorcerers, adulterers, and all who refuse to walk in ways of truth. Into the terrestrial will go all those who are honorable, who have been morally clean, but who would not receive the gospel; also those who die without law.

To enter the celestial and obtain exaltation it is necessary that the whole law be kept. The word of the Lord is as follows:

Therefore, it must needs be sanctified from all unrighteousness, that it may be prepared for the celestial glory; . . .

And they who are not sanctified through the law which I have given unto you, even the law of Christ, must inherit another king-

4D&C 41:1.

dom, even that of a terrestrial kingdom, or that of a telestial kingdom.[5]

To become sanctified there are certain definite covenants we must keep in faithfulness, living by "every word that proceedeth forth from the mouth of God."[6]

They are they who receive the testimony of Jesus, and believed on his name and were baptized after the manner of his burial, . . .

That by keeping the commandments they might be washed and cleansed from all their sins and receive the Holy Spirit by the laying on of the hands of him who is ordained and sealed unto this power;

And who overcome by faith and are sealed by the Holy Spirit of promise which the Father sheds forth upon all those who are just and true.[7]

And they who are not sealed by the Holy Spirit of promise and who are not just and true, need not expect these great blessings.

Never Too Early to Serve the Lord

No person can begin too early to serve the Lord. Parents are instructed to teach their children from infancy, with the warnings that they will be held accountable if they fail to do so. If a child is taught in righteousness from birth it will most likely be a follower of righteousness always. They who refuse to seek the Lord early are forsaken in the hour of their trouble. Read the history of Israel; of the Nephites. How often when they rebelled were they punished? How slow was the Lord to hear their cries when trouble came upon them because of their sins? "They were slow to hearken unto the voice of the Lord their God; therefore, the Lord their God is slow to hearken unto their prayers, to answer them in the day of their trouble."[8] So spake the Lord to modern Israel.

---

[5]D&C 88:18, 21.
[6]D&C 84:44.
[7]D&C 76:51-53. Also see verses 54-60.
[8]D&C 101:7.

Do you desire to enter into the celestial kingdom and receive eternal life? Then be willing to keep all of the commandments the Lord may give you. Baptism and confirmation are the ordinances by which we come into the kingdom of God. But these ordinances of themselves will not grant us a place of exaltation!

Each person baptized into the Church is under obligation to keep the commandments of the Lord. He is under covenant, for baptism is a "new and an everlasting covenant."[9] When he has proved himself by a worthy life, having been faithful in all things required of him, then it is his privilege to receive other covenants and to take upon himself other obligations which will make of him an heir, and he will become a member of the "Church of the Firstborn." "They are they into whose hands the Father has given all things." He will receive of the Father's fulness and of his glory. Is this worth having? It cannot be obtained without some effort. We frequently hear quoted these words of the Lord to Joseph Smith: "It is impossible for a man to be saved in ignorance."[10] In ignorance of what? the philosophies of the world? NO! In ignorance of the gospel truth—the saving principles and ordinances by which salvation comes! These must not only be understood, but they must be lived! Knowledge of them will not in itself save us! Obedience thereto will! And then will come the fulness of knowledge, bringing with it wisdom, power and dominion. And the fulness of these blessings can only be obtained in the temple of the Lord!

We are told that the fear (love) of the Lord is the beginning of knowledge; but fools despise wisdom and instruction.

Also I give unto you a commandment that ye shall continue in prayer and fasting from this time forth.

---

[9]D&C 22:1.
[10]D&C 131:6.

And I give unto you a commandment that you shall teach one
another the doctrine of the kingdom.[11]

Do not let us forget the words of Alma:

For behold, this life is the time for men to prepare to meet God;
yea, behold the day of this life is the day for men to perform their
labors.

And now, as I said unto you before, as ye have had so many
witnesses, therefore, I beseech of you that ye do not procrastinate the
day of your repentance until the end; for after this day of life, which
is given us to prepare for eternity, behold, if we do not improve our
time while in this life, then cometh the night of darkness wherein
there can be no labor performed.

Ye cannot say, when ye are brought to that awful crisis, that
I will repent, that I will return to my God. Nay, ye cannot say this;
for that same spirit which doth possess your bodies at the time that
ye go out of this life, that same spirit will have power to possess your
body in that eternal world.[12]

The Lord is always merciful and kind. If we draw near
unto him, he will draw near unto us.

Seek me diligently and ye shall find me; ask, and ye shall receive;
knock, and it shall be opened unto you.[13]

Our chief trouble is we do not seek diligently. Our
seeking is superficial; we seem to think the Lord is bound
to hear us without our putting forth much effort. Let diligence and love be our guides, and we shall find the path of
eternal life.—(*Conference Report,* April 6, 1969.)

---

[11]D&C 88:76-77.
[12]Alma 34:32-34.
[13]D&C 88:63.

*All sin, no matter what nature it is, is a viola-
tion of a constituted law or commandment and
hence is worthy of punishment unless the price
is paid. That price could be in physical or
mental suffering or by otherwise paying the
debt. The scriptures inform us that for every
sin there must be compensation, either by repentance or punishment.*

Forgiveness for Sin

The dictionary gives us the following interpretation of the committing of sin: Sin is the transgression of a rule or requirement; neglect or disregard of a divine law or commandment.

Some sins are more serious than others and less easily repented of. There are sins that cannot be forgiven, such as murder, without the punishment of the guilty with the shedding of blood.[1] All sin, no matter what nature it is, is a violation of a constituted law or commandment and hence is worthy of punishment unless the price is paid. That price could be in physical or mental suffering or by otherwise paying the debt. The scriptures inform us that for every sin there must be compensation, either by repentance or punishment.

Cannot Look Upon Sin without Recompense

Naturally the Lord cannot look upon sin with the "least degree of allowance." Justice demands that there must be recompense for the violation of any divine law. A human being may receive forgiveness for the transgression of divine

---
[1]Genesis 9:6.

law through repentance and a faithful turning away from sin.

There are some sins which, according to the scriptures, are worthy of death of the transgressor. This is a divine law. Compensation must be made in some way for every sin. For this reason our Redeemer, Jesus Christ, came into this world and suffered a painful death to atone for the sins of those who will repent and keep his commandments. This is called vicarious redemption from sin.

All those who repent and accept the gospel are redeemed without having to pay a price in torment or punishment. In regard to this great blessing that comes to us, the Lord said by revelation to the Prophet Joseph Smith:

> For behold, I, God, have suffered these things for all, that they might not suffer if they would repent;
> But if they would not repent they must suffer even as I;
> Which suffering caused myself, even God, the greatest of all, to tremble because of pain, and to bleed at every pore, and to suffer both body and spirit—and would that I might not drink the bitter cup, and shrink—
> Nevertheless, glory be to the Father, and I partook and finished my preparations unto the children of men.[2]

Divine Law of Compensation

The divine law of compensation demanded that an atonement must be made for every sin or there is no forgiveness. In his great mercy the Son of God came into this world and offered himself a sacrifice to redeem all mankind from Adam's fall and to redeem every man from his individual sins on condition of his faithful repentance and acceptance of the divine plan of salvation. Moreover, he came to restore the dead to immortality. This restoration is not only for those who accept the gospel of Jesus Christ; it also extends to every living thing upon the face of the earth and

---

[2]D&C 19:16-19.

even to the earth itself, for the earth, like all creatures upon her face, must pass through the ordeal of death and be renewed in a resurrection based on the atonement of our Savior. So the scriptures, given by divine commandment, inform us that this earth is also to be redeemed and will become a celestial body and the abode of the righteous.— (*The Improvement Era*, August 1966.)

It is true that a country cannot get ahead of its religion. The higher our ideals, the nearer we observe divine law, and the stronger are our spiritual forces. No Christian country can forsake the divinity of Jesus Christ and not suffer.

"Blessed Is the Nation Whose God Is the Lord"

"Blessed is the nation whose God is the Lord, and the people whom he hath chosen for his own inheritance."[1] So said the Psalmist. This saying it would be well for the people of America to remember.

No nation has been more greatly blessed than has the United States. We live in a land which has been called choice above all other lands by divine pronouncement. The Lord has watched over it with a jealous care and has commanded its people to serve him lest his wrath be kindled against them and his blessings be withdrawn. Our government came into existence through divine guidance. The inspiration of the Lord rested upon the patriots who established it. He inspired them through the dark days of their struggle for independence and through the critical period which followed that struggle when they framed our glorious Constitution which guarantees to all the self-evident truth proclaimed in the Declaration of Independence, "that all men are created equal: that they are endowed by their Creator with certain inalienable rights; that among these

[1]Psalm 33:12.

are life, liberty, and the pursuit of happiness." That is to say, it is the right of every soul to have equal and unrestricted justice before the law, equal rights to worship according to the dictates of conscience, and to labor according to the individual inclinations, independently of coercion or compulsion.

That this might be, the Lord has said, "I established the Constitution of this land, by the hands of wise men whom I raised up unto this very purpose, and redeemed the land by the shedding of blood."[2]

Founders Were Men of Humble Faith

The founders of this nation were men of humble faith. Many of them saw in vision a glorious destiny for our government, provided we would faithfully continue in the path of justice and right with contrite spirits and humble hearts, accepting the divine truths which are found in the Holy Scriptures. The appeal of these men has echoed down the passing years with prophetic warning to the succeding generations, pleading with them to be true to all these standards which lay at the foundation of our government. This country was founded as a Christian nation, with the acceptance of Jesus Christ as the Redeemer of the world. It was predicted by a prophet of old that this land would be a land of liberty, and it would be fortified against all other nations as long as its inhabitants would serve Jesus Christ. But should they stray from the Son of God, it would cease to be a land of liberty and his anger be kindled against them.[3]

It is a sad reflection, but one that cannot be successfully refuted, that we have forgotten the admonition which has come down to us, just as Israel forgot the commandments which would have blessed that nation in the land of Canaan forever had they been observed. In forsaking these laws we stand in danger of punishment as the people of

[2]D&C 101:80.
[3]2 Nephi 1:7.

Israel stood in danger of punishment, because they forsook
the Lord and failed to repent and accept the warnings of
their prophets.

Since the days of our fathers there has been a gradual
straying from the sacred teachings which we have received.
In later years we have, in fact, fulfilled the prophecy of Paul.

This know also, that in the last days perilous times shall come.
For men shall be lovers of their own selves, covetous, boasters,
proud, blasphemers, disobedient to parents, unthankful, unholy.
Without natural affection, trucebreakers, false accusers, incon-
tinent, fierce, despisers of those that are good.
Traitors, heady, highminded, lovers of pleasure more than lovers
of God;
Having a form of godliness, but denying the power thereof: . . .[4]

A Severe Indictment

This is a very severe indictment made by Paul; but can
we honestly deny the charge? The Ten Commandments are
just as much the word of the Lord today as they were when
written by the finger of God on Sinai. They have not been
abrogated; they have not been modified and are binding
upon the people with all the force which accompanied them
when first uttered. As sure as we live we are to be judged
by them and all other divine commandments, for God will
not permit us to mock him and hold his laws in contempt
with impunity.

Have not the people of this land ignored the first commandment?

. . . Thou shalt love the Lord thy God with all thy heart, and
with all thy soul, and with all thy mind.
This is the first and great commandment.
And the second is like unto it, Thou shalt love thy neighbor
as thyself.
On these two commandments hang all the law and the prophets.[5]

[4]II Timothy 3:1-5.
[5]Matthew 22:37-40.

In other words, all that has been revealed for the salvation of man from the beginning to our own time is circumscribed, included in and a part of these two great laws. If we love the Lord with all the heart, with all the soul, and with all the mind, and our neighbor as ourselves, then there is nothing more to be desired. Then we will be in harmony with the total of sacred law. If we were willing to live in harmony with these two great commandments—and we must do so eventually if we are worthy to live in the presence of God—then wickedness, jealousy, ambition, covetousness, bloodshed and all sin of every nature would be banished from the earth. Then would come a day of eternal peace and happiness. What a glorious day that would be! We have been endowed with sufficient reason to know that such a state is most desirable and would establish among men the Fatherhood of God and the perfect brotherhood of man.

Messenger Sent from Presence of God

But as a people have we not forsaken these commandments? Can we say that we love the Lord with all the soul? Can we say we are as solicitous for the welfare of our neighbor as we are for our own? As we look about us we cannot fail to see the selfishness, the unbelief, blasphemy and love of evil which are found everywhere among the people, all revealing to us our weakness and unwillingness to obey these laws. We are not ignorant of the things of God, for they have been made known to us from the days of Adam until now and are recorded in the Holy Scriptures. Messengers from the presence of God have been sent to the earth from the beginning to establish in the hearts of men and to reveal to them all that is essential for man's salvation. If any among us are ignorant of these things it is due to wilful rebellion.

The Son of God came to earth to show us by example the way to eternal life, and was himself free from sin. We cannot excuse ourselves for the violation of the laws of God on the ground of ignorance. With all of these commandments before us we are moral agents responsible to the Most High and under obligation to be obedient. Nevertheless, because of the love of the things of the world and the enticing influence of the powers of darkness, we have departed from the strait path which leads to life and which our Lord has said few men find because they love darkness rather than light, their deeds being evil. We have permitted the philosophies of men, which deny the divinity of Jesus Christ and mock at the sacred ordinances of the gospel, to enter into our schools, our businesses and our homes, thus weakening our faith and our reverence for our Creator. We have forgotten that man was created in the image of God, that the scriptures declare that we are his offspring, and that we are commanded to seek first the kingdom of God and his righteousness.

Are We Keeping Our Bodies Clean?

Are we keeping our bodies clean and free from all contaminating influences? We are informed that no unclean thing can inherit the kingdom of God, that "he that is unjust, let him be unjust still: and he which is filthy, let him be filthy still: and he that is righteous, let him be righteous still: and he that is holy, let him be holy still."[6] So it will be in the judgment. Every man shall receive a reward according to his works. Unfortunately there are many selfish, greedy, agencies at work playing upon the credulity and ignorance of the people, enticing them to indulge in many evil habits which weaken and impair their vitality and drive them from the spiritual guidance promised them through their humility and faith.

---

[6]Revelation 22:11.

Have we observed the Sabbath day and kept it holy? Is it not a fact that we have looked upon this law as being obsolete; something suited, perhaps, to the needs of a primitive people, who, like little children, need special care, but not necessary for us to observe in this modern world of superior wisdom? Is it not the fact that through the length and breadth of our land, this sacred commandment has been treated, and is being treated, with absolute contempt? Have we not made of it a day of pleasure, of indulgence, and have we not lost all love for its sacredness? How can we expect the Lord to bless us when we ignore so universally this holy law?

Have We Forgotten to Pray?

Have we forgotten to pray and to thank the Lord for his mercies and for his guidance in all that we do? If at times we have been requested to seek the help of the Lord in this great struggle which has deluged the world, have we prayed in the true spirit of prayer? What good does it do for us to petition the Lord, if we have no intention of keeping his commandments? Such praying is hollow mockery, and an insult before the throne of grace. How dare we presume to expect a favorable answer if such is the case?

Seek ye the Lord while he may be found, call ye upon him while he is near:

Let the wicked forsake his way, and the unrighteous man his thoughts: and let him return unto the Lord, and he will have mercy upon him; and to our God, for he will abundantly pardon.[7]

So said Isaiah. But is not the Lord always near when we petition him? Verily no! He has said,

They were slow to hearken unto the voice of the Lord their God; therefore, the Lord their God is slow to hearken unto their prayers, to answer them in the day of their trouble.

[7]Isaiah 55:6-7.

In the day of their peace they esteemed lightly my counsel; but, in the day of their trouble, of necessity they feel after me.[8]

If we draw near unto him, he will draw near unto us and we will not be forsaken, but if we do not draw near to him we have no promise that he will answer us in our rebellion.

Are we free from all covetousness? Do we refrain from desiring to possess unjustly the property of others? Have we permitted the lusts of the flesh and the desire to possess that which is not our honest due, to canker our souls?

Have we not come to look upon the sacred and holy bonds of matrimony as merely a civil contract which may be broken at will on the slightest whim by either covenanting party? Has not divorce become a blot upon the nation? How can we reconcile our practices and the statutes of many states with the commandments given us by Jesus Christ in relation to the marriage covenant? The home is the foundation of civilization and vital to the safety of our country. When the home is destroyed, the foundation of the country is in danger of destruction. Such has been the history of the past among nations. Marriage is a sacred ordinance instituted before death came into the world when the Lord said, "It is not good that the man should be alone; I will make him an help meet for him."[9]

Children Have Right to Blessings

Throughout our land we see the tragedy of broken homes, fathers and mothers separated, children denied the natural affections. Children have a right to the blessings coming from this sacred union. They are entitled to the love and care of faithful parents and the happiness and devotion which true worship brings. When these blessings are lost the whole community suffers and the integrity of

[8]D&C 101:7-8.
[9]Abraham 5:14.

government is weakened. It is a shame and a disgrace that so much evil is coming out of broken homes, and this comes largely because we have forgotten God and our obligations to serve and honor him. Truly we have room for repentance and a return to the simple worship of true Christianity.

It is true that a country cannot get ahead of its religion. The higher our ideals, the nearer we observe divine law, and the stronger are our spiritual forces. No Christian country can forsake the divinity of Jesus Christ and not suffer. In those lands in Europe where paganism has superseded the Christian ideals, there is bound to come decay and eventually, if there is no repentance, their former greatness will be forgotten. Jesus said: "And why call ye me Lord, Lord, and do not the things which I say?"[10]

But someone will say: "Are we not living in the most enlightened age the world has ever seen? Is it not true that great progress is being made to lessen the burdens and increase the happiness of man?" Yes, this is true in regard to many material things. Great progress has been made in mechanics, chemistry, physics, surgery and other things. Men have built great telescopes that have brought the hidden galaxies to view. They have, by the aid of the microscope, discovered vast worlds of micro-organisms, some of which are as deadly as are men towards their fellowmen. They have discovered means to control disease; they have, by the aid of anesthesia, made men insensible to pain, thus permitting major and delicate operations which could not otherwise be performed. They have invented machines more sensitive than the human touch, more farseeing than the human eye. They have controlled elements and made machinery that can move mountains and many other things have they done too numerous to mention. Yes, this is a wonderful age. However, all of these discoveries and inventions have not drawn men nearer to God, nor created in

---

[10]Luke 6:46.

their hearts humility and the spirit of repentance, but to the contrary, to their condemnation. Nearly everything, it seems, which has been given that should be a blessing to men, has been turned to evil.

Many of these discoveries and inventions are now being used to bring destruction to the human race. They are being used in the most cruel, most inhuman, godless war this world has ever seen. They are employed by criminals to aid them in their crimes, by the ambitious in their efforts to destroy the agency of man, and by despots who are endeavoring to subjugate the world to an unholy, wicked rule.

Faith Has Not Increased in the World

Faith has not increased in the world, nor has righteousness, nor obedience to God. What the world needs today is to draw nearer to the Lord. We need more humble abiding faith in our Redeemer, more love in our hearts for our Eternal Father and for our fellowmen. Yes, this is a good time, a vital time, if we are to survive the forces of evil, for every man to forsake the paths of sin and turn unto the Lord who will abundantly pardon. If we will do this we may in confidence call upon the Lord and he will be near. He will help us fight our battle to cleanse the world of despotism and make it a fit abode for all who love the principles of truth and righteousness. "Blessed is the nation whose God is the Lord." Let us make our nation all that it was destined to be, and this will come if we will humble ourselves and learn to be obedient to divine law.

Joseph Smith was chosen to stand at the head of the work of the Lord in the last days, and his work was assigned to him through the fore-knowledge of our Eternal Father in the eternities before he was born. He came in the spirit of Elias to prepare the way for the coming of our Lord. No prophet since the days of Adam, save of course, our Redeemer, has been given a greater mission.

The Historical Background of the Prophet Joseph Smith

In the far distant past before the foundations of this earth were laid, a grand council was held in heaven. At that council plans were perfected and an organization formed for the government of this earth during its mortal probation. Our Eternal Father, knowing the end from the beginning, chose from among the spirits those to be his rulers and prophets to assist in carrying through his eternal purposes on this earth in relation to the final destiny of men. All this the Lord revealed to Abraham, who declared that among these assembled spirits were "many of the noble and great ones."

And God saw these souls that they were good, and he stood in the midst of them, and he said: These I will make my rulers; for he stood among those that were spirits, and he saw that they were good; and he said unto me: Abraham, thou art one of them; thou wast chosen before thou wast born.[1]

Abraham was not the only prophet thus selected before he was born. Similar information is recorded of

---

[1] Abraham 3:23.

Jeremiah and other prophets, and we have good reason to believe that all the prophets were likewise called and fore-ordained.

Michael Was Progenitor of the Human Family

In this grand council, Michael was chosen to come as the progenitor of the human family and to bring mortality into the world. Jesus Christ was chosen to come in the meridian of time to redeem man from the mortal state, and, on condition of repentance and faithfulness to the eternal plan, to extend redemption from individual sin. Abraham was appointed to become the "father of the faithful," and the founder of the house of Israel. Moses was chosen to lead Israel from Egyptian bondage, and Joseph Smith to stand at the head of the greatest of all dispensations, that of the fulness of times.

In this grand council, we are informed, "the morning stars sang together, and all the sons of God shouted for joy," because they were to receive the privilege of coming to this earth and partake of all the vicissitudes of mortality, fraught with such glorious and momentous possibilities.

Speaking of the appointment of Joseph Smith in this grand council, President Brigham Young has said:

It was decreed in the councils of eternity, long before the foundations of the earth were laid, that he, Joseph Smith, should be the man, in the last dispensation of this world, to bring forth the word of God to the people, and receive the fulness of the keys and power of the priesthood of the Son of God. The Lord had his eyes upon him, and upon his father, and upon his father's father, and upon their progenitors clear back to Abraham, and from Abraham to the flood, from the flood to Enoch, and from Enoch to Adam. He has watched the family and that blood as it has circulated from its fountain to the birth of that man. He was fore-ordained in eternity to preside over this last dispensation.[2]

------

[2]*Journal of Discourses*, 7:289.

Named Sixteen Centuries before Birth

Joseph, son of Jacob, spoke of Joseph Smith and named him more than sixteen centuries before the birth of our Lord, and his glorious mission was foreshadowed and his greatness declared by this worthy son of Israel, in the following words:

A seer shall the Lord my God raise up, who shall be a choice seer unto the fruit of thy loins.

Thus saith the Lord God of my fathers unto me, A choice seer will I raise up out of the fruit of thy loins, and he shall be esteemed highly among the fruit of thy loins, his brethren; and unto him will I give commandments that he shall do a work for the fruit of thy loins.

And he shall bring them to the knowledge of the covenants which I have made with thy father; and he shall do whatsoever work I shall command him.

And I will make him great in mine eyes, for he shall do my work; and he shall be great like unto him whom I have said I would raise up unto you, to deliver my people, O house of Israel, out of the land of Egypt; for a seer will I raise up to deliver my people out of the land of Egypt; and he shall be called Moses. And by this name he shall know that he is of thy house; for he shall be nursed by the king's daughter, and shall be called her son.

And again, a seer will I raise up out of the fruit of thy loins, and unto him will I give power to bring forth my word unto the seed of thy loins; and not to the bringing forth of my word only, saith the Lord, but to the convincing them of my word, which shall have already gone forth among them in the last days;

Wherefore the fruit of thy loins shall write, and the fruit of the loins of Judah shall write; and that which shall be written by the fruit of thy loins, and also that which shall be written by the fruit of the loins of Judah, shall grow together unto the confounding of false doctrines, and laying down of contentions, and establishing peace among the fruit of thy loins, and bringing them to a knowledge of their fathers in the latter days; and also to the knowledge of my covenants, saith the Lord.

And out of weakness shall he be made strong, in that day when my work shall go forth among all my people, which shall restore them, who are of the house of Israel, in the last days.

And that seer will I bless, and they that seek to destroy him shall be confounded; for this promise I give unto you; for I will remember you from generation to generation; and his name shall be called Joseph, and it shall be after the name of his father; and he shall be like unto you; for the thing which the Lord shall bring forth by his hand shall bring my people unto salvation.

And the Lord sware unto Joseph, that he would preserve his seed for ever, saying, I will raise up Moses, and a rod shall be in his hand, and he shall gather together my people, and he shall lead them as a flock, and he shall smite the waters of the Red Sea with his rod.

And he shall have judgment, and shall write the word of the Lord. And he shall not speak many words, for I will write unto him my law by the finger of my own hand. And I will make a spokesman for him, and his name shall be called Aaron.

And it shall be done unto thee in the last days also, even as I have sworn. Therefore, Joseph said unto his brethren, God will surely visit you, and bring you out of this land, unto the land which he sware unto Abraham, and unto Isaac, and to Jacob.

And Joseph confirmed many other things unto his brethren, and took an oath of the children of Israel, saying unto them, God will surely visit you, and ye shall carry up my bones from hence.[3]

In this manner the Lord spoke to Joseph, son of Jacob, and we have lived to see these words fulfilled.

Mentioned by Other Ancient Prophets

This choice seer has been mentioned by other ancient prophets who have declared also his work. Isaiah declared that in the days of this seer, when the people had closed their eyes, and had rejected the prophets, and covered the seers, the work of this choice seer would commence, and the Lord would—

. . . bring forth unto you the words of a book; and they shall be the words of them which have slumbered.

And behold the book shall be sealed; and in the book shall be a revelation from God, from the beginning of the world to the ending thereof.

---

[3]Holy Scriptures, Inspired Version, Genesis 50:26-37.

Wherefore because of the things which are sealed up, the things which are sealed shall not be delivered in the day of the wickedness and abominations of the people. Wherefore, the book shall be kept from them.

But the book shall be delivered unto a man, and he shall deliver the words of the book, which are the words of those who have slumbered in the dust; and he shall deliver these words unto another, but the words that are sealed he shall not deliver, neither shall he deliver the book. . . .

And again it shall come to pass, that the Lord shall say unto him that shall read the words that shall be delivered him, Forasmuch as this people draw near unto me with their mouth, and with their lips do honour me, but have removed their hearts far from me, and their fear toward me is taught by the precepts of men, therefore I will proceed to do a marvelous work among this people; yea, a marvelous work and a wonder; for the wisdom of their wise and learned shall perish, and the understanding of the prudent shall be hid.[4]

Many other prophets have spoken of the work of this modern seer, but we need not take time to quote them.

Joseph Smith Chosen

From what is here given we see that Joseph Smith was chosen to stand at the head of the work of the Lord in the last days, and his work was assigned to him through the fore-knowledge of our Eternal Father in the eternities before he was born. He came in the spirit of Elias to prepare the way for the coming of our Lord. No prophet since the days of Adam, save, of course, our Redeemer, has been given a greater mission, but of that mission it is not my place to speak. I am dealing only with the historical phases of that mission.

Joseph Smith was born in Sharon, Windsor County, Vermont, December 23, 1805. He was the third son and fourth child of Joseph and Lucy Mack Smith. His parents were devout, humble believers in the mission of our Lord. Joseph's mother was the daughter of Solomon Mack and

---

[4]*Ibid.*, Isaiah 29:11-14, 26.

Lydia Gates. Solomon's grandfather was born in Inverness, Scotland, March 6, 1653. The Mack and Gates families were well-respected in their communities and several members had distinguished themselves in the Revolutionary War.

On his paternal side, Joseph Smith was a descendant of Robert Smith who came from England in 1638. We have no record of Robert's parents, but President George A. Smith once said that the Prophet had declared that the family was related to Captain John Smith of early American history. Some slight indication of this is found in the fact that Robert Smith came from that part of Lincolnshire where Captain John Smith was born.

Robert landed in Boston and a few years later moved to Rowley and purchased one hundred eight acres of land in that part which later became the township of Boxford. He married Mary French, daughter of Thomas and Mary French. They were the parents of ten children.

Samuel, son of Robert, was born January 26, 1666. He married Rebecca, daughter of John Curtis and moved to Topsfield and there became an influential member of the community and was highly respected, holding several positions of trust. He was the father of nine children.

His son, Samuel, was born January 26, 1714, and became one of the most influential citizens of Massachusetts. The greater part of his life was spent in the service of the people. In the stormy days of the American Revolution he cast his lot with the Colonial forces. From 1760 to the year 1783, he was constantly in the service of his country. He was a member of the General Court, or House of Representatives, for four terms. He was a delegate to the Provincial Congress at Concord, in 1774 and again in 1775, and he bore arms during the Revolution. He married Priscilla, daughter of Zacheus Gould. His wife died shortly after the birth of their son Asael. Samuel married again, the cousin of his first wife, also named Priscilla. At his death in

November, 1785, the Salem *Gazette* spoke of him in these words:

Died—At Topsfield, on Monday, the 14th instant, Samuel Smith, esquire. So amiable and worthy a character as he evidently appeared, both in public and private, will render the memory of him ever precious. For a number of years he represented the town in the General Court, where he was esteemed a man of integrity and uprightness. His usefulness among those with whom he was more immediately conversant was eminent. He was a sincere friend to the liberties of his country, and a strenuous advocate for the doctrines of Christianity.

The memory of the just be blessed.

Asael, grandfather of the Prophet, was born in Topsfield, March 7, 1744. He married Mary Duty of Windham, New Hampshire, and later moved to that place. During the Revolution he followed his honored father, and served faithfully with the Colonial forces. After the death of his father he returned to Topsfield and made his home on the family estate, where some of his children were born, notably, Joseph, father of the Prophet.

Asael was a man of liberal views. He had outstanding literary ability. Some of his views, far in advance of his time, have come down to us and are cherished by members of the family. He was very frank and outspoken and wrote the things he firmly believed, without fear or favor. Many years before his death he wrote a document of sound advice for the guidance of his family. This advice could be followed very profitably by his descendants to this day. He was a devout believer in the atoning sacrifice of our Redeemer, but could not conform to the dogmas and religious notions of his day which brought down the wrath of some pious hypocrites upon his head. Time has vindicated his sound judgment. One item of interest in his remarkable epistle to his family I will here present.

And first to you, my dear wife, I do with all the strength and power that is in me, beseeching God who is the husband of the widow, to take care of you and not to leave you nor forsake you, nor suffer you to leave nor forsake Him, nor His ways. Put your whole trust solely in Him; He never did nor never will forsake any that trust in Him. . . . And now, my dear children, let me pour out my heart to you and speak first of immortality in your souls. Trifle not in this point; the soul is immortal; you have to deal with an infinite Majesty! you go upon life and death, therefore in this point be serious. Do all to God in a serious manner; when you make your address to His great Majesty, be in good earnest. Trifle not with His name, nor with His attributes, nor call him to witness to anything but in absolute truth, nor then, but when sound judgment and reason or serious consideration require it.[5]

He had a good sense of humor which he mingled with his seriousness, but he knew when properly to use it. When, on one occasion, he declared his possessions to the tax assessor, he couched his statement in the following words:

I have two poles, tho' one is poor;
I have three cows and want five more;
I have no horse, but fifteen sheep;
No more than these this year I keep.
Steers, that's two years old, one pair;
Two calves I have, all over hair;
Three heffers two years old, I own;
One heffer calf that's poorly grone.
My land is acres eighty-two,
Which search the record youle find true
And this is all I have in store;
I'll thank you if you'le tax no more.[6]

Prophetic Statement of Asael Smith

In his declining years he moved to Stockholm, St. Lawrence County, New York, and made his home with his son Silas. In stature he was tall and he possessed unusual strength. On one occasion he said:

---

[5]Smith, *Life of Joseph F. Smith* (Salt Lake City: Deseret Book Co.), p. 24.
[6]*Ibid.*, p. 21.

It has been borne in upon my soul that one of my descendants will promulgate a work to revolutionize the world of religious faith.[7]

It is hardly possible that he expected to live to see his prophetic inspiration fulfilled, but he did. In his declining years, his son, Joseph, and grandson, Don Carlos, came to visit him bringing a copy of the Book of Mormon. He readily accepted their message and that of his grandson, Joseph, but was not baptized because of enfeebled health. He died a short time later, October 31, 1830, when eighty-six years of age. His wife, Mary Duty Smith, joined the Church, moved to Kirtland where she died full of faith in the mission of her grandson, Joseph Smith.

Joseph Smith, Senior, was the first to accept the message of the Prophet. His life was from that time forth, interwoven in the history of the Church. He was the first Patriarch ordained in this dispensation, receiving that office by divine right as the firstborn descendants of Ephraim.

All of these persons were highly respected and honored by their fellow citizens, until the knowledge went forth that the Lord had spoken to the youthful Prophet. From that day forth vicious and evil persons did everything in their power to destroy the character of Joseph Smith and his forebears, thus fulfilling the prophetic words of Moroni when he first came to the bedside of Joseph Smith with the definite call to his important mission.

Only a Few of the Highlights

These are a few of the highlights in the background of the history of Joseph Smith, the Seer, whom the Eternal Father and his beloved Son appointed before he was born, to stand at the head of the glorious dispensation of the fulness of times when the Son of God shall come to take his rightful place as King of kings.

---

[7]*Essentials in Church History* (Salt Lake City: Deseret Book Co., 1967 edition), p. 25.

It is very proper that a building of this kind should be erected on BYU campus to the name and honor of Joseph Smith. May those who teach and those who come here for instruction, never forget the magnitude and glorious nature of this work which the Lord entrusted to the hands of Joseph Smith, and may those eternal principles never be forsaken or marred by the philosophies of men. Let us remember that Joseph Smith, the humble farmer boy, was trained and instructed as, perhaps, no other prophet was ever taught and trained, by divine instructors sent from the throne and presence of our Eternal Father.—(*The Improvement Era,* December, 1941.)

A BRIEF CHRONOLOGY OF THE LIFE
OF THE PROPHET JOSEPH SMITH

December 23, 1805—Born at Sharon, Windsor County, Vermont, the son of Joseph and Lucy Mack Smith.

About 1818—Moved to Smith farm at Manchester, near Palmyra.

Spring 1820—Received the vision of the Father and the Son in a grove of trees on the Smith farm.

September 21-22, 1823—Visitation by the Angel Moroni.

January 18, 1827—Married Emma Hale.

September 22, 1827—Received custody of the Book of Mormon plates.

April 7, 1829—Oliver Cowdery began as Joseph's scribe.

May 15, 1829—John the Baptist restored the Aaronic Priesthood.

May-June 1829—Peter, James, and John conferred the Melchizedek Priesthood.

Late March-early April 1830—Book of Mormon came from the press.

April 6, 1830—The Church organized at Peter Whitmer's home, Fayette, New York.

January-February 1831—Moved to Kirtland, Ohio.

August 3, 1831—Dedicated site for temple at Independence, Missouri.

November 8, 1832—Visited by Brigham Young, Heber C. Kimball, and others from Vermont.

February 27, 1833—Received revelation on the Word of Wisdom.

March 8-18, 1833—Organized First Presidency of the Church.

October 5, 1833—Went on mission to Canada.

February 14, 1835—Twelve Apostles called at Kirtland.

February 28, 1835—The Seventy called at Kirtland.

March 27, 1836—Dedicated the Kirtland Temple.

About June 1, 1837—Called Heber C. Kimball to undertake a mission to England.

January 12, 1838—Flees from Kirtland with Sidney Rigdon "to escape mob violence."

Winter 1838-39—In the Liberty Jail in Missouri.

May 1, 1839—Arranged land purchases for the future site of Nauvoo.

April 15, 1840—Sent Orson Hyde to Palestine to dedicate that land.

December 16, 1840—Nauvoo charter passed the Illinois Legislature.

February 3, 1841—Presented ordinances establishing Nauvoo Legion and University.

December 24, 1841—Announced plans for an immigration agency to be established for Church immigrants in England.

March 1, 1842—Began publishing the Book of Abraham in the *Times and Seasons*.

March 17, 1842—Organized the Relief Society of the Church.

May 4, 1842—Gave the temple endowment to a selected group meeting in the private office of his store in Nauvoo.

August 6, 1842—Prophesied that the Saints will remove to the Rocky Mountains.

June 27, 1844—Killed by the mob at Carthage, Illinois, shortly after 5:15 p.m.—(*The Improvement Era*, December 1955.)

Do I believe that the Prophet saw the Father and the Son? I certainly do. I know it. I do not need a vision. Reason teaches that to me. And then I have that knowledge also by the guidance of the Spirit of the Lord. The Lord has made it known to me.

Joseph Smith's First Prayer

I want to thank this choir for giving me a text, "Joseph Smith's First Prayer." I wonder, brethren, particularly you brethren, and our sisters, too, if we have fully realized the importance of that First Vision, the coming of the Father and the Son to the Prophet Joseph Smith, just a boy?

The world has not realized it, or they would repent of their sins. For some fifteen hundred years or more, perhaps, the world had lost the truth in relation to the Father and the Son and in the year 325, at a conclave that was held, they adopted a new idea entirely in regard to God and confused the Father and the Son, and the Christian world, from that day down until now, has looked upon the Father and the Son as being mysterious—I cannot say individuals, nor can I say substance, but some sort of spirit without separation and the idea of the separate individuals, Father and Son, from that day on ceased to exist.

Now, if the Prophet was telling a falsehood when he went into the woods to pray, he never would have come out and said that he had seen a vision of the Father and the Son and that they were separate Personages, and that the Father introduced the Son and then told the Prophet to address his question to the Son, who would give him the answer. The Prophet never would have thought of such a thing as that, had it been a fraud.

Facts Prove Authenticity of First Vision

If he had come out of the woods saying he had seen a vision, had it been untrue never would he have thought of separating Father and Son, nor would he have ever thought of having the Father introduce the Son and for him to put his question to the Son to receive his answer. He never could have thought of it; for that was the farthest thing from the ideas existing in the world in the year 1820.

The very fact that the Prophet made that statement that he saw the Father and the Son and they were glorious Personages, and that the Father spoke to him and introduced the Son, but did not ask him what he wanted, is one of the most significant things that ever occurred in the history of this world. The Prophet, if he had been telling an untruth, even if he had thought that the Father and the Son were separate Personages, would have made another very serious error, if he had lied about it. More than likely he would have said he saw the Father and the Son and the Father asked him what he wanted, and the Father gave him the answer. If Joseph Smith had said a thing like that, it would have been fatal to his story. He did not make a mistake.

It was Jesus who answered his question, and the Father introduced his Son, just as he did at the baptism of the Savior and just as he did to the three, Peter, James, and John, on the Mount, and the Savior gave the answer, as all answers have come from our Father in heaven from the beginning, since Adam was driven out of the Garden of Eden, down to this day. They have all come through the Son.

Joseph Smith Did Not Err

Now, the Prophet made no mistake, and a boy of his age would not have known; he would have fallen into a trap, just as sure as we live, if it were untrue.

Do I believe that the Prophet saw the Father and the Son? I certainly do. I know it. I do not need a vision. Reason teaches that to me. And then, I have that knowledge also by the guidance of the Spirit of the Lord. The Lord has made it known to me. So I thanked the choir, as I sat here wondering what I would say.

I have that absolute confidence in every vision, in every manifestation, in every revelation that has come to us through the Prophet Joseph Smith. I know he spoke the truth. And the evidence is made manifest in every act where there has been a manifestation from the heavens, either by the Son of God, himself, or by his servants the prophets of old. Everything has worked out harmoniously and according to the revelations we find in the Old Testament and in the New. There were no mistakes made.

On the third day of April, 1836, certain heavenly messengers appeared to the Prophet and to Oliver Cowdery. First came the Son of God himself. And they described him. Then the Lord sent certain messengers with keys to restore pertaining to the restoration of all things. Moses came and gave to the Prophet the keys of the gathering of Israel, otherwise you would not be here today, and through those keys the gospel is being preached in all the world, and scattered Israel is being gathered out again according to the fulfilment, that is, in fulfilment of the promises that were made by the Lord to his ancient prophets, that he would gather Israel in the latter days.

Elias came and restored the gospel of Abraham. Who

was Elias? That question is frequently asked. Well, Elias was Noah, who came and restored his keys.[1]

Appearance of the Prophet Elijah

Elijah came and restored his keys, opening the way for the preaching of the gospel to the dead and the performing of the ordinances in the temples of the Lord, for the dead. The prophecy of Malachi was fulfilled, at least the beginning of it, and the keys were again given through the coming of Elijah, which turned the hearts of the fathers to the children and the hearts of the children to the fathers so that we can go into the temple and do the work for our dead.

There is nothing, in my judgment, that has been revealed that is more apparent of its fulfilment than the coming of Elijah, for this spirit has gone forth into the world. It is not confined to the members of the Church, and I am sorry to say, it does not rest upon the members of the Church as fully as it ought to, but it has gone forth into the world so that there are thousands of those who do not belong to the Church, whose hearts have been turned to their fathers and who are seeking out the records of their dead, and preparing them so that we, their children, that is, the children of the dead, may go into the temples of the Lord and perform the labors that will give unto those who had no opportunity, when they were living, to receive the gospel of Jesus Christ, to give them that liberty and the privilege, that they, too,

---

[1]"The priesthood was first given to Adam; he obtained the First Presidency and held the keys of it from generation to generation. He obtained it in the Creation, before the world was formed, as in Gen. 1:26, 27, 28. He had dominion given him over every living creature. He is Michael the Archangel, spoken of in the scriptures. Then to Noah, who is Gabriel; he stands next in authority to Adam in the priesthood; he was called of God to this office, and was the father of all living in his day, and to him was given the dominion. These men held keys first on earth, and then in heaven." (DHC 3:385-386.) It was Gabriel who appeared to Zacharias and promised him a son, and who appeared to Mary and announced the coming of the Son of God as recorded by Luke. It was also Gabriel as an Elias who is mentioned in the Doctrine and Covenants, section 27, verse 7. It was Gabriel, or Noah, who stands next to Michael or Adam in the priesthood.

might be numbered in the house of Israel and receive the blessings of eternal life.

Do I love the Prophet Joseph Smith? Yes, I do, as my father did before me. I love him because he was the servant of God and because of the restoration of the gospel and because of the benefits and blessings that have come to me and mine, and to you and yours, through the blessings that were bestowed upon this man and those who were associated with him in the restoration of the dispensation of the fulness of times.—(Conference Report, April 1960.)

Concerning seeking for knowledge of countries and kingdoms, the Lord gave a revelation which we call Section 88, or the Olive Leaf, in order that the members of the Church might be inspired to seek for knowledge and an understanding of the things pertaining to this earth and, likewise, to the eternities.

The School of the Prophets

It was suggested that I say something about the School of the Prophets at this session. I should like to preface my remarks with a few remarks about the Prophet Joseph Smith and his interest in education. He never had much opportunity for schooling, that is, for going to school as other boys and girls go to school. He had to learn at his Mother's knee, but he had the best teachers that ever any man had. He became the most profound, the best informed, the greatest of all teachers of these modern days; for he was taught by angels and by the Lord Jesus Christ himself. And he was always interested in education and in seeing that the members of the Church had every opportunity which circumstances permitted to receive training in the things pertaining to this world, as well as to things pertaining to the world to come.

One of the first projects undertaken in the city of Nauvoo was the establishment of a university. But long before that time some of our brethren, Parley P. Pratt and William Phelps, were appointed to prepare text books that could be used not only by the children, but also by the elders of Israel. Even earlier, shortly after the organization of the Church, a school was established; in fact, two of them

were established.   One of these schools was the School of
the Elders, where teachers were brought to teach the elders
of this Church not only the ordinary branches of education,
but also to teach them some of the foreign languages, principally Hebrew and German.   This School of the Elders
was established in Kirtland long before the temple was
built.   Concerning seeking for knowledge of countries and
kingdoms, the Lord gave a revelation which we call Section
88, or the Olive Leaf, in order that the members of the
Church might be inspired to seek for knowledge and an
understanding of the things pertaining to this earth and,
likewise, to the eternities.

Hebrew Language Taught

In this school, a Jewish scholar was appointed, or
called, to teach the brethren Hebrew.   It is my opinion
that the Prophet felt the Hebrew language to be, perhaps,
of more importance than any other language for our people
to learn.   The Bible comes from the Hebrew people.   The
Lord calls attention to this fact in the Book of Mormon,
speaking particularly of the Jews.   But that term *Jew* meant
more than just the descendants of Judah.   It had reference
to the tribes of the Hebrew nation, to the children of Israel.

On January 14, 1833, the Prophet sent a letter to William W. Phelps, who was in Missouri, in which the following appears:

> . . . You will see that the Lord commanded us, in Kirtland, to
> build a house of God, and establish a School of the Prophets. This is
> the word of the Lord to us, and we must, yea, the Lord helping us,
> we will obey: as on conditions of our obedience he has promised us
> great things; yea, even a visit from the heavens to honor us with his
> own presence. . . .[1]

Now that is a reference to the School of the Prophets.
This school is distinct from the School of the Elders, where

---

[1]*DHC* Vol. I, p. 316.

the Hebrew scholar, Dr. Joshua Seixas taught Hebrew. I
shall read, before I am through, some of the statements in
the revelation regarding these two schools.

In another communication, written by commandment
of Elders Orson Hyde and Hyrum Smith, this is recorded:

> We now close our epistle by saying unto you, that the Lord has
> commanded us to purify ourselves to wash our hands and our feet,
> that he may testify to his Father and our Father, to his God and
> our God, that we are clean from the blood of this generation; and
> before we could wash our hands and our feet, we were constrained
> to write this letter. Therefore, with the feelings of inexpressible
> anxiety for your welfare, we say again, Repent, repent, or Zion
> must suffer. . . .[2]

In the winter of 1832-33, the Prophet wrote again:
"We spent in translating the scriptures (that is, the time),
the School of the Prophets and sitting in conference, I had
many glorious seasons of refreshing." So you see this
School of the Prophets was organized, as was the other
school, very shortly after the organization of the Church.

Circumstances Did Not Permit Continuance

The School of the Prophets and the school where the
ordinary branches of learning were taught continued in
Kirtland until the exodus from there. I am sorry to say
that it was not continued in Nauvoo, nor in Missouri, because circumstances did not permit. Because of the per-
secutions, and the drivings, and all the conditions that the
brethren had to face, this school was not continued. However, the Prophet, from time to time, gave instruction. He
gathered the brethren together, and instructed them, and
—as I have already said—prepared for a university, and
appointed some of our prominent, educated men to take
charge in the City of Nauvoo.

---

[2]*DHC* Vol. I, p. 320.

It was for this school that the Lectures on Faith, which were delivered to the elders, were prepared. I suppose that the rising generation knows little about the Lectures on Faith. They used to appear in the Doctrine and Covenants, not as revelations but as "helps" in the study of faith. They continued in the Doctrine and Covenants for many years, until about 1920. But when they got out the new edition in double columns, the Lectures on Faith were removed. Some people have wondered about that. The reason they were taken out was that they were not revelations; they were only "helps." A great many members of the Church have had an idea that they were revelations and that a mistake was made in taking them out of the Doctrine and Covenants. But when they were received and ordered placed in the Doctrine and Covenants, it was made very plain that they were added merely as "helps" to assist us in the study of faith. The brethren felt justified in removing them from the Doctrine and Covenants, thus leaving in the Doctrine and Covenants only the revelations of Jesus Christ.

In my own judgment, these Lectures on Faith are of great value and should be studied. I think they can be obtained in printed form. They were not taken out of the Doctrine and Covenants because they contained false doctrine, and I consider them to be of extreme value in the study of the gospel of Jesus Christ. These lectures were compiled, as I say, in this school, the School of the Prophets; and the Prophet Joseph Smith prepared them. There may have been some suggestions in them that came from some other brethren, but the Prophet himself revised and prepared these Lectures on Faith for publication; and they were studied in the School of the Prophets.

School Not New to This Dispensation

The School of the Prophets is not something new to this dispensation. In ancient Israel, especially in the days of Samuel, Elijah, and Elisha, we hear of the activities of this school. We can read in I Samuel 10 that after Samuel had anointed Saul to be king of Israel, the Spirit of the Lord came upon Saul, and he joined a company of the sons of the prophets, and he prophesied. In II Kings 2, we read of the School of the Prophets, the sons of the prophets. We read about them at the time that Elijah was taken into heaven; they had followed Elijah and after he was taken away they followed Elisha. Then we read, "And fifty men of the sons of the prophets went and stood to view afar off: and they two (Elijah and Elisha) stood by Jordan."[3] These sons of the prophets discovered that the power of Elijah was upon Elisha; and so, after Elijah was taken, they followed Elisha. It seems, to me, quite evident that there were a number of very choice young men who followed these two great prophets and were taught by them.

We read of the sons of the prophets in other parts of our scriptures, how certain of these young prophets were sent with special missions to anoint and to bless certain individuals. Now, the influence is very strong. It seems to me at least, that these young men who were called the sons of the prophets were not Levites. You know the Lord took away Moses and the higher priesthood, the Melchizedek Priesthood, from Israel and left with them the Aaronic Priesthood and the carnal law. And so the sons of Aaron became the priests of the people and ministered to them, looked after their wants—but in their restricted way, because as the Lord has pointed out in Section 84 of the Doctrine and Covenants, they were subject to the preparatory gospel of faith, repentance, and baptism, and they had no power to lay on hands for the gift of the Holy Ghost. There were other things, too, that they could not do; and so the Lord had to keep someone with the Melchizedek Priesthood, although it was not scattered among the tribes of Israel. Most of those who held the higher priesthood were not of

---

[3]II Kings 2:7.

the tribe of Levi.   Some were, but others came from other tribes.   These prophets gathered around them choice young men and taught them, instructed them; and they followed in the footsteps of these prophets and became known as the sons of the prophets.   It was a group of these young men who followed Elijah, and who followed Elisha, and who were present on the occasion when Saul was anointed king of Israel.

Now, all of the Melchizedek Priesthood was not given to everyone.   It was confined to a select few.   Of these few that were some who came out of the other tribes of Israel, who followed the prophets, and, by their faith and understanding, became prophets themselves.   Just how many of them were given the authority to officiate in the higher ordinances, the Lord has not revealed.   It was only by special appointment that this priesthood was given to any of the prophets.

These students of Elisha and Elijah, and a few others, were chosen, then, by revelation and commissioned, at least many of them, to anoint and to bless; and they were sent to deliver prophetic messages from time to time.   The object with which the school was organized in this dispensation is plainly stated in the revelation found in Section 88. None could join except he were clean from the blood of this generation, and the only way he could be cleansed was to be obedient to the covenants of the gospel and to labor in behalf of his fellows for their salvation.   Thus, the preaching of the gospel was by a requirement made of those who desired to join this school, the School of the Prophets.

School Organized in Salt Lake City

This school was organized in Salt Lake City, after the saints came to these valleys, under the direction of President Brigham Young.   It continued for some time, but there came a time when some of the members who attended became rebellious.   Dissension broke out, and the spirit of apostasy entered into the hearts of some of these brethren who assembled to receive divine instruction. And so this School of the Prophets was closed, and from that time until now, in the form in which it then existed, has never again been brought into existence. The School of the Prophets, as far as we have a School of the Prophets today, is confined to the First Presidency and the Council of the Twelve.

Now, in regard to these two schools, I want to read what the Lord said to the Prophet by revelation:

Organize yourselves; prepare every needful thing, and establish a house, even a house of prayer, a house of fasting, a house of faith, a house of learning, a house of glory, a house of order, a house of God;

That your incomings may be in the name of the Lord, that your outgoings may be in the name of the Lord, that all your salutations may be in the name of the Lord, with uplifted hands unto the Most High.

Therefore, cease from all your light speeches, from all laughter, (that is, loud laughter—boisterous laughter), from all your pride and light-mindedness, and from all your wicked doings.

Appoint among yourselves a teacher, and let not all be spokesmen at once; but let one speak at a time and let all listen unto his sayings, that when all have spoken that all may be edified of all, and that every man may have an equal privilege.

See that ye love one another; cease to be covetous; learn to impart one to another as the gospel requires.

Cease to be idle; cease to be unclean; cease to find fault one with another; cease to sleep longer than is needful; retire to thy bed early, that ye may not be weary; arise early, that your bodies and your minds may be invigorated.

That is good counsel for all of us today.

And above all things, clothe yourselves with the bond of charity, as with a mantle, which is the bond of perfectness and peace.

Pray always, that ye may not faint, until I come. Behold, and lo, I will come quickly, and receive you unto myself. Amen.

And again, the order of the house prepared for the presidency of the school of the prophets, established for their instruction in all things that are expedient for them, even for all the officers of the church, or in other words, those who are called to the ministry in the church, beginning at the high priests, even down to the deacons—

And this shall be the order of the house of the presidency of
the school: He that is appointed to be president, or teacher, shall
be found standing in his place, in the house which shall be prepared for him.

Therefore, he shall be first in the house of God, in a place
that the congregation in the house may hear his words carefully and
distinctly, not with loud speech.

And when he cometh into the house of God, for he should be
first in the house — behold, this is beautiful, that he may be an
example—

Let him offer himself in prayer upon his knees before God, in
token or remembrance of the everlasting covenant.

And when any shall come in after him, let the teacher arise,
and with uplifted hands to heaven, yea, even directly, salute his
brother or brethren with these words.

Art thou a brother or brethren? I salute you in the name of
the Lord Jesus Christ, in token of remembrance of the everlasting
covenant, in which covenant I receive you to fellowship, in a determination that is fixed, immovable, and unchangeable, to be your
friend and brother through the grace of God in the bonds of love,
to walk in all commandments of God blameless, in thanksgiving,
forever and ever. Amen.

And he that is found unworthy of this salutation shall not have
place among you; for ye shall not suffer that mine house shall be
polluted by him.

And he that cometh in and is faithful before me, and is a
brother, or if they be brethren, they shall salute the president or
teacher with uplifted hands to heaven, with this same prayer and
covenant, or by saying Amen, in token of the same.

Behold, verily, I say unto you, this is an ensample unto you for
a salutation to one another in the house of God, in the school of
the prophets.

And ye are called to do this by prayer and thanksgiving, as the
Spirit shall give utterance in all your doings in the house of the
Lord, in the school of the prophets, that it may become a sanctuary,
a tabernacle of the Holy Spirit to your edification.[4]

Now other instructions were given too. I said that
there was a school of learning. Let me read a verse or two,
here, in regard to it:

---

[4]D&C 88:119-137.

Also, I give unto you a commandment that ye shall continue in prayer and fasting from this time forth.

And I give unto you a commandment that you shall teach one another the doctrine of the kingdom.

Teach ye diligently and my grace shall attend you, that you may be instructed more perfectly in theory, in principle, in doctrine, in the law of the gospel, in all things that pertain unto the kingdom of God, that are expedient for you to understand.

Now this is the instruction that was given to the elders who had been out preaching the gospel, and who had been called in to be endowed that they might go out with more power. To continue this quotation:

Of things both in heaven and in the earth, and under the earth; things which have been, things which are, things which must shortly come to pass; things which are at home, things which are abroad; the wars and the perplexities of the nations, and the judgments which are on the land; and a knowledge also of countries and of kingdoms.[5]

I think that covers about everything you are taught here in this university. And the Lord has called upon us to teach these things. But whether we come to school here to be taught from textbooks that are published by those who are not of the Church or to be taught from textbooks that are published by those who belong to the Church, we should come in that same spirit of faith, with a desire in our hearts to seek the truth, to draw nearer to God our Eternal Father, and to worship him in the name of his Son, Jesus Christ.

I am grateful for the opportunity of meeting with all you good people who have assembled at this grand gathering of Leadership Week to be instructed by those who are appointed to give instruction, from time to time, while you are here. The Lord bless you, in the name of the Lord Jesus Christ, Amen—(Address presented at Brigham Young University Leadership Week, June 18, 1956.)

[5]D&C 88:76-79.

*Priesthood is divine authority which is con-
ferred upon men that they may officiate in
the ordinances of the gospel. In other words,
priesthood is a part of God's own power, which
he bestows upon his chosen servants that they
may act in his name in proclaiming the gospel
and officiating in all the ordinances thereof.*

Priesthood in Relation to History

Let us consider briefly what the priesthood is and something in relation to its history. President Joseph F. Smith has given us this definition:

It is nothing more nor less than the power of God delegated to man by which man can act in the earth for the salvation of the human family, in the name of the Father and the Son and the Holy Ghost, and act legitimately; not assuming that authority, nor borrowing it from generations that are dead and gone, but authority that has been given in this day in which we live by ministering angels and spirits from above, direct from the presence of God. . . . It is the same power and priesthood that was committed to the disciples of Christ while he was upon the earth; that whatsoever they should bind on earth should be bound in heaven and whatsoever they should loose on earth should be loosed in heaven.[1]

President Lorenzo Snow defined it as follows:

The priesthood or authority in which we stand is the medium or channel through which our Heavenly Father has purposed to communicate light, intelligence, gifts, powers, and spiritual and temporal salvation unto the present generation.[2]

However the priesthood is far more than this. It is the great power by and through which our Eternal Father

[1]*Conference Report,* October, 1904.
[2]*Millennial Star,* May, 1841.

and his Son Jesus Christ perform their work throughout
the universe. The greatness and glory of the priesthood,
we in our limited sphere, do not fully understand. We read
in the word of the Lord, that

> . . . judgment goeth before the face of him who sitteth upon the
> throne and governeth and executeth all things.
> He comprehendeth all things, and all things are before him,
> and all things are round about him; and he is above all things, and
> in all things, and is through all things, and is round about all things;
> and all things are by him, and of him, even God, forever and for-
> ever.[3]

A Law Given unto All Things

He it is who has given "a law unto all things, by which
they move in their times and in their seasons." It is by this
divine power that our Heavenly Father rules in and controls
the universe.

In the beginning, as far as this world is concerned, the
priesthood was first given to Adam. On this the Prophet
Joseph Smith said:

> The priesthood was first given to Adam; he obtained the First
> Presidency, and held the keys of it from generation to generation.
> He obtained it in the Creation, before the world was formed, as in
> Genesis 1:26-27, 28. He held dominion given him over every living
> creature. He is Michael the Archangel, spoken of in the scriptures.
> Then to Noah, who is Gabriel; he stands next in authority to Adam
> in the priesthood; he was called of God to this office, and was the
> father of all living in this day, and to him was given the Dominion.
> These men held keys first on earth, and then in heaven.[4]
> The priesthood is an everlasting principle, and existed with God
> from eternity, and will to eternity, without beginning of days or end
> of years. The keys have to be brought from heaven whenever the
> gospel is sent. When they are revealed from heaven, it is by Adam's
> authority.[5]

---

[3]D&C 88:40-41.
  [4]*Teachings of the Prophet Joseph Smith* (Salt Lake City: Deseret Book Co.),
p. 157.
    [5]*Ibid.*, p. 157.

Priesthood of Adam Was Patriarchal

The priesthood of Adam, and from Adam to Moses, was the patriarchal order. Of this order the Lord has said: "The order of this priesthood was confirmed to be handed down from Father to son, and rightly belongs to the literal descendants of the chosen seed, to whom the promises were made." This order was instituted in the days of Adam, and came down by lineage, the keys evidently being held by the following prophets to the days of Noah: Adam, Seth, Enos, Cainan, Mahalaleel, Jared, Enoch, Methuselah, Lamech and Noah.

This same priesthood continued, principally through the seed of Abraham, until the days of Moses. The Lord offered it to Israel in the days of Moses, but they were not prepared nor worthy to receive it. He would have made of all the tribes a royal priesthood, but they rebelled. Therefore the Melchizedek Priesthood, for that was the name by which it was called since the days of Melchizedek, was taken away from Israel and the Aaronic Priesthood was given with the law of Moses added as a "schoolmaster," and with this the tribes of Israel had to be content. During all of these years from the time of Moses to the coming of our Lord, it was necessary that there be some prophets who held the Melchizedek Priesthood, therefore the Lord raised up prophets in Israel on whom the Higher Priesthood was conferred but each ordination was a special call. In relation to this the Prophet Joseph Smith said:

Was the Priesthood of Melchizedek taken away when Moses died? All priesthood is Melchizedek, but there are different portions or degrees of it. That portion which brought Moses to speak with God face to face was taken away; but that which brought the ministry of angels remained. All of the prophets had the Melchizedek Priesthood and were ordained by God himself.[6]

---

[6]*Ibid.,* pp. 180-181.

The prophets who held the Melchizedek Priesthood, with a few exceptions, following the departure of Moses, were more or less restricted in their jurisdiction. It was essential that the Melchizedek Priesthood be in Israel after Moses was taken, in order that the gift of the Holy Ghost could be given, but the tribes of Israel had forfeited their right to it because of their rebellion. For instance the Prophet Elijah held the keys of the sealing power and was, according to the word of the Lord, the last of those prophets, until the coming of Jesus Christ, to hold the keys of that authority. Therefore there were restrictions placed upon other prophets although they were blessed with the Melchizedek Priesthood.

The Calling of the Twelve

When the Savior entered his ministry, one of the early things he did was to call twelve men. It is written that he "gave them power against unclean spirits, to cast them out, and to heal all manner of sickness and all manner of disease." The names of these twelve are familiar to most all. They were: Simon, whom he called Peter, and Andrew his brother; James, the son of Zebedee, and John his brother; Philip, and Bartholomew; Thomas, and Matthew the publican; James, the son of Alphaeus, and Lebbaeus, whose surname was Thaddaeus; Simon the Canaanite, and Judas Iscariot. While the record does not say so, it is very evident that the Savior conferred upon them the apostleship, with its keys and authorities. Later he said to them:

> Verily I say unto you, Whatsoever ye shall bind on earth shall be bound in heaven; and whatsoever ye shall loose on earth shall be loosed in heaven.[7]

It is believed by some, because of what the Lord said to Peter at Caesarea Philippi, that this authority to bind and loose was a gift to Peter only. This however, is not

---
[7]Matthew 18:18.

the case, for this commission was given to the entire Twelve. In fact, each received the fulness of the apostleship so that each, should the time come, could serve as the senior, or president of the Church in his turn. The order in the Church today is based on that same principle. Moreover, the Lord selected Peter, James, and John and set them at the front to act as a First Presidency after his departure. Evidence of this is found in the fact that on several occasions the Savior took these three with him to attend to special duties. They were with him on the Mount of Transfiguration. There according to the Prophet Joseph Smith, the Lord with Moses and Elias ministered unto them and gave them keys of the priesthood.

> The priesthood is everlasting. The Savior, Moses, and Elias, gave the keys to Peter, James and John, on the mount, when they were transfigured before him. The priesthood is everlasting—without beginning of days or end of years; without father, mother etc. If there is no change of ordinances, there is no change of priesthood. Wherever the ordinances of the gospel are administered, there is the priesthood.
>
> How have we come at the priesthood in the last days? It came down, down, in regular succession. Peter, James, and John had it given to them and they gave it to others. Christ is the Great High Priest; Adam next. Paul speaks of the Church coming to an innumerable company of angels—to God the Judge of all—the spirits of the just men made perfect; to Jesus the Mediator of the new Covenant.[8]

Peter, James, and John Given Special Authority

The fact that Peter, James, and John were separated from the other apostles and given special authority, was the forerunner of the quorum of the First Presidency in our day. It should be perfectly clear from what is written that these three apostles formed such a presidency. Therefore on the death of Peter and James, it was John who by right of seniority became the presiding officer in the Church. Then, it is very apparent to Latter-day Saints that these three were a

---

[8]*Teachings of the Prophet Joseph Smith*, p. 158.

Presidency due to the fact that all three came to the Prophet Joseph Smith and Oliver Cowdery and conferred upon them the Melchizedek Priesthood.

According to the teachings of Paul, it was the intention that when vacancies occurred in the Council of the Twelve, that these vacancies should be filled, for he declared to the Saints in his day at Ephesus, while arguing for the unity of the Church:

> And he gave some apostles; and some, prophets; and some, evangelists, and some, pastors and teachers;
> For the perfecting of the saints, for the work of the ministry, for the edifying of the body of Christ:
> Till we all come in the unity of the faith, and of the knowledge of the Son of God, unto a perfect man, unto the measure of the stature of the fulness of Christ.[9]

We know also that after the fall of Judas, the disciples met and by the inspiration of the Lord selected Matthias to fill that vacancy. We know also that it was but a short time following the death of the Lord, that James, one of the three, was killed. That Paul was called to be an apostle is evident from many of his epistles and Barnabas was also so called. We look upon James who wrote the epistle and Jude as being apostles. If so, then they must have taken the places of others who had passed away. The question is a sound one that the apostles in that day were intended to be in the Church through the years, but apostasy stepped in and the ways of the Lord were perverted.

Chosen by Command of the Lord

In our day, by command of the Lord, men have been chosen to carry on the work of the Twelve whenever vacancies occur. In the Book of Mormon we read that this was the custom among the Nephites. It was never intended that there should be but twelve men called to this position and

---

[9]Ephesians 4:11-13.

no more when vacancies occurred. Our scripture is perfectly clear on this point.

One of the first intimations that there were to be chosen twelve apostles in this dispensation, is found in the revelation given at Fayette, New York, in June, 1829, where the three witnesses were appointed to search out the Twelve, seventeen years before the Twelve were called. This is a wonderful revelation of counsel intended for the Twelve. The brethren selected for this important calling were men who had proved their integrity in Zion's Camp. On the fourteenth day of February, 1835, the Prophet called the brethren who had gone to Missouri in Zion's Camp to assemble, for he had blessings for them. He stated that the object of the meeting was to choose men for important positions in the ministry. He had been commanded by the Lord to call men of integrity and faith, among these would be twelve to be ordained as apostles in the Church. These men were, according to revelation, to be selected by the three witnesses of the Book of Mormon. After the usual opening exercises, the three witnesses were blessed by the laying on of hands by the First Presidency that they might have the inspiration to make the selections. The names in the order in which they were selected are as follows:

1. Lyman E. Johnson
2. Brigham Young
3. Heber C. Kimball
4. Orson Hyde
5. David W. Patten
6. Luke S. Johnson
7. William E. McLellin
8. John F. Boynton
9. Orson Pratt
10. William Smith
11. Thomas B. Marsh
12. Parley P. Pratt

Later these brethren were arranged in order of precedence according to their age as follows:

1. Thomas B. Marsh
2. David W. Patten
3. Brigham Young
4. Heber C. Kimball
5. Orson Hyde
6. William E. McLellin

7. Parley P. Pratt	10. Orson Pratt
8. Luke S. Johnson	11. John F. Boynton
9. William Smith	12. Lyman E. Johnson

After the selection the witnesses according to their divine appointment ordained these brethren. The first three were ordained at this meeting and on the following day all the others, except Thomas B. Marsh, Parley P. Pratt and Orson Pratt. Elders Marsh and Orson Pratt were on a mission and Parley P. Pratt did not arrive until late in April. At this solemn gathering a charge was given to these apostles. March 12, 1835 the apostles met in council and petitioned the First Presidency to seek for them a revelation that would guide them in their labors. The answer to their petition came March 28, 1835, when the great revelation on priesthood was received (Sec. 107).

I do not understand how any member of the Church can read this revelation without being thoroughly convinced of its divine origin. It should be thoroughly studied in the spirit of humility and faith by every member of the Church holding the priesthood. In fact, such a study is imperative if we wish to know something of the greatness, glory and responsibilities of the priesthood. It is difficult to believe that any person can read this inspired document and not be definitely convinced of the prophetic powers of the Prophet Joseph Smith. Without this revelation we would still be groping in the dark in relation to our duties and the divine organization of the priesthood of the Church.

Causes of Apostasy

It is true that a few years later, several of these men who had been honored by a call to become special witnesses for Christ, with the divine injunction to carry the message of the restored gospel to all the world, fell away. Of course they had pledged themselves by solemn covenant to take upon them the name of Jesus Christ and serve him diligently in this calling and without fear or favor of men, go into all the world, no matter what the hardships might be and sacredly perform their duty. I am fully convinced that they were good men; that they had faithfully performed their labor which laid the foundation for their call to this sacred ministry. Yet they fell from this high and holy calling. What were the reasons? First the severe opposition which they met, but more particularly because, when adverse circumstances came, they commenced to complain. Then, added to this, the false rumors afloat that leading brethren had not been true to sacred trusts and feeling that they the disgruntled members had been injured in financial ventures. It was a period of great financial depression and universal reverses and there were some who failed to have the clear vision to help them weather the storm. Unjust accusations arose in their souls against the Prophet and some of the brethren who remained faithful and true. All of these and other conditions preyed upon their souls, and as they gave way to this sin, the Spirit of the Lord withdrew and they were left to themselves, and darkness replaced the light which was formerly in their souls.

One of these original brethren returned years later, fully repentant, seeking forgiveness and when reinstated in the Church remained faithful and true to the end. The others apparently never overcame their bitterness. Yet the story is told of one of these that years later he had the privilege of associating with his former companions and talking over the experiences which he had when faithfully performing his duty, he made a remark something like this: "I would give everything in the world, if I could feel as I did when I was associated with you." But he did not, and perhaps could not, repent; for repentance is a gift of God.

Naturally, when these brethren fell others were selected to take their places. It seems strange that men can have the guidance of the Spirit of the Lord and then fall away, but such things have happened from the very beginning. The examples of these unfaithful men, and their miserable end, should impress every member of the Church that humility, faith, and obedience should be at the very foundation of their character. No man is tempted beyond his capacity or power to resist. It is only when one yields to temptation or wanders, oh so slightly from the path of rectitude, that Satan obtains the advantage and destroys one's faith. So many times we have been warned that it is "he who endures to the end, that shall be saved."

The Lord Gave Warning

The Lord gave a warning to the members of the Church at the very time of its organization to walk in paths of righteousness in deep humility, with "a broken heart and a contrite spirit."

> But we know also, that sanctification through the grace of our Lord and Savior Jesus Christ is just and true, to all those who love and serve God with all their mights, minds, and strength.
> But there is a possibility that man may fall from grace and depart from the living God;
> Therefore let the church take heed and pray always, lest they fall into temptation.
> Yea, and even let those who are sanctified take heed also.[10]

The failure of men to live up to their covenants—men who one time were filled with light and truth—should be to us a constant warning. We have been warned constantly that it is he who endures to the end that shall be saved.

But let us return to those who, even under these difficult and most trying circumstances, remained faithful and true. Brigham Young, Heber C. Kimball, David W. Patten, and the faithful men called to succeed those who fell, John Taylor, Wilford Woodruff, Willard Richards and many others. No men passed through more by way of persecution,

---

[10]D&C 20:31-34.

ridicule, hatred than did these men who under all the circumstances that confronted them remained loyal and true. These are the men who remained loyal to the Prophet Joseph Smith and his brother Hyrum and were willing, if circumstances required it, to have died with them. The Lord will place within the reach of every honest soul who is willing to seek the truth a testimony of his divine truth.

Let us consider briefly the great responsibilities which devolve upon the apostles. They are special witnesses for Jesus Christ. It is their right to know the truth and have an abiding witness, and this is an exacting duty upon them, to know that Jesus Christ is in very deed the Only Begotten Son of God, the Redeemer of the world and the Savior of all those who will confess their sins, repent and keep his commandments.

The question frequently arises: "Is it necessary for the members of the Council of the Twelve to see the Savior in order to be an apostle?" It is their privilege to see him if occasion requires, but the Lord has taught that there is a stronger witness than seeing a personage, even of the Son of God, in a vision. I wish we could get this clear in the minds of members of the Church. The Savior said:

Wherefore I say unto you, all manner of sin and blasphemy shall be forgiven unto men: but the blasphemy against the Holy Ghost shall not be forgiven unto men.

And whosoever speaketh a word against the Son of man, it shall be forgiven him, but whosoever speaketh against the Holy Ghost, it shall not be forgiven him, neither in this world, neither in the world to come.[11]

Therefore the seeing, even the Savior, does not leave as deep an impression in the mind as does the testimony of the Holy Ghost to the spirit. Both Peter and Paul understood this. Here are the words of Paul:

----

[11]Matthew 12:31-32.

For it is impossible for those who were once enlightened, and have tasted of the heavenly gift, and were made partakers of the Holy Ghost.

And have tasted the good word of God, and the powers of the world to come.

If they shall fall away, to renew them again unto repentance; seeing they crucify to themselves the Son of God afresh, and put him to an open shame.[12]

What Is the Lesson To Be Learned?

What is the lesson to be learned from this? That the impressions on the soul that come from the Holy Ghost are far more significant than a vision. It is where Spirit speaks to spirit, and the imprint upon the soul is far more difficult to erase. Every member of the Church should have the impressions on his soul made by the Holy Ghost that Jesus is the Son of God indelibly pictured so that they cannot be forgotten. We read that it is the Spirit that giveth life. In the revelation on priesthood there are three quorums mentioned that have special authority. First the First Presidency, and of this quorum we have the following:

Of the Melchizedek Priesthood, three Presiding High Priests, chosen by the body appointed and ordained to that office, and upheld by the confidence, faith, and prayer of the church, form a quorum of the Presidency of the Church.

The twelve traveling councilors are called to be the Twelve Apostles, or special witnesses of the name of Christ in all the world —thus differing in the duties of their calling.

And they form a quorum, equal in authority and power to the three presidents previously mentioned.

The Seventy are also called to preach the gospel, and to be especial witnesses unto the Gentiles and in all the world—thus differing from other officers in the church in the duties of their calling.

And they form a quorum, equal in authority to that of the Twelve special witnesses just named.

And every decision made by either of these quorums must be by the unanimous voice of the same; that is, every member in each

---

[12]Hebrews 6:4-6.

quorum must be agreed to its decisions, in order to make their decision of the same power or validity one with the other—

A majority may form a quorum when circumstances render it impossible to be otherwise—

Unless this is the case, their decisions are not entitled to the same blessings which the decisions of a quorum of three presidents were anciently, who were ordained after the order of Melchizedek, and were righteous and holy men.[13]

Only One Quorum Presides at a Time

Of course there cannot be three quorums of equal authority at the same time. Such a thing could lead to confusion if each of the three, or even two of them, made adverse decisions. The natural interpretation of this is, and is well understood, that only in the destruction of the first quorum—the Presidency of the Church, would the second, or apostles, step forth to make a decision. This has happened each time that the First Presidency has been disorganized by the death of the President, and then only until a new First Presidency was organized would the Council of the Twelve exercise this authority. Should the time ever arise, which is unlikely, that both the Council of the First Presidency and the Council of the Twelve were destroyed, would the seventy step forth to make a decision for the Church, then they would drop back to their normal position.

The Twelve are a Traveling Presiding High Council, to officiate in the name of the Lord, under the direction of the Presidency of the Church, agreeable to the institution of heaven; to build up the church, and regulate all the affairs of the same in all nations, first to the Gentiles and then to the Jews;

The Seventy are to act in the name of the Lord, under the direction of the Twelve or the traveling high council, in building up the church and regulating all of the affairs of the same in all nations, first unto the Gentiles and then to the Jews.

The Twelve being sent out, holding the keys, to open the door by the proclamation of the gospel of Jesus Christ, and first unto the Gentiles and then unto the Jews. . . .

---

[13]D&C 107:22-29.

It is the duty of the traveling high council to call upon the Seventy, when they need assistance, to fill the several calls for preaching and administering the gospel, instead of any others.

It is the duty of the Twelve, in all large branches of the church to ordain evangelical ministers, as they shall be designated unto them by revelation.[14]

Thus the request of the original Twelve to obtain knowledge concerning their duties was given by revelation from the Lord.—(Address to seminary and institute faculty, Brigham Young University, June 18, 1958.)

---

[14]D&C 107:33-35, 38-39.

The great revelation on priesthood and patriar-
chal descent was given to the Prophet by the
Lord and reveals its descent from the beginning
of time.

The Patriarchal Priesthood

After the organization of the Council of the Twelve Apostles in Kirtland in 1835, the members of that council were called to go into the mission field. March 28th of that year they came to the Prophet seeking a revelation in relation to their duties that they might understand more perfectly what the Lord required at their hands. In answer to this request, the great revelation on priesthood (D&C 107) was received. In this revelation certain knowledge was revealed concerning the Patriarchal Priesthood and its descent from the beginning of time. Regarding this priesthood the Lord said:

It is the duty of the Twelve, in all large branches of the church, to ordain evangelical ministers, as they shall be designated unto them by revelation—

The order of this priesthood was confirmed to be handed down from father to son, and rightly belongs to the literal descendants of the chosen seed, to whom the promises were made.

This order was instituted in the days of Adam, and came down by lineage in the following manner:

From Adam to Seth, who was ordained by Adam at the age of sixty-nine years, and was blessed by him three years previous to his [Adam's] death, and received the promise of God by his father, that his posterity should be the chosen of the Lord, and that they should be preserved unto the end of the earth;

Because he [Seth] was a perfect man, and his likeness was the express likeness of his father, insomuch that he seemed to be like unto his father in all things, and could be distinguished from him only by his age.[1]

Other Patriarchs

In the following verses are named the other patriarchs from Seth to Noah, with the ages of each when ordained. In Genesis we find the descent continued as follows: Shem, Arphaxad, Salah, Eber, Peleg, Reu, Serug, Nahor, Terah, Abraham.[2] The father of Abraham from what we learn in the Book of Abraham, turned to the worship of idols; therefore he either lost his priesthood or it passed him by; nevertheless the descent came through him to Abraham. From Abraham the birthright went to Isaac and from him to Jacob, who was named Israel. From Israel it went to Joseph, the firstborn son of Rachel. The reason for this birthright not going to Israel's oldest son or to any of Joseph's older brothers was evidently because each had forfeited it by transgression. Therefore the birthright and the Patriarchal Priesthood continued through the seed of Joseph. Just why it was continued through Ephraim rather than through Manasseh, his older brother, we have not been informed, but we may be sure that the Lord had sufficient reason. From that time until now, this birthright has been vested in the descendants of Ephraim.[3]

In the dispensation of the fulness of times in which we live, the Lord revealed that this birthright of the first-born in Israel belonged to Joseph Smith, the father of the Prophet, and he was the first patriarch ordained in this dispensation. After his death the office and priesthood was conferred upon

---

[1]D&C 107:39-43.
[2]Genesis 11:10-26.
[3]I Chronicles 51:2; Jeremiah 31:9; D&C 133:30-34.

Hyrum Smith, the Prophet's oldest living brother. There is an interesting statement in a revelation given to Hyrum Smith in April 1830, a few days after the organization of the Church. In this revelation the Lord said to him:

Behold, I speak unto you, Hyrum, a few words; for thou also art under no condemnation, and thy heart is open, and thy tongue loosed; and thy calling is . . . unto the church forever, and this because of thy family.[4]

Authority of Hyrum Smith's Descendants

This appears to be a clear intimation that he and his descendants after him should hold this patriarchal authority.

After the death of the Patriarch Joseph Smith, Sr., Hyrum Smith, who was serving as second counselor in the First Presidency of the Church, was called to take the office of patriarch, and the Lord said:

And again, verily I say unto you, let my servant William [Law] be appointed, ordained, and anointed, as a counselor unto my servant Joseph, in the room of my servant Hyrum, that my servant Hyrum may take the office of Priesthood and Patriarch, which was appointed unto him by his father, by blessing, and also by right;

That from henceforth he shall hold the keys of the patriarchal blessings upon the heads of all my people.

That whosoever he blesses shall be blessed, and whosoever he curses shall be cursed; that whatsoever he shall bind on earth shall be bound in heaven; and whatsoever he shall loose on earth shall be loosed in heaven.[5]

In the same blessing and appointment an additional authority was conferred upon Hyrum Smith, for he was appointed to be an assistant President of the Church in the place of Oliver Cowdery, and all the keys and authorities that were given to Oliver were transferred to Hyrum Smith.[6]

Today in each stake of Zion a patriarch is ordained, in some cases more than one. The patriarchs are authorized to

---

4D&C 23:3.
5D&C 124:91-93. See also verses 93-125.
6D&C 124:94-95.

give blessings to all faithful members of the Church, within the borders of the stake in which they live, who come properly recommended by their bishops.

PATRIARCHS TO THE CHURCH

1. Joseph Smith, Sr. Born July 12, 1771, at Topsfield, Mass., ordained December 18, 1833, under the hands of Joseph Smith, Jr., Oliver Cowdery, Sidney Rigdon, and Frederick G. Williams; died September 14, 1840, at Nauvoo, Illinois.

2. Hyrum Smith. Born February 9, 1800 at Tunbridge, Vermont, ordained January 24, 1841 by Joseph Smith, Jr.; died a martyr June 27, 1844, at Carthage Jail, Illinois.

4. John Smith. Born September 22, 1832, at Kirtland, Ohio, ordained February 18, 1855; died November 6, 1911, at Salt Lake City.

5. Hyrum G. Smith. Born July 8, 1879 at South Jordan, Utah, ordained May 9, 1912; died February 4, 1932 at Salt Lake City.

6. Joseph F. Smith. Born January 30, 1899 at Salt Lake City, ordained October 8, 1942; released October 6, 1946 because of ill health.

7. Eldred Gee Smith. Born January 9, 1907 at Lehi, Utah, ordained April 10, 1947.—(*The Improvement Era*, November, 1956.)

We have these two great responsibilities—every man holding the priesthood—first, to seek our own salvation; and second, our duty to our fellowmen. I take it that my first duty is, so far as I am individually concerned, to seek my own salvation. That is your individual duty first, and so with every member of this Church.

The Duties of the Priesthood in Temple Work

Every married man stands at the head of his household, that is, his immediate family. Thus I, for instance, will stand at the head of my family group by virtue of the sealing for time and eternity, and my children will belong to me. I will belong to my parents in their family group. My father likewise with his brothers and sisters will belong to his father's unit in that family group, and his father to his father before him—all linked together generation to generation like a chain. So it will be of the righteous from the days of Adam down—Adam standing at the head as Michael, having authority and jurisdiction over his posterity in this large family group who have kept the commandments of God. Now that is the order of the priesthood.

Of course there will be chains that will be broken, links that will be missing, because we cannot force people into the kingdom. Those who are unworthy to be joined in this grouping of families will have to stand aside, and those who are worthy will be brought together, and the chain will go on just the same. This is what was meant by Malachi in saying that Elijah should come to turn the heart of the children to their fathers lest the earth be smitten with a curse.

Elijah Held Keys of Sealing Power

Elijah held the keys of the sealing power. Some of us do not understand what this means. I know a great many people have an idea that Elijah had a mission peculiar to the dead, but this was not so. In his day there was no work done for the dead, but he held the fulness of the priesthood, the sealing power, and by virtue of that sealing power, or the keys of the priesthood which he held, he restored to Joseph Smith and Oliver Cowdery the sealing power by virtue of which in this dispensation the work can be done for the dead just the same as it is done for the living.

The duty of a man in his own family is to see that he and his wife are sealed at the altar. If married out in the world before they joined the Church, or if they have been in the Church and have been unable to go to the temple, it is that man's duty to go to the temple, have his wife sealed to him, and have their children sealed, so that the family group, that unit to which he belongs, is made intact in order that it will continue throughout all eternity. That is the first duty that a man owes to himself, to his wife, and to his children. He receives this blessing by virtue of the priesthood.

Then it is his duty to seek his record as far back as he can go and do the same thing for each unit. He should begin with his father and mother and their children, and his grandfather and his children, great-grandfather and his children, and have the work done in like manner, linking each generation with the one that goes before. That is the responsibility resting upon every man who is at the head of a household in this Church.

Responsible for Our Own Families

The Lord has not placed upon any man in this Church the responsibility of doing the temple work for his neighbor. If you want to help your neighbor, there is no objection. If he needs help and you can help him, he will appreciate it. But your responsibility is to do your own work for your own line, going from father to son or from son to father, clear back as far as you are able to carry this record. When you do that, then you place yourself in line, through the fulness of the priesthood, eventually to receive the fulness of the glory of God.

That is what temple work is for. Temple work is for the purpose of giving to every man and to every woman the blessings of the higher ordinances of the gospel that are essential to salvation in the kingdom of God. There is not an ordinance performed in the temple that does not pertain to this mortal life. When we go into the temple and act for somebody else, we are treating that person as if we were that person living here, doing for him just what he would have to do if he were in mortal life. Thus we bring to pass his salvation, and we learn through these keys the knowledge of God which is made manifest through these ordinances, these blessings, these signs, all that is given to us in the temple of the Lord.

Two Great Responsibilities

We have these two great responsibilities—every man holding the priesthood—first, to seek our own salvation; and, second, our duty to our fellowmen. I take it that my first duty is, so far as I am individually concerned, to seek my own salvation. That is your individual duty first, and so with every member of this Church. Our duty to our fellowmen in the world is a responsibility resting especially on the shoulders of the men holding the priesthood. Our duty is to preach the gospel, to teach the nations of the earth,

to go out and bring people into the Church. That duty is
upon the Church. The Lord has arranged it so that certain
men are called to certain offices in the Church with that
peculiar duty on their shoulders. The Twelve, the seventies,
are the missionaries of the Church, but every man in the
Church has this responsibility as a man holding the priesthood.

Of course, the Lord says that our greatest individual
responsibility is to seek after our dead; but as men holding
the priesthood our responsibility is—so far as temple work
is concerned—to teach, to instruct, to persuade, to prevail
upon men and women who are not inclined to take advantage of their opportunities and receive these blessings for
themselves, to go into the temple where they can do this
work. That is our responsibility as men holding the priesthood. It does not make any difference whether we are high
priests, seventies, or elders. We are trying to place this burden especially upon the high priests of the Church. The
seventies preach the gospel—that is where they belong—the
elders are ministers at home, the high priests are ministers
at home, and we are also trying to train them to take upon
themselves this responsibility of teaching their fellowmen
in all that pertains to exaltation and to help prepare them
to go to the temple to do these labors in behalf of their dead.
This is our responsibility, and it is a great responsibility.

Vicarious Work Is Foundation of Salvation

Vicarious work is the foundation of salvation. There is
no salvation without vicarious work. If Christ had not felt
in his heart a love for us, if there had not been that love of
the Father to sacrifice his Son for us, and if the Son had
not been willing, there would have been no salvation for us.
We would be subject to Satan forever, as Lehi says in the
Book of Mormon. The Father, through his love for us,
called upon the Savior who was willing, of course, to come

into this world to act vicariously for me and for you. He came and offered himself as a sacrifice to save me and save you from a condition where we could not help ourselves.

Temple work is a vicarious work. We may, without any suffering so far as we are concerned, act as saviors on Mount Zion by going into the temple and doing for our dead the things they cannot do for themselves. But there are thousands of Latter-day Saints who seem to be uncertain about this. They are willing to go to meeting, willing to pay their tithing, and attend to the regular duties of the Church, but they do not seem to feel or understand the importance of receiving the blessings in the temple of the Lord which will bring them into exaltation. It is a strange thing. People seem to be content just to slide along without taking advantage of the opportunities presented to them and without receiving these necessary covenants that will bring them back into the presence of God as sons and daughters. Now that is our duty as men holding the priesthood: To teach them and make them understand the importance of this.

We will go to them as missionaries; we will labor with them; we will try to show them, we will try to convince them, we will try to persuade them to go to the temple for their own salvation and for the salvation of their dead; and when we have done that, we have done our duty. So I want to say that to all those who are engaged in the genealogical work in the stakes of Zion, that work of persuasion is assigned to you. We want you as men holding the priesthood, and the sisters laboring with you, to persuade, to teach, to do everything in your power by persuasion and by teaching the members of the Church to get them to the temple to do the thing that will bring them the fulness of the glory of God.—(*The Utah Genealogical and Historical Magazine,* Vol. 30, pp. 1-4.)

Never before in the history of the Church has the responsibility that has been given to the priesthood been more necessary of fulfilment than today. Never before have we been under greater obligation to serve the Lord, and keep his commandments, and magnify the callings that have been assigned to us.

Your Priesthood Responsibilities

This is a wonderful sight to me, as I look to the other end of this building, and in the gallery, and back of men, and see all of you brethren who hold divine authority. I have thought that the best thing I could do would be to prepare something that had to do with this divine authority with which the Lord has blessed us.

Authority is an eternal principle operative throughout the universe. To the "utmost bounds" of space, all things are governed by law emanating from the Lord our God. On Kolob and other giant governing stars, and in the tiny electron, infinitely small and of which all things are composed, divine authority is manifest in the form of immutable law. All space is filled with matter, and that matter is controlled and directed by an all-wise and omniscient Creator.

Priesthood Is Divine Authority

Priesthood is divine authority that is conferred upon men, that they may officiate in the ordinances of the gospel. In other words, priesthood is a part of God's own power that he bestows upon his chosen servants, that they may act in his name in proclaiming the gospel and officiating in all the ordinances thereof. All such official acts performed by these duly authorized servants are recognized by the author of our salvation.

Man cannot act legally in the name of the Lord unless he is vested with the priesthood, which is divine authority. No man has the power or the right to take this honor to himself. Unless he is called of God, as was Aaron, he has no authority to officiate in any of the ordinances of the gospel; should he do so, his act is not valid or recognized in the heavens. The Lord has said that his house is a house of order, and he has given the commandment that no man shall come unto the Father but by his divine law, which is established in the heavens.

All men who assume authority but who have not been properly called will have to answer for their acts in the day of judgment. Nothing that they perform in the name of the Lord is valid, for it lacks the stamp of divine authority. To deceive and lead others to believe that unauthorized acts are valid when performed in the name of the Lord is a grievous sin in the sight of God.

The Question of Priesthood

The question of priesthood, or divine authority, is a vital one, since it concerns the salvation of each of us. It is impossible for a man to enter the kingdom of God without complying with the laws of that kingdom. Only authorized officers may properly officiate in rites and ceremonies of his kingdom. No man has the right to assume the authority and officiate without being ordained to the ministry. To do so is an unauthorized and illegal act.

With regard to the holding of the priesthood in the pre-existence, I will say that there was an organization there just as well as an organization here, and men there held authority. Men chosen to positions of trust in the spirit world held the priesthood.

Adam received the holy priesthood and was commanded by the Lord to teach his children the principles of the gospel. Moreover, Adam was baptized for the remission of his sins, for the same principles by which men are saved now were the principles by which men were saved in the beginning. In that day all those who repented and were baptized received the gifts of the Holy Ghost by the laying on of hands. Adam made all these things known to his sons and daughters.

A False Notion Prevails Today

A false notion prevails today that men may assume the authority to speak and officiate in the name of the Lord Jesus Christ when they have not been divinely called. The commission given by our Lord to his disciples nearly two thousand years ago does not authorize any man today to officiate in the ordinances of the gospel or to preach and expound the scriptures by divine authority. The Bible does not and cannot give to any man this right to exercise the functions of the priesthood. This can only come, as in days of old, by authority from the Son of God or his properly constituted representatives. There is a perfect order in the kingdom of God, and he recognizes the authority of his servants.

It is our duty to save the world. That is our mission, insofar as they will listen unto us and receive our testimony. All those who reject the testimony of the elders of Israel will be held responsible and will have to give an accounting for their stewardship, just as we will have to give an accounting of our stewardship as elders and teachers of the people.

Never before in the history of the Church has the responsibility that has been given to the priesthood been more necessary of fulfilment than today. Never before have we been under greater obligation to serve the Lord, and keep his commandments, and magnify the callings that have been assigned to us.

The World Is Torn Asunder

The world today is torn asunder. Evil is rampant upon the face of the earth. The members of the Church need to be humble and prayerful and diligent. We who have been called to these positions in the priesthood have the responsibility upon our shoulders to teach and direct the members of the Church in righteousness.

If we do not serve the Lord with all our heart, might, mind, and strength, if we are not loyal to this calling that we have received, we are not going to be blameless when we stand before the judgment seat. It is a very serious thing to hold the priesthood.

Brethren of the priesthood, these are your responsibilities. The Council of the Twelve did not place them upon you; the Presidency of the Church did not place them upon you. It is true that they, or their representatives, called you and ordained you to the ministry, but the responsibility to perform this labor came to you from the Son of God. You are his servants. You will be held accountable to him for your stewardship, and unless you magnify your callings and prove yourselves worthy and faithful in all things, you will not stand blameless before him at the last day.

May the Lord bless you good brethren, holders of the priesthood, and may you magnify your callings in the Church, and may the Lord bless you in all that you do is my humble prayer.—(*Conference Report*, priesthood session, October, 1966.)

*Every man who is ordained to the priesthood
has authority to officiate in some capacity in
the Church. For without priesthood there could
be no Church, and if there were no priesthood,
no official act could be performed in the name
of the Lord. Men would be left in darkness
without an understanding of the truth, for the
power of God could not be made manifest.*

The Keys of the Priesthood

I am sure that we all know the fifth Article of Faith, that a man must be called of God, by prophecy.

In the month of February 1835, the Twelve Apostles in this dispensation were called. As early as June, 1829, it was made known to Joseph Smith by revelation that Twelve Apostles would be chosen. This information came before the organization of the Church and Oliver Cowdery and David Whitmer were then appointed to "search out the Twelve" when the time should come for them to be chosen. One month after the apostles had been chosen, the Twelve in council sought information by revelation, that they might have a better understanding of their calling. In their behalf Joseph Smith sought the Lord and received the revelation on priesthood.[1]

This revelation gives us light in relation to the priesthood and the various offices which grow out of it, which the Church did not have previous to that time. It was made known that there were in the Church two priesthoods, or grand divisions of priesthood, the Melchizedek and the Aaronic, including the Levitical.

[1]D&C 107.

Why the first is called the Melchizedek Priesthood is because Melchizedek was such a great high priest.

Before his day it was called the *Holy Priesthood after the Order of the Son of God.*

But out of respect or reverence to the name of the Supreme Being, to avoid the too frequent repetition of his name, they, the church, in ancient days, called that priesthood after Melchizedek, or the Melchizedek Priesthood.[2]

This Information Was New

This information was all new, only general statements pertaining to this truth having been revealed before that time, and the world knew nothing of it. There are some further phases of the priesthood, however, that we should clearly understand.

Every man who is ordained to the priesthood has authority to officiate in some capacity in the Church. For without priesthood there could be no Church, and if there were no priesthood, no official act could be performed in the name of the Lord. Men would be left in darkness without an understanding of the truth, for the power of God could not be made manifest.

This greater priesthood administereth the gospel and holdeth the key of the mysteries of the kingdom, even the key of the knowledge of God.

Therefore, in the ordinances thereof, the power of godliness is manifest.

And without the ordinances thereof, and the authority of the Priesthood, the power of godliness is not manifest unto men in the flesh.[3]

So the Lord taught us through Joseph Smith.

This Holy Priesthood, which is eternal, is the authority which prevails in all the universe. The ordinances of the gospel are made valid through its power and without it the

---

[2]D&C 107:2-4.
[3]D&C 84:19-21.

knowledge of God could not be made manifest. It is by this authority and through the ordinances that man is able to know of God. Without the priesthood it would be impossible for man to gain the knowledge which would bring him into the presence of the Father.

Is there any wonder, then, that the world, deprived of the priesthood, is in such spiritual confusion? Men may search and they may study, but they will never come to a knowledge of God until they receive the gospel and obtain light through the power of the priesthood and the ordinances of the gospel.

See the sad condition of those who once belonged to the Church, but have fallen away, how they have lost the key to spiritual knowledge! Certain organizations have been formed from time to time by those who have gone out of the Church, but the light which they formerly had has left them. They are soon left to grope in spiritual darkness, because the "power of godliness" ceases to be with them. When the light goes out, then darkness of the worst kind enters in. As Alma said, they are bound by the chains of hell.

Difference Between an Office and Keys in the Priesthood

There is a difference between receiving an office in the priesthood and in receiving the keys of the priesthood. This we should clearly understand. Peter, James, and John conferred upon Joseph Smith and Oliver Cowdery the Melchizedek Priesthood. Before that time John the Baptist came and conferred upon them the Aaronic Priesthood. But it was necessary for Elias, who lived in the days of Abraham, to come and restore the keys of his dispensation; for Moses to come and restore the keys of the gathering of Israel; and for Elijah to come and restore the keys of the sealing power, by which the hearts of the fathers and the children are turned to each other. In fact it was necessary that the keys of all the dispensations should be restored in this dispensation of the fulness of times, and so the Prophet Joseph Smith has recorded it: D&C 128:20-21. Please read it.

From this description we discover that all who held keys of authority in dispensations from the days of Adam down, came in this dispensation and declared their keys, their honors and priesthood. All of this had to be done for this is the dispensation of restoration.

President Joseph F. Smith has given us a very clear understanding of what is meant by keys of priesthood in the book, *Gospel Doctrine,* on p. 168.

So we learn that while all men hold the priesthood who are ordained to any office, yet there are special, or directing authorities, bestowed upon those who are called to preside. These authorities are called keys. The bishop of a ward has the power to direct the members of his ward, for he holds the keys of presidency there, and he acts both as bishop and as the president of the ward by virtue of his high priesthood. Now, in his ward may live an apostle, but as a member of the ward the apostle is under the jurisdiction of his bishop. For instance, should be desire to baptize one of his children, it would be his duty to obtain the permission of his bishop, for that is the order of the Church. The bishop holds the keys for the performance of all ordinances in his ward, but he may delegate authority for administering these to others.

President Holds All the Keys

The President of the Church, as the Prophet Joseph Smith has clearly stated, holds the keys over all the Church. There is only one at a time on earth who has this power.[4] No man can officiate in and confer the blessings of the temple without the authority to do so being delegated to him by the President of the Church. No man can officiate in any capacity in this Church, without the virtue accompanying him in that act, as it is obtained through the power

---

[4]D&C 132:7.

and keys held by the President of the Church. The President has power, if the Lord should direct him to do so, to call home all the missionaries in the world. He could say that there shall be no more preaching of the gospel to the nations. He could forbid the official act of baptizing, or of ordaining to the priesthood, anywhere in the world, if the Lord should so direct. This authority is vested in him, for he holds all the keys of the priesthood. If by virtue of his keys he should say that certain privileges should be withdrawn from the people, then no man would have authority to officiate in conferring those particular privileges. Should any one attempt to do so, the act would be invalid, and the one so attempting to officiate would have to answer before the bar of God, if not before the Church, and would be found in transgression.

Let it be understood that no man has authority to perform the sealing of wives to husbands, for time and for eternity, outside a temple, because all such ordinances pertain to the house of the Lord, and the privilege of performing this ordinance elsewhere has been withdrawn by the one holding these keys. Neither can any man officiate in these, or other sealings, unless he has been called and set apart and had that authority given him by the President of the Church in whom those keys are vested.[5]

When men are commissioned by the one who holds these keys, then their acts are valid. That which they do is sealed and ratified in the Church both on earth and in the heavens. When the apostles or other brethren visit the stakes of Zion and are appointed to set in order anything requiring attention there, they do it by virtue of the commission, or authority, delegated to them by the President of the Church. This same principles applies in the lesser degree in stakes and in wards.

I hope and pray that what I have said to you good

---

[5]D&C 132:7.

brethren will be of assistance to you, and may the blessings of the Lord be with you I humbly pray, in the name of Jesus Christ, our Redeemer. Amen.—(General Priesthood Conference, May 8, 1967.)

In the dispensation of the fulness of times, the Lord has not only restored what was given to Israel when Christ came, but he has added keys and authorities, which were intended for the dispensation of the fulness of times, and which were not exercised before the resurrection of the Son of God. . . . Today the Lord has given us more than has been given to other generations.

"Ye Are a Chosen Generation"

When I was invited to speak tonight, I was furnished a little slip of paper on which was printed the words of Peter, which I shall read. I suppose this is to be my text.

> But ye are a chosen generation, a royal priesthood, an holy nation, a peculiar people; that ye should shew forth the praises of him who hath called you out of darkness into his marvellous light.[1]

That is a wonderful statement that ought to stir the souls of all the brethren holding the priesthood within the Church.

When Adam was on the face of the earth, the Lord gave him the priesthood—the Melchizedek Priesthood as we call it today, but that was before the birth of Melchizedek. So it was called the Priesthood after the Order of the Son of God. That priesthood continued with the servants of the Lord, the patriarchs, until the flood. It was carried through the flood by Noah and it was the same priesthood that was given to the prophets from that time on until the days of Moses.

When Israel came out of the land of Egypt and was in the wilderness, Moses went up into the mountain and spent

---

[1] I Peter 2:9.

some time there with the Lord, and the Lord wrote the law on tables of stone.

Israelites Forgot Promises

Moses was gone 40 days; so when he returned, he found the children of Israel in confusion. They had forgotten the promises of the Lord and his goodness to them in bringing them out of Egypt. They hearkened after the things of Egypt and asked Aaron to make them gods that they might worship them. Moses had disappeared, and they thought he was dead. So Aaron was prevailed upon and he took their gold—gold which they had taken away from the Egyptians when they left—and he made a golden calf. The bull was one of the gods of Egypt, and so they were harking back to the religion of Egypt.

When Moses came down out of the mountain and saw these people, the children of Israel to whom the Lord had shown his hand so many times and whom he had blessed miraculously in the wilderness, he took the tablets and threw them down and demolished them. Then he came in his anger and tried to straighten Israel out; after which he went back up into the mountain again at the command of the Lord, and the Lord wrote some other tablets.

The Bible does not tell us the correct story because of mistranslations. It reads this way:

And the Lord said unto Moses, Hew thee two tables of stone like unto the first: and I will write upon these tables the words that were in the first tables, which thou brakest.

And be ready in the morning, and come up in the morning unto mount Sinai, and present thyself there to me in the top of the mount.[2]

Anger Expressed by the Lord

Moses went up into the mountain. The Lord expressed

---

[2]Exodus 34:1-2.

his anger at Israel, and so he wrote with his finger again on other tablets.

In reading the Bible, you would think that he sent Moses down with the same things on the second tables that were on the first ones. In large measure, that is true; but the Lord made some changes of vital importance.

When he wrote the first tables, it was his intention to make of Israel a royal priesthood and give the Melchizedek Priesthood to all the tribes of Israel. But in his anger, because of their rebellion, he did not send the same writings that he sent before—not in all particulars. The Lord made some changes; and he added the law, which was known as the law of Moses, the law of carnal commandments. He took away from Israel the promises of the Higher Priesthood, the Melchizedek Priesthood, and said in his anger that they should not have it.

And so down through the ages, Israel had to go without the Melchizedek Priesthood. They had the Aaronic Priesthood, but the Melchizedek was withheld from them with some exceptions. There had to be, of course, some prophets in Israel with the Melchizedek Priesthood, because there were certain ordinances that the Melchizedek Priesthood had to perform. But he denied that priesthood to Israel in general.

He called certain men and made them his prophets and gave them keys of authority in the Melchizedek Priesthood to perform such ordinances as had to be performed; but he did not give the priesthood to all the tribes of Israel, as was first intended. He chose the seed of Aaron, the Levites, I should say, because Aaron was one of the seed of Levi. He made the Levites the priests in Israel. He denied the priesthood to all the other tribes of Israel. That priesthood which was given to them was the Aaronic Priesthood, named after Aaron, who became the chief priest of that order. Moses, of course, held the Melchizedek Priesthood.

Israel Restricted in Priesthood

Israel had to be content with the Aaronic Priesthood and with one tribe having the authority to administer. The other tribes were denied this blessing because of their great rebellion. That condition continued until the days of the coming of the Son of God.

Following is a short statement showing what was revealed to the Prophet Joseph Smith about the priesthood and about the plates that Moses brought back the second time. The Lord said:

> . . . I will give unto them the law as at the first, but it shall be after the law of a carnal commandment; for I have sworn in my wrath, that they shall not enter into my presence, into my rest, in the days of their pilgrimage. Therefore do as I have commanded thee, and be ready in the morning, and come up in the morning unto mount Sinai, and present thyself there to me, in the top of the mount.[3]

So Moses received these other tables which denied to the children of Israel all the privileges that had been on the first and the authority that had been promised; and this because of the hardness of their hearts and their failure to keep the commandments of the Lord.

Paul has something to say about this in his writings in the book of Hebrews:

> Wherefore (as the Holy Ghost saith, To day if ye will hear his voice,
> Harden not your hearts, as in the provocation, in the day of temptation in the wilderness:
> When your fathers tempted me, proved me, and saw my works forty years.
> Wherefore I was grieved with that generation, and said, They do always err in their heart; and they have not known my ways.
> So I sware in my wrath, They shall not enter into my rest.)
> Take heed, brethren, lest there be in any of you an evil heart of unbelief, in departing from the living God.

---

[3]Inspired Version of the Holy Scriptures, Exodus 34:2.

But exhort one another daily, while it is called To day; lest any of you be hardened through the deceitfulness of sin.

For we are made partakers of Christ, if we hold the beginning of our confidence stedfast unto the end;

While it is said, To day if ye will hear his voice, harden not your hearts, as in the provocation.

For some, when they had heard, did provoke: howbeit not all that came out of Egypt by Moses.

But with whom was he grieved forty years? was it not with them that had sinned, whose carcases fell in the wilderness?[4]

The Lord's Anger Was Kindled

So the Lord's anger was kindled against them and that was the condition that prevailed from the days that Israel entered into the land of Palestine until the coming of Jesus Christ. When Jesus Christ came, he restored the Melchizedek Priesthood, or the higher priesthood. He called 12 men and ordained them apostles. He called other men and gave them authority in the Melchizedek Priesthood. Again it was restored, and given for the first time to Israel, as a people, since the days when they made the calf and bowed down to worship it.

Following is what the Lord said to the Prophet Joseph Smith as recorded in Section 84 of the Doctrine and Covenants. In the first part of this revelation, the Lord tells us about the priesthood which he gave to the ancient prophets. Then he tells how the priesthood came down from generation to generation:

. . . From Noah till Enoch, through the lineage of their fathers;

And from Enoch to Abel, who was slain by the conspiracy of his brother, who received the priesthood by the commandments of God, by the hand of his father Adam, who was the first man—

Which priesthood continueth in the church of God in all generations, and is without beginning of days or end of years.

And the Lord confirmed a priesthood also upon Aaron and his seed, throughout all their generations, which priesthood also con-

---

[4]Hebrews 3:7-17.

tinueth and abideth forever with the priesthood which is after the holiest order of God.

And this greater priesthood administereth the gospel and holdeth the key of the mysteries of the kingdom, even the key of the knowledge of God.

Therefore, in the ordinances thereof, the power of godliness is manifest.

And without the ordinances thereof, and the authority of the priesthood, the power of godliness is not manifest unto men in the flesh;

For without this no man can see the face of God, even the Father, and live.

Now this Moses plainly taught to the children of Israel in the wilderness, and sought diligently to sanctify his people that they might behold the face of God.[5]

In the Old Testament, back in those early days recorded in the Book of Exodus, the people wanted to see the Lord. But because of their wickedness, he only showed them his back parts. They could not look upon his face. He revealed himself to Moses from time to time, but the children of Israel, because of their rebellion could not look upon his face. They could not stand his presence. Now to continue from the Doctrine and Covenants:

But they hardened their hearts and could not endure his presence; therefore, the Lord in his wrath, for his anger was kindled against them, swore that they should not enter into his rest while in the wilderness, which rest is the fulness of his glory.

Therefore, he took Moses out of their midst, and the Holy Priesthood also;

And the lesser priesthood continued, which priesthood holdeth the key of the ministering of angels and the preparatory gospel;

Which gospel is the gospel of repentance and of baptism, and the remission of sins, and the law of carnal commandments, which the Lord in his wrath caused to continue with the house of Aaron among the children of Israel until John, whom God raised up, being filled with the Holy Ghost from his mother's womb.[6]

---

[5]D&C 84:15-23.
[6]D&C 84:24-27.

Added Keys and Authorities

In the dispensation of the fulness of times, the Lord has not only restored what was given to Israel when Christ came, but he has added keys and authorities which were intended for the dispensation of the fulness of times, and which were not exercised before the resurrection of the Son of God. After his resurrection, these things were, of course, permissible, and the privileges were granted to the people who repented of their sins.

Today the Lord has given us more than has been given to other generations. Not only did he send John the Baptist with the Aaronic Priesthood, the keys of which he held, but he sent Peter, James, and John to confer upon Joseph Smith and Oliver Cowdery the Melchizedek Priesthood. But for our dispensation these blessings were not quite enough.

The Melchizedek Priesthood is the power of God by which ordinances are performed—ordinances and ordinations. But there had to be in this dispensation other authorities restored. It was necessary, for instance, for Noah to come and restore the keys of his dispensation; and before him, Michael or Adam came with the keys of his dispensation. Then the Lord sent other prophets to the Prophet Joseph Smith and Oliver Cowdery—always to the two of them—restoring keys and authorities of a special nature pertaining to the dispensation of the fulness of times.

Today we have in the Church all the authority, all the power, all the priesthood, including the keys of authority, that were held by the various prophets of old, for the completion of the work of the kingdom of God in the dispensation of the fulness of times. Everything is here. The ancient prophets came from Adam down to Moroni, each in his turn restoring keys, authorities, and priesthood

to Joseph Smith and Oliver Cowdery, because everything
of that nature is essential for the dispensation in which
we live.

Now we have the Aaronic Priesthood in addition to
that priesthood which was spoken of by Peter. Israel could
have this lesser priesthood, and did have it through the
Levites before the coming of Christ. Peter called upon the
people in his day to receive the royal priesthood, which is
the Melchizedek Priesthood, and to magnify their callings
in it in that dispensation. In this present dispensation, all
the keys and all the authorities of all the ancient prophets
from Adam down to the present day have been restored
and given to the Church. They were given originally to
the Prophet Joseph Smith and to Oliver Cowdery. And
from them the keys were given to the Council of the Twelve.

Keys Held by President

There is one thing that I want to say that I think is
not generally understood, and that is this: Only one man
at a time on the face of the earth holds the keys of the
Melchizedek Priesthood—just one, and that is the President of the Church. "Well," you say, "do not the Twelve
have authority?" Yes. And the Council of the Twelve
have had hands laid upon their heads to receive all the
keys and the powers and authorities that pertain to the
priesthood, but they can exercise them only as that power
is delegated to them by the President of the Church. In
other words, the President of the Church holds the keys of
the priesthood; and we, the Council of the Twelve, with all
the authority that is placed upon us, could not act without
the sanction of the President of the Church. Neither
could a bishop in his ward nor a president of a stake nor
anybody else, because the President of the Church holds
the keys. And there is only one person on earth at a time
who holds those keys.

Here is another thing that I would like to make clear. The Prophet Joseph Smith, before his death, was commanded by the Lord to confer the keys and the authorities and the powers—all of them—upon the twelve apostles. And when a man is ordained an apostle today, he is given all the authority and the power, all the keys and everything. That has been done ever since the days when the Lord told the Prophet Joseph Smith to confer the keys. But here is a great point, they can exercise the keys and the power and authority only in their turn. In other words, every member of the Council of the Twelve has the authority in him, should he become President of the Church, to exercise all the keys and powers of the priesthood. As long as the President of the Church is active, he holds the keys and there can not be two holding the same power at the same time.

Any man holding the office of elder in this Church, or seventy or high priest or whatever else it is, holds that authority by the sanction of the President of this Church. All that is recorded in the Doctrine and Covenants:

And verily I say unto you, that the conditions of this law are these: All covenants, contracts, bonds, obligations, oaths, vows, performances, connections, associations, or expectations, that are not made and entered into and sealed by the Holy Spirit of promise, of him who is anointed, both as well for time and for all eternity, and that too most holy, by revelation and commandment through the medium of mine anointed, whom I have appointed on the earth to hold this power (and I have appointed unto my servant Joseph to hold this power in the last days, and there is never but one on the earth at a time on whom this power and the keys of this priesthood are conferred), are of no efficacy, virtue, or force in and after the resurrection from the dead; for all contracts that are not made unto this end have an end when men are dead.[7]

So, while each of the Council of the Twelve holds this priesthood, and has this authority, it is dormant. He exer-

---

[7]D&C 132:7.

cises authority that is sanctioned to him by the President of
the Church. So does a bishop in the ward and the president
of a stake and everyone else. And the President of the
Church has the right, if there is reason for it, to withdraw
the keys from men who hold keys of authority today. No
man can perform a marriage ceremony in the temple unless
the President of the Church has given him the authority to
do so. The marriage is for time and all eternity. The President is the only one who has that power, and he delegates
it. Every man who performs marriage ceremonies for time
and eternity in the temple for the living and the dead has
the President's hands laid upon his head. The President
can delegate that authority for it is his right and privilege;
he holds those keys and nobody can exercise them without
his sanction.—(Sunday School Conference Address, October
9, 1960.)

There are fundamental teachings of the gospel of Jesus Christ that have been expressed many times by the prophets of old and our Redeemer when they were on the earth. It is a fact that no unclean thing can inherit the kingdom of God and obtain what is known as eternal life.

No Unclean Thing
Can Inherit the Kingdom

When I was a boy, too young to hold the Aaronic Priesthood, my father placed a copy of the Book of Mormon in my hands with the request that I read it. I received this Nephite record with thanksgiving and applied myself to the task which had been assigned to me. There are certain passages that have been stamped on my mind and I have never forgotten them. One of these is in the 27th chapter of Third Nephi.[1] It is the word of our Redeemer to the Nephites as he taught them after his resurrection. It is as follows:

And no unclean thing can enter into his kingdom; therefore nothing entereth into his rest save it be those who have washed their garments in my blood, because of their faith, and the repentance of all their sins, and their faithfulness unto the end.

Now this is the comandment: Repent, all ye ends of the earth, and come unto me and be baptized in my name, that ye may be sanctified by the reception of the Holy Ghost, that ye may stand spotless before me at the last day.

The other passage is in the book of Alma and is as follows:

---

[1] 3 Nephi 27:19-20.

Do not suppose, because it has been spoken concerning restoration, that ye shall be restored from sin to happiness. Behold, I say unto you, wickedness never was happiness.[2]

Life's Counsel and Guidance

These two passages I have tried to follow all the days of my life, and I have felt to thank the Lord for this counsel and guidance, and I have endeavored to stamp these sayings on my mind and on the minds of many others. What a wonderful guide these teachings can be to us, if we can get them firmly fixed in our minds. These thoughts are of course not peculiar to the Book of Mormon. They are fundamental teachings of the gospel of Jesus Christ and have been expressed many times by the prophets of old and our Redeemer when they were on the earth.

It is a fact that no unclean thing can inherit the kingdom of God and obtain what is known as eternal life. This is to say the Redeemer of this world, through the great sacrifice which he made, opened the graves and restored all mortal things, both mankind, the fowls of the air, fishes of the sea and every creature that partook or partakes of death through the fall of Adam. In the Book of John, we have the definite statement of our Redeemer proclaiming this truth as follows:

Marvel not at this: for the hour is coming, in the which all that are in the graves shall hear his voice,

And shall come forth; they that have done good, unto the resurrection of life; and they that have done evil, unto the resurrection of damnation.[3]

Permit me to quote some other passages of scripture from the revelations that have come to us by divine decree in this dispensation. This is from the Doctrine and Covenants:

[2]Alma 41:10.
[3]John 5:28-29.

And again, verily, verily, I say unto you that when the thousand years are ended, and men again begin to deny their God, then will I spare the earth but for a little season;

And the end shall come, and the heaven and the earth shall be consumed and pass away, and there shall be a new heaven and a new earth.

For all old things shall pass away, and all things shall become new, even the heaven and the earth, and all the fulness thereof, both men and beasts, the fowls of the air and the fishes of the sea;

And not one hair, neither mote, shall be lost, for it is the workmanship of mine hand.[4]

The Lord's Words to the Prophet Joseph Smith

Again the Lord spoke to the Prophet Joseph Smith in a revelation in answer to the question,

What are we to understand by the four beasts spoken of in the same verse? (Rev. 4:6.)

They are figurative expressions, used by the Revelator, John, in describing heaven, the paradise of God, the happiness of men, and of beasts, and of creeping things, and of the fowls of the air; that which is spiritual being in the likeness of that which is temporal; and that which is temporal in the likeness of that which is spiritual; the spirit of man in the likeness of his person, as also the spirit of the beast, and every other creature which God has created.[5]

There is a strange doctrine in the world concerning the resurrection even among those who believe there will be a reuniting of spirit and body, which is to the effect that only the righteous will come forth, to receive rewards of exaltation. This however, is a misunderstanding. Through the atonement wrought by the Son of God, our Savior, the resurrection is a complete restoration of all things mortal, even of this earth itself, on which we stand. The earth is to be purified and become the abode of the righteous. Peter understood this doctrine and in his second epistle made the following statement:

[4]D&C 29:22-25.
[5]D&C 77:2-3.

But the day of the Lord will come as a thief in the night; in the which the heavens shall pass away with a great noise, and the elements shall melt with fervent heat, the earth also and the works that are therein shall be burned up.

Seeing that all these things shall be dissolved, what manner of persons ought ye to be in the holy conversation and godliness,

Looking for and hasting unto the coming of the day of God, wherein the heavens being on fire shall be dissolved, and the elements shall melt with fervent heat?

Nevertheless we, according to his promise, look for new heavens and a new earth, wherein dwelleth righteousness.[6]

The New Heaven and New Earth

Let us not misunderstand this expression. The new heaven and new earth will be the same heaven and the same earth on which we now sojourn, for this earth is to receive the resurrection after this day of mortality and be the abode of the righteous in eternity. Without the revelations of the Lord given to men, this truth would not be made known. Neither would we have knowledge of the final glory to which this earth will be assigned. Even now, where men are without the divine guidance and revelation, this truth would not be known.

I am very grateful to my Eternal Father for the privilege that has been granted to me to come into this world in this dispensation when once again the fulness of the gospel has been revealed. I have been grateful and have thanked the Lord many times for the privilege which came to me to live in the present dispensation and that I was not born two or three hundred years ago, or the great period when the fulness of the gospel was not had among men and they were running as the scriptures say "to and fro," seeking for the truth which could not be found because of the deep spiritual darkness which covered the entire earth. This condition was not the fault of the Lord but the fault of mankind, for they

---

[6]II Peter 3:10-13.

had been offered the fulness of the gospel but in course of time they refused to have it. Their teachers turned away and caused to enter into the Church false doctrines and false ordinances and worse than all, a false conception in relation to God our Eternal Father and his Son Jesus Christ. It was a day when there was no one left in mortality with the divine power to officiate in the vital and saving ordinances of the gospel—a day when false ordinances and false instructors came upon the scene. This condition left the entire Christian world in a state of confusion, without divine inspiration so that the notion prevailed universally that the heavens were closed, that communication with the Father and his Beloved Son had ceased, and that angels for a long long past had ceased to visit mortal man on the face of the earth. Under such conditions it was a natural thought encouraged by clergy that our Eternal Father had ceased to commune with his children on the earth. Moreover the false notion became prevalent that mortal man was left with the teachings of the Bible and that it contained all of the revelation that mankind needed to insure his salvation in the kingdom of God.

Satan Rejoiced

Under such conditions and practice no doubt Satan rejoiced; false teachers arose, and the people, no matter how devout they were, found themselves in spiritual darkness. Moreover, for a long time the edict went forth that mortal men who had not been prepared for the clergy should not seek for knowledge or search the scriptures for this was the sole responsibility of the clergy. Therefore I am exceedingly grateful for the Prophet Joseph Smith and the coming of the Father and the Son to him to direct him in the course he should take. Moreover, I am grateful that the time came for the restoration of divine truth and the power of the holy priesthood that the inhabitants of the world could find the path to eternal life, and the ordinances of the holy priesthood could again be exercised in behalf of the salvation of all mankind.

On January 22, 1834, The Prophet Joseph Smith said:

The great plan of salvation is a theme which ought to occupy our strict attention, and be regarded as one of heaven's best gifts to mankind. No consideration whatever ought to deter us from showing ourselves approved in the sight of God, according to His divine requirement. Men frequently forget that they are dependent upon heaven for every blessing which they are permitted to enjoy, and that for every opportunity granted them they are to give an account. You know, brethren and sisters, that when the Master in the Savior's parable of the stewards called his servants before him he gave them several talents to improve on while he should tarry abroad for a little season, and when he returned he called for an accounting. So it is now, our Master is absent only for a little season, and at the end of it, He will call each to render an account; and where the five talents were bestowed, ten will be required; and he that has made no improvement will be cast out as an unprofitable servant, while the faithful will enjoy everlasting honors. Therefore we earnestly implore the grace of our Father to rest upon you, through Jesus Christ His Son, that you may not faint in the hour of temptation, nor be overcome in the time of persecution.[7]

I would like to quote a few remarks of divine truth from the lips of President David O. McKay:

No man can disobey the word of God and not suffer for so doing.

No sin, however secret, can escape retribution. True, you may lie and not be detected; you may violate virtue without it being known by anyone who would scandalize you; yet you cannot escape the judgment that follows such transgression. The lie is lodged in the recesses of your mind, an impairment of your character that will reflect sometime, somehow in your countenance or bearing. Your mortal turpitude though only you, your accomplice, and God may ever know it, will canker your soul.[8]

---

[7]*Teachings of the Prophet Joseph Smith*, p. 68.
[8]*Gospel Ideals*, p. 383.

I will close these remarks by reading a poem which I think is very appropriate, entitled:

THE GUY IN THE MIRROR

When you get what you want in your struggle for self,
And the world makes you king for a day,
Then go to the mirror and look at yourself and see what that guy
   has to say,
For it isn't a man's father, or mother, or wife,
Whose judgment upon you must pass;
The feller whose verdict counts most in his life
Is the guy staring back from the glass.
He's the fellow to please, never mind all the rest
For he's with you clear up to the end.
And you've passed your most dangerous, difficult test,
If the guy in the glass is your friend.
You may be like Jack Horner and "chisel" a plumb,
And think you're a wonderful guy,
But the man in the glass says you're only a bum,
If you can't look him straight in the eye.
You can fool the whole world down the pathway of years,
And get pats on the back as you pass,
But your final reward will be heartaches or tears
If you've cheated the guy in the glass.

—Anonymous
—(*Conference Report,* October, 1964.)

We believe that we were created in the image of God, so stated in the Bible, in the Doctrine and Covenants, in the Pearl of Great Price, and also . . . the Book of Mormon. We are his sons and his daughters. We were created in his image . . . There could be no intelligence in a Supreme Being who had each time an earth is formed to leave everything to chance hoping that in some great period of time from an amoeba, creatures would be developed, fit to possess an eternal spirit in his image.

Our Relationship to God

I cannot tell you how happy I am to have this opportunity of meeting with you.

My theme today, that is, the thread that will run through it, is our relationship to God. I want to make a few preliminary remarks. We are all members of The Church of Jesus Christ of Latter-day Saints, I hope, and I think I am right in having that hope, and that we all have a testimony of the truth—that is, of the restoration of the gospel.

There are certain things that must be considered fundamental with us. First we must accept Jesus Christ as the Only Begotten Son of God in the flesh. We must accept God as our Father, the Father of our Spirits. We must put our faith in and accept the revelations in what we call the Standard Works of the Church. We cannot have in our minds any doubts in relation to the First Vision, the coming of the Father and the Son. That is absolutely fundamental.

We Must Accept Church Teachings

We must accept the coming of Moroni and the revealing of the Book of Mormon and its translation by the gift and power of God. We must believe in the coming of John the Baptist to restore the Aaronic Priesthood. We must believe in the coming of Peter, James, and John with the keys of the Melchizedek Priesthood and the conferring of those keys upon the heads of Joseph Smith and Oliver Cowdery, and the command given unto them to organize the Church.

We must believe, there can be no doubts in our minds, as to the reason for the restoration—that it is because of the universal apostasy, that spread over the Christian world, which made it necessary for the reopening of the heavens.

Now, I have written here a few things that I consider to be fundamental, some of which I want to read to you. These are on pages 50 and 51 in the book.[1]

Eternal Father Immortal

God, our Eternal Father, is an immortal, exalted man with a body of flesh and bones, and an eternal spirit inseparably connected that cannot be divided and cannot die. That is a fundamental doctrine of the Church.

The presiding authority in the universe is God the Father, his Son, Jesus Christ, and the Holy Ghost.

The earth on which we dwell, at the word of the Father, was created by the Son before he obtained his tabernacle of flesh and bones.

Adam was the first man on the earth, and Eve, his wife, was the first woman. They were created in the image of God. When Adam and Eve were placed in Eden they were not subject to the power of death, and could have lived in the state of innocence in which they were forever, had they not violated the law given them in the Garden.

The earth also was pronounced good, and would have remained in that same state forever had it not been changed to meet Adam's fallen condition. All things on the face of

---

[1]*Man: His Origin and Destiny*, pp. 50-51.

the earth also would have remained in that same condition had not Adam transgressed the law. By partaking of the forbidden fruit and thus violating the law under which he was placed, his nature was changed, and he became subject to: first, spiritual death, which is banishment from the presence of God; second, temporal death, which is separation of spirit and body.

This death also came to Eve his wife. Had Adam and Eve not transgressed the law given in Eden, they would have had no children. Because of this transgression bringing mortality, the children of Adam and Eve inherited mortal bodies and became subject to the mortal death.

Because Adam transgressed the law, the Lord changed the earth to suit the mortal condition, and all things on the face of the earth became subject to mortality as did the earth also.

Need for Atonement

To defeat the power which death had gained, it became necessary that an infinite atonement be offered to repay the debt and thereby restore Adam and Eve and all of their posterity and all things to immortal life through the resurrection.

To accomplish this, Jesus Christ, who created the earth, volunteered, and was chosen to come to earth as that infinite sacrifice. According to eternal law this sacrifice had to be made by a God who was not subject to death, yet had the power to die and take up his body by inherent right. Being the Only Begotten Son of God in the flesh, our Redeemer obtained from his Father the mastery over death, and from his mother he inherited the power to die.

The atonement by the Son of God is of a two-fold nature. First, it redeems all creatures who are subject to mortality through the fall, and restores them to immortality without any act whatever on their part. Hence, every soul

born into this world shall receive the resurrection of the
body, the body and spirit being reunited, never again to be
divided.

Second, it redeems every soul from the penalties of his
own transgressions on the condition that he accepts the plan
of salvation and is obedient to all the laws and commandments of God, and that he endures in faithfulness to the end.
None but the truly repentant are entitled to this forgiveness
of sin.

There are definite laws which are known as the gospel
of Jesus Christ, and must be obeyed in order to obtain this
salvation. The first or foundation principles, which must
be received and obeyed, are these: faith in God and the
atonement of Jesus Christ; repentance from all sins; baptism by one having authority in water by immersion for
the remission of sins; laying on of hands by one holding authority for the gift of the Holy Ghost; a contrite spirit and
a humble heart; obedience to every other ordinance and
principle of the gospel appertaining to the blessings of eternal life; and faithfulness to the end.

All men will be judged according to their individual
work, and none will be required to pay the debt of another.

All of those things are absolutely fundamental. I have
given references for all of the things that I have mentioned.

In the Image of God

We believe that we were created in the image of God,
so stated in the Bible, in the Doctrine and Covenants, in
the Pearl of Great Price, and also, not quite so definitely, in
the Book of Mormon. We are his sons and his daughters.
We were created in his image.

I think you have on your papers references from these
scriptures, and they are all before you.

Now, children of God also inhabit other earths, and
they also are in the image of God. References to that are

found in Moses 1, verses 33 to 39; Doctrine and Covenants 76, verses 22 and 24; and Ether, the third chapter, where the Savior appeared to the Brother of Jared and manifested to him his body which is the body of the spirit, and where he taught the Brother of Jared that as he appeared to him in the spirit, so would he appear to men on the earth in the flesh, and that all men were created in that image, and that is a fundamental doctrine of the Church.

The world today, even the so-called Christian world, does not accept that doctrine. To them God is not a personal being. Man is not created in his image. As one great religious teacher said, "If we are created in the likeness of God, it is in reason not in body," then he went on to argue that it must be in reason because God has no body. If you analyze that you will see how foolish it is, because man's reason is very faulty, and every man goes his own way, following his reason, and surely God is not a God of confusion.

Let me spend a little time here in regard to those sons and daughters of God who dwell on other earths. In the vision given to Moses as recorded in the first chapter of the Book of Moses in the Pearl of Great Price we read, beginning with Verse 33 — we should go even higher than that to get the full import of this, but I will begin with the thirty-third verse. The Lord says:

And worlds without number have I created; and I also created them for mine own purpose; and by the Son I created them, which is mine Only Begotten.

Then further down, when Moses asked him for a little information regarding our earth, the Lord said to him:

The heavens, they are many, and they cannot be numbered unto man; but they are numbered unto me, for they are mine.

And as one earth shall pass away, and the heavens thereof even shall another come; and there is no end to my works, neither to my words.

An Interpretation

Before I read the next verse let me make a comment. In regard to earth's passing away, the Lord does not mean to place an interpretation upon the world's passing away like that which is placed upon worlds passing away by our scientific brethren, by our astronomers and others who look into the heavens and see these great bodies and tell us they are dying, that our Sun eventually will become cold, having spent its energy. I am glad to know they are beginning to change their views, some of them, on that. But that has been the doctrine. They teach that this earth will die after a certain great period of years, and will revolve through the heavens a dead, lifeless, cold, useless body.

The Lord has told us otherwise. This earth will not have that end.

I shall not turn to read passages of scripture, but you can turn to Section 88 of the Doctrine and Covenants, and therein you will find recorded the destiny of this earth. It is going to die. Peter said it would die, as other earths have died and passed away, but it will receive a resurrection, be glorified and placed in the heavens where it belongs as a celestial body, just like other worlds have done.

Now I am going to make a statement here in contradiction of the teaching of the philosophers and the scientists who set forth that doctrine, that the earth will become lifeless, and I am going to tell you a little incident that took place here at the summer school a few years ago, a conversation that I had with Dr. Carl Eyring.

We were up in the summer school on the mountainside, and he had a telescope in the middle of the day which showed the planet, Venus. He wanted to know if I wanted to see it, and I told him "yes," so I went and had a look at Venus, which through the telescope looked much like our moon in one of its quarters.

As we walked away we talked about the planets, and how wonderful it was that we had instruments which would reveal these things to us, and I said: "Brother Eyring, I do not have the idea that you scientists have about the sun."

"Well, is that so? What is your idea?"

I said, "You have never seen the sun. Neither has any other mortal man."

"Why, what do you mean?"

I said, "All you see when you look at the sun through smoked glasses or any way that you can look at the sun, is the cloud that surrounds it. Every eclipse of the sun shows that."

He said, "I guess that is right." Well, what is the sun?

"It is not a dying world. Of course, it is full of energy. God is full of energy, and should we mortals stand in his presence, unless his spirit was upon us to protect us we would be consumed. That is how much energy there is in a celestial body.

Sun—An Immortal World

I said, "The sun is a body that has gone on to its fulness. It has reached its glory. It is an immortal world." The bell rang and we had no further time for discussion, but that doctrine was taught by the Prophet Joseph Smith. I am sorry, I do not have that reference with me.

We look into the heavens and we see worlds that have gone on to their glory. Some of them may be terrestrial worlds, telestial, some celestial worlds, and so the Lord here says worlds after they are created will pass away. Of course they will. This earth will pass away, for God never made anything to be destroyed or come to naught, and so these worlds that pass away receive their resurrection as this earth will receive its resurrection. Now I will read the next verse:

For behold, this is my work and my glory—to bring to pass
the immortality and eternal life of man.[2]

This is the great work of the Lord, and so he is peopling
worlds and after they have been celestialized or received the
resurrection, with their inhabitants, they will endure forever.

Now, let us consider a statement in Section 76 of the
Doctrine and Covenants. This is a vision given to the
Prophet Joseph Smith and to Sidney Rigdon. They say:

For we saw him, even on the right hand of God; and we heard
the voice bearing record that he is the Only Begotten of the Father—
That by him, and through him, the worlds are and were created,
(not this world only) and the inhabitants thereof are begotten sons
and daughters unto God.[3]

If we had the opportunity of visiting some of these
other worlds, what would we find? Human beings just
like we are, for they were created in the image of God. That
is what we would find. Not only would we find human
beings, we would find vegetation, we would find animals.

I am not taking time to read from Section 77. You can
read it, where the Prophet, interpreting certain passages in
the Book of Revelations calls attention to the fact that there
are animals that have received their resurrection. These
are animals in the presence of God. They get a resurrection. Everything gets a resurrection, for everything that has
been created has a soul. By that I mean just what the Lord
defines the soul to be—spirit and body—and in the resurrection they become inseparably connected.

Now let us read the third chapter of Moses in the ninth
verse. I am passing by references to man being a soul as we
find it in Verse 1. I will refer to that a little later. But in
the ninth verse:

---

[2]Moses 1:39.
[3]D&C 76:23-24.

And out of the ground made I, the Lord God, to grow every tree naturally, that is pleasant to the sight of man; and man could behold it.   And it became also a living soul.

Spiritual Creation

Now he is speaking about a spiritual creation, the trees, the vegetation, created spiritually, and then placed on the earth to become living souls just as well as men do.

Now we will turn to another passage.   Verse 19 of the same chapter:

And out of the ground I, the Lord God, formed every beast of the field, and every fowl of the air; and commanded that they should come unto Adam, to see what he would call them; and they were also living souls; for I, God, breathed into them the breath of life and commanded that whatsoever Adam called every living creature, that should be the name thereof.

So here we find that the animals, and the plants, the vegetation, became living souls, and were created spiritually before they were naturally upon the earth.   These are very significant expressions, and I am stressing them as evidence that contradicts and confutes the organic theory of evolution.

What do they teach?   That man has evolved, come to what he is, by accident?   Some evolutionary scientists have said man is an accident.   All life is an accident upon the earth.   Sir James Jeans has said that.   We are just a by-product, something that happened and likely could not happen anywhere else in the universe.   Just a by-product, you people here, sons and daughters of God.   That is all they can give you.

Well now, in Section 29 of the Doctrine and Covenants we have something more:

And again, verily, verily, I say unto you that when the thousand years are ended, and men again begin to deny their God, then will I spare the earth but for a little season.

And the end shall come, and the heaven and the earth shall
be consumed and pass away, and there shall be a new heaven and
a new earth.[4]

That is the celestialized earth.

For all old things shall pass away, and all things shall become
new, even the heaven and the earth, [and that means the heaven
of our earth], and also the fulness thereof, both men and beasts, the
fowls of the air, and the fishes of the sea.

And not one hair, neither mote, shall be lost, for it is the workmanship of mine hand.[5]

Word of the Lord

There is the word of the Lord. Do we believe the revelations in the Doctrine and Covenants, in the Pearl of
Great Price, Book of Mormon, the Bible, or are we to dis-
card all that because some men, "educated beyond their intelligence," so Golden Kimball said of them, teach a contrary doctrine? "Educated beyond their intelligence"—
there is a difference between intelligence and knowledge.
We confuse them, and that which we think is knowledge
sometimes is not.

Well anyway, all of these things were created spiritually before they were naturally in the earth, and that is also
recorded in the third chapter of the Book of Moses.

Evolution teaches production and development of all
things by chance, development of the smallest germ to a
man created in the image of God, requiring several billions
of years for that development. Moreover, this process would,
if true, produce on other earths, passing through similar
conditions, beings of a most hideous and dreadful nature
imaginable. As they teach it has produced some very
hideous beings on this earth.

There could be no intelligence in a Supreme Being who
had each time an earth is formed to leave everything to

[4]D&C 29:22-23.
[5]D&C 29:24-25.

chance hoping that in some great period of time from an amoeba, creatures would be developed, fit to possess an eternal spirit in his image.

I want you to get that! The idea, for us, sons and daughters of God, to be led astray by these theories of men into thinking that things began way back in that far distant time by some chance, suddenly appearing. Why, conditions today are far more favorable to spontaneous life than they were according to the teachings of science, millions of years ago, and have not men struggled and done everything that they knew how to do to find spontaneous life, and in searching for it they have always been defeated.

Man, His Origin and Destiny

So I state, and have the evidence in this book. They have never found life coming only from antecedent life. God is the author of life, and that is one secret he has not revealed to man. It is absolutely ridiculous to think this universe created by God as he tells us here, came by chance, and that every time a new earth comes to take the place of one that has gone on, he has to start by hoping that some time some germ will happen to appear spontaneously upon it.

You cannot believe in a God like that, can you? We are transplanted beings. Adam was transplanted. I do not want to get a misunderstanding when I say that. He did not come here a resurrected being. He did not die on some other earth and then come here to die again, to be changed to mortality again, for the resurrected being cannot die. The Lord has told us so in the eleventh chapter of John, in the 63rd Section of the Doctrine and Covenants, in the 88th Section of the Doctrine and Covenants, in other places he has told us—in the eleventh chapter of the Book of Alma, the twelfth chapter of the Book of Alma, and in other places—that the resurrected being does not die.

Christ says that they who believe in him pass from death unto life, celestialized, immortalized, and Adam got his body from the dust of the earth. Read the 12th verse in the 77th Section of the Doctrine and Covenants. Read the first two or three verses and you will find that every creature on the face of the earth has a spirit, and that his body was created in the image of his spirit. Things do not come by chance. All living things are entitled to the everlasting life through the restoration from mortal death based on the statement of Jesus Christ.

All Creation Restored

The Savior is not going to save only mankind. Everything God has created must be restored, and so I read it to you in the 27th Section of the Doctrine and Covenants, and it is all going to be restored—everything the Lord has created that has been changed and become mortal and subject to death through Adam's transgression. Everything that has life and created in the image of its spirit, and is a living soul, and therefore entitled to the resurrection.

Why? Because when Adam fell the Lord cursed the earth, brought a fall upon it and it is passing through one week, seven days of a thousand years, of mortal or temporal existence. Doctrine and Covenants: Verse 6, Section 77.

In the few remaining minutes, I want to read the seventh verse, which I skipped, in the third chapter of Moses:

And I, the Lord God, formed man from the dust of the ground, and breathed into his nostrils the breath of life; and man became a living soul, [that is, the spirit and body were united], *the first flesh upon the earth, the first man also;* nevertheless, all things were before created; but spiritually were they created and made according to my word.

And in Verse 5 the Lord tells you that spiritual creation was in heaven. So, Adam was the first man upon the earth, according to the Lord's statement, and the first flesh also. That needs a little explanation.

Adam did not come to this earth until it was prepared for him. The animals were here. Plants were here. The Lord did not bring him here to a desolate world, and then bring other creatures. It was all prepared for him, just according to the order that is written in our scriptures, and when it was all ready for Adam he was placed upon the earth.

Then what is meant by the "first flesh"? It is simple when you understand it. Adam was the first of all creatures to fall and become flesh, and flesh in this sense means mortality, and all through our scriptures the Lord speaks of this life as flesh, while we are here in the flesh, so Adam became the first flesh. There was no other mortal creature before him, and there was no mortal death until he brought it, and the scriptures tell you that. It is here written, and that is the gospel of Jesus Christ.

Men Must Repent

I will turn to the Book of Moses again, and we will discuss here the word of the Lord to Adam as recorded by Enoch. Enoch is telling what the Lord taught Adam. This is in the sixth chapter of Moses. I am going to begin with Verse 56:

> And it is given unto them to know good from evil; wherefore they are agents unto themselves, and I have given unto you another law and commandment.
>
> Wherefore [and he is talking to Adam], teach it unto your children, that all men everywhere, must repent, or they can in nowise inherit the kingdom of God, for no unclean thing can dwell there, or dwell in his presence; for, in the language of Adam, Man of Holiness is his name, and the name of his Only Begotten is the Son of Man, even Jesus Christ, a righteous Judge, who shall come in the meridian of time.
>
> Therefore I give unto you a commandment, to teach these things freely unto your children, saying:

That by reason of transgression cometh the fall, which fall bringeth death, and inasmuch as ye were born into the world by water, and blood, and the spirit, which I have made, and so became of dust a living soul, even so ye must be born again into the kingdom of heaven, of water, and of the Spirit, and be cleansed by blood, even the blood of mine Only Begotten.

Here the Lord says to Adam that through the fall came death, and other statements of that kind are given in these scriptures.

Now the Lord speaks here about our being cleansed by blood. If I had more than the alloted time, Brother Lee, I could tell them something interesting about blood, but I will cut it short.

Cleansed by Blood

We are cleansed by blood. The Savior had to have blood in his body. He got it from his mother, not his Father. There is no blood in a celestial being, nor an immortal being. Blood is the life of the mortal body. Read the first verses of the ninth chapter of Genesis. Write down also the seventeenth chapter of Leviticus, beginning with the tenth verse. You will find that blood is the life of mortality. There was no blood in Adam's body until he partook of the forbidden fruit, then blood became the life-giving influence, or force, fluid, in the mortal body.

The Savior had to pay the price on the cross to atone for Adam's transgression by the shedding of his blood and giving it back. So, by the blood we are cleansed. The Savior could not have been put to death by hanging on a tree, or by being smothered, drowned, or something of that kind. They had to shed his blood, and he gave back the life-giving power or influence which belongs to mortality. He paid the price, the debt that Adam owed. He paid the debt that we owe. He redeemed every creature from death and has restored them to life that will be everlasting by the shedding of his blood. When you partake of the sacrament think of that. We drink the water in remembrance of his blood, the bread because of his broken body. The blood plays a very important place in our mortal existence, and in the atonement of Jesus Christ, and by it we are blessed.

We are sanctified by the Spirit but it is the blood that cleanses us—his blood. Not mine, not yours, but the giving back what Adam received in the fall. That was the punishment. The Lord said "You shall surely die, From earth you came. To earth you shall go," speaking of his body. He had to die.

If you will read in the second chapter of Second Nephi, and in the ninth chapter of Second Nephi, you will find that after we die we would remain dead an awful long time —forever—if it had not been for the atonement of Jesus Christ.

Now, evolution leads men away from God. Men who have had faith in God, when they have become converted to that theory, forsake him. Charles Darwin was a religious man when he started out. I have told in this book something about what happened to him, and how his feelings changed, and what was beautiful to him in the beginning ceased to be beautiful to him thereafter.

Let us seek for the guidance of the Spirit of the Lord, and we will be taught and will be led in all truth, the truth that will make us free—(Lecture to seminary and institute teachers held at Brigham Young University, June 25, 1954.)

No judge in this world in any court of the land can annul a marriage for time and all eternity. He may separate the husband and wife by legal enactments, but he cannot separate husband and wife so far as the next world is concerned. Only the President of the Church has authority to cancel sealings.

The Eternity of Temple Marriage

I trust that I may have the guidance of the Spirit of the Lord in what I may say.

I will commence by quoting from the nineteenth chapter of Matthew:

The Pharisees also came unto him, tempting him, and saying unto him, Is it lawful for a man to put away his wife for every cause?

And he answered and said unto them, Have ye not read, that he which made them at the beginning made them male and female,

And said, For this cause shall a man leave father and mother, and shall cleave to his wife: and they twain shall be one flesh?

Wherefore they are no more twain, but one flesh. What therefore God hath joined together, let not man put asunder.[1]

In The Church of Jesus Christ of Latter-day Saints, marriage is performed for those who love the truth and desire to belong to the family of God, as spoken of by Paul in the third chapter of Ephesians, wherein he says:

For this cause I bow my knees unto the Father of our Lord Jesus Christ,

Of whom the whole family in heaven and earth is named.[2]

---

[1]Matthew 19:3-6.
[2]Ephesians 3:14-15.

Is There a Family in Heaven?

Is there a family in heaven and in earth? Yes. That family is composed of those who go to the temple of the Lord and there are sealed or married for time and for all eternity according to the law of the Lord. Marriage is to be eternal, just as the Lord declares here in the words that I have read, and when a man and a woman go to the house of the Lord and are married for time and for all eternity, they take upon them certain covenants that they will be true and faithful in that union. Those covenants are made in the presence of God and angels at the altar in the temple of the Lord. How, then, can a man and a woman with the love of God in their hearts ever turn away from the solemn covenants that they make that they will be true and faithful all the days of their lives in mortality and that their faithfulness will continue after death? That is the covenant that they make.

Now, the Lord says further in answer to the Pharisees query:

> They say unto him, Why did Moses then command to give a writing of divorcement, and to put her away?
>
> He saith unto them, Moses because of the hardness of your hearts suffered you to put away your wives: but from the beginning it was not so.
>
> And I say unto you, Whosoever shall put away his wife, except it be for fornication, and shall marry another, committeth adultery: and whoso marrieth her which is put away doth commit adultery.
>
> His disciples say unto him. If the case of the man be so with his wife, it is not good to marry.[3]

Evidently they did not get the full significance of the Savior's words.

In the temple of the Lord, a couple goes to be sealed or married for time and all eternity. Children born in that union will be the children of that father and mother

---
[3]Matthew 19:7-10.

not only in mortal life but in all eternity, and they become members of the family of God in heaven and on earth, as spoken of by Paul, and that family order should never be broken. The Lord tried to impress this upon his disciples that it was only because of the hardness of the hearts of the people, because they failed to keep the commandments that the Lord had given them that Moses granted the putting away of the wife. Today the laws are different, and sometimes men put away their wives, and sometimes wives put away their husbands, but a marriage in the temple of the Lord should be one that should be considered sacred and holy, never to be violated in any way whatsoever, because it means that those who enter into such a covenant shall continue after death and have eternal increase and build a kingdom.

Divorce Is a Result of Violations

If there is ever a divorce between a man and a woman married in the temple for time and all eternity, it is because they, one or the other or both, have violated the covenants that they made at the altar of the Lord, otherwise they could not separate, and the Lord never intended that a man and a woman be separated in death, but that this marriage was one for eternity. There was no separation in death, and one of the greatest sins that can be committed is for a man and a woman to separate after they have been sealed in the house of the Lord to become sons and daughters of God and members of his household, and to have children come to them, sent by divine approval to be in that household not only for time but for all eternity.

Now how in the world a man and a woman can go to the temple and there be sealed and make their solemn covenants that they will be true and faithful before the Lord, and then the time comes when one of them is dissatisfied, maybe both, and they want to separate! They are committing one of the great crimes that could be committed, if they have children. Those children born to them have a right to the companionship of father and mother, and father and mother are under obligations before their Eternal Father to be true to each other and raise those children in light and truth, that they may in the eternities to come, be one—a family within the great family of God, as spoken of by Paul.

It is only because of transgression on the part of the wife or of the husband, or perhaps on the part of both, when a couple has been married in the temple of the Lord, and then separate. If they were true to their covenants, to the obligations that they have made to each other at the altar in the house of the Lord, they could not separate, and if they have children, they are not only committing a crime against themselves, but they are harming those children and robbing them of blessings that they were born entitled to receive.

Law of Marriage Is Still True Today

The Savior is very emphatic in his answer to these Pharisees. If the law was true in the days of the Savior, and his words are according to the law, then it seems to me that law has not changed in the dispensation of the fulness of times. It is only through sin and the transgression of the law that a separation can come that would divide father and mother and leave the children stranded and perhaps to be received into some other family by adoption, because parents have lost their faith and have turned away from the covenants they solemnly made before God and angels.

How members of the Church can do such a thing appears to be as a mystery. It can be explained, of course. They do it because they have lost the spirit of the gospel. That divorce comes to them because they are not keeping the commandments that the Lord gave to them, because they have permitted darkness to enter into their souls.

I think I can say here safely and truthfully that no judge in this world in any court of the land can annul a marriage for time and all eternity. He may separate the husband and wife by legal enactments so far as this world is concerned, but he cannot separate that husband and wife so far as the next world is concerned. Only the President of the Church has authority to cancel sealings, and when the man and his wife lose their faith and go to the courts and get a separation, and then go out and marry according to the laws of the land, they are not culpable before the law of the land, but they are before the kingdom of God and what the Savior says here in this revelation is absolutely true:

> . . . Whosoever shall put away his wife, except it be for fornication, and shall marry another, committeth adultery: and whoso marrieth her which is put away doth commit adultery.[4]—(*Conference Report*, April 1961.)

---

[4]Matthew 19:9.

Why do we build temples? It is because the Lord commands it. For what purpose are they built? In order that sacred ordinances and covenants necessary to the exaltation in the celestial kingdom may be bestowed upon all those who are worthy of the exaltation.

The Salt Lake Temple

April 6, 1953, commemorated one hundred years since the laying of the cornerstones of the Salt Lake Temple. This was a solemn occasion, for the members of the Church understood the significance of temples and the eternal nature of the ordinances to be performed in them. The Saints had been driven from their homes after erecting a sacred temple to the name of the Lord in which the ordinances of exaltation belong, and they longed for the time to come when another house of the Lord should stand in which they could go and receive these sacred blessings.

During the westward journey the building of a temple was frequently discussed. On the evening of July 28, 1847, President Brigham Young, with some of the apostles and Thomas Bullock, the clerk, walked from the camp in Salt Lake Valley to the site chosen for the temple. There President Young raised his hands and said: "Here is the forty acres[1] for a temple, and the city can be laid out perfectly square north and south, east and west." Ground was broken in February 1853, for the foundation, and on the morning of April 6, 1853, several thousand members of the Church assembled where President Young made some preliminary

---

[1] Later the size of the site was reduced to ten acres.

remarks after which the General Authorities and other of-
ficials took their places around the foundation, and the ceremonies proceeded as follows:

The First Presidency with the Patriarch, John Smith,
laid the first, or southeast cornerstone, in accordance with
the pattern, given by the Prophet Joseph Smith, and President Young gave the oration saying:

> We dedicate the southeast cornerstone of the temple to the
> Most High God. May it remain in place till it has done its work,
> and until he who has inspired our hearts to fulfil the prophecies of
> his holy prophets, that the house of the Lord should be reared in
> the "tops of the mountains" shall be satisfied, and say it is enough.

Dedicatory Prayer

President Heber C. Kimball offered the prayer of
dedication at this stone, and the assembly then gathered
at the southwest cornerstone, which was laid by the Presiding Bishopric, followed by the oration by Bishop Edward
Hunter and a prayer of dedication by Bishop Alfred Cor-
don. Then the northwest cornerstone was laid by the
presidency of the high priests, and President John Young
of that quorum delivered the oration. Elder George B.
Wallace offered the prayer of dedication. The last, or
northeast cornerstone, was laid by the Council of the Twelve
Apostles. Elder Parley P. Pratt delivered the oration, and
the prayer of dedication was offered by Elder Orson Hyde.

At the afternoon services President Brigham Young
made the following remarks:

> I scarcely ever say much about revelations, or visions, but suf-
> fice it to say, five years ago last July [1847], I was here and saw
> in the spirit the temple not ten feet from where we have laid the
> chief cornerstone. I have not inquired what kind of a temple
> we should build. Why? Because it was represented before me,
> I never looked upon that ground, but the vision of it was there. I
> see it as plainly as if it was in reality before me. Wait until it is

done. I will say, however, that it will have six towers, to begin with, instead of one. Now do not any of you apostatize because it will have six towers, and Joseph only built one. It is easier for us to build sixteen, than it was for him to build one. The time will come when there will be one in the center of temples we shall build, and on the top groves and fish ponds.

A Grand Edifice of Stone

As a boy I used to go up to the temple block and watch the men carving the hard granite stones and raise and place each in its chosen spot, and to me this was indeed a slow process. In my boyhood anxiety I wondered if I would live to see the temple finished. I also frequently visited the blacksmith shop farther up the street on North Temple where the tools were sharpened. In the summers much of my time was spent in Little Cottonwood Canyon, and there I watched the men digging and blasting the great granite blocks and preparing them for delivery to the temple. I can remember the days of the ox teams and how they tugged with their heavy loads, and how at intervals down the canyon road rough-cut blocks had skidded from the wagons and were lost. As I grew, my patience became more reasonable, and I saw the grand edifice rise stone upon stone until all were laid perfectly in their places, and the building was ready for dedication.

It was my privilege to be present in April 1892, at the ceremonies of the laying of the capstone.

In the general assembly in the Tabernacle, President Lorenzo Snow of the Council of the Twelve explained to the congregation the order of the ceremony to be held at the laying of the stone and taught the assembled Saints how to proceed with the Hosannah Shout. After remarks by President Wilford Woodruff the congregation proceeded to the southwest corner of the temple where a platform for the General Authorities had been built. After appropriate exercises, President Woodruff pushed an elec-

tric button, and the capstone was laid. Then followed the
Hosannah Shout. Elder Francis M. Lyman of the Council of the Twelve moved that efforts be made to finish the
temple so that it could be dedicated on April 6, 1893. This
motion was received with enthusiasm by the vast assembly
of about forty thousand.

On April 6, 1893 the temple was ready for dedication.
President Wilford Woodruff offered the dedicatory prayer
which was followed by the Hosannah Shout led by President Lorenzo Snow. These services were repeated almost daily until April 24. Thirty-one meetings were held,
and a total of seventy-five thousand people had the privilege of attending. As a young man holding the Aaronic
Priesthood, it was my privilege to be present at the opening session. With others holding the Aaronic Priesthood
I had a place in the gallery on the north side of the assembly room. I was greatly impressed with the wonderful spirit of these exercises and have looked back to that
day many times with deep feelings of satisfaction.

Commencement of Ordinance Work

Tuesday, May 23, 1893, the temple was opened for
ordinance work under the direction of the First Presidency,
Wilford Woodruff, George Q. Cannon, and Joseph F. Smith,
and the great wish of President Brigham Young had been
fulfilled. This, of course, was not the first temple in Utah
to be erected, but it was the one above all others for which
the members of the Church had longed. Nor was it the
last to be built, and President Brigham Young predicted
that the time would come when temples would be erected
all over the land of Zion and in foreign lands.

Why do we build temples? It is because the Lord
commands it. For what purpose are they built? In order
that sacred ordinances and covenants necessary to the exaltation in the celestial kingdom may be bestowed upon

all those who are worthy of the exaltation. In relation to these blessings the Lord has said:

> That by keeping the commandments they might be washed and cleansed from all their sins, and receive the Holy Spirit by the laying on of the hands of him who is ordained and sealed unto this power;
> And who overcome by faith, and are sealed by the Holy Spirit of promise, which the Father sheds forth upon all those who are just and true.
> They are they who are the church of the Firstborn.
> They are they into whose hands the Father has given all things—
> They are they who are priests and kings, who have received of his fulness, and of his glory.[2]

None Enter Temples Except Those Prepared

We can discern from this that according to the letter of the commandment, none are entitled to enter the temple and receive these ordinances except those who have prepared themselves for exaltation by the keeping of all of the commandments and have prepared themselves by faith and faithfulness to be so endowed. This strictness is not always followed and many are privileged to receive some of these ordinances on the promise of faithfulness thereafter.

So important did the Lord consider the need of a temple in Israel, he commanded Moses to build one while the children of Israel were in the wilderness. This was built of the most costly materials that the Israelites could produce. It was a portable building that could be taken down and set up as the camp of Israel moved in their journey from place to place. It is frequently spoken of as the tabernacle. It was to this building that Samuel was taken by his mother in his childhood. In the days of Solomon, Israel was commanded to build a permanent temple which

[2]D&C 76:52-56.

served them until through their rebellion and corruption
it was destroyed by Nebuchadnezzar at the time of the
captivity.   On the return of the Jews from this bondage, by
decree of Cyrus the Persian, the temple was rebuilt.   Later
it was neglected, and then it was repaired and partially re-
constructed in the days of Herod.   This was the temple
as our Savior found it.

Baptism for the Dead

Since the resurrection of our Savior, baptism for the
dead has been performed.   This ordinance belongs to the
temples as do all the ordinances pertaining to the salvation
of the worthy dead.   At the time of the building of the
Nauvoo Temple, the Lord said:

> For therein are the keys of the holy priesthood ordained, that
> you may receive honor and glory. . . .
> For it is ordained that in Zion and in her stakes, and in Jeru-
> salem, those places which I have appointed for refuge, shall be the
> places for your baptisms for your dead.
> And again, verily I say unto you, how shall your washings be
> acceptable unto me, except ye perform them in a house which you
> have built to my name?
> For, for this cause I commanded Moses that he should build
> a tabernacle, that they should bear it with them in the wilderness,
> and to build a house in the land of promise, that those ordinances
> might be revealed which had been hid from before the world was.[3]

Today it is the privilege of the Latter-day Saints to go
to this sacred house, and there receive all of these blessings
in fulfilment of the promise of the Lord through Jeremiah.
—(*The Improvement Era,* April 1953.)

---

[3]D&C 124:34, 36-38.

It might seem to some that the Lord was rather harsh with Israel by . . . leaving them with the law of Moses but denying them the fulness of the gospel. However, a closer study of the situation will show that the Lord used wisdom in making these restrictions. Evidently the time had not come for the complete restoration. . . .

The Two Tables of Stone Written by the Finger of God

It is true that when Moses broke the first tables, the Lord prepared other tables "like unto the first." It is unfortunate that the Lord had to modify the second tables, because in some respects they were not exactly like the first. We have learned through modern revelation that parts of the first recorded counsel were changed. For instance, here is part of the counsel the Lord gave to Moses after the breaking of the tables, found in the scriptures revealed to the Prophet Joseph Smith:

And the Lord said to Moses, Hew thee two other tables of stone, like unto the first, and I will write upon them also, the words of the law, according as they were written at first on the tables which thou brakest; but it shall not be according to the first, for I will take away the priesthood out of their midst; therefore my holy order, and the ordinances thereof shall not go before them; for my presence shall not go up in their midst, lest I destroy them.

But I will give unto them the law as at the first, but it shall be after the law of a carnal commandment; for I have sworn in my wrath, that they shall not enter into my presence, into my rest, in the days of their pilgrimage. Therefore do as I have commanded thee, and be ready in the morning, and come up in the morning unto mount Sinai, and present thyself there to me, in the top of the mount.

And no man shall come up with thee, neither let any man be seen throughout all the mount; neither let the flocks nor herds feed before that mount.

And Moses hewed two tables of stone like unto the first; and he rose up early in the morning, and went up unto mount Sinai, as the Lord had commanded him, and took in his hand the two tables of stone.

And the Lord descended in the cloud, and stood before him there, and proclaimed the name of the Lord.

And the Lord passed by before him, and proclaimed, The Lord, The Lord God, merciful and gracious, long-suffering, and abundant in goodness and truth,

Keeping mercy for thousands, forgiving iniquity and transgression and sin, and that will by no means clear the rebellious. visiting the iniquity of the fathers upon the children, and upon the children's children, unto the third and to the fourth generation.

And Moses made haste, and bowed his head towards the earth and worshipped.[1]

Agreement in Scripture

So we read in the Prophet's edition of the Bible. This agrees perfectly with what the Lord has given us by revelation in the Doctrine and Covenants:

And this greater priesthood administereth the gospel and holdeth the key of the mysteries of the kingdom, even the key of the knowledge of God.

Therefore, in the ordinances thereof, the power of godliness is manifest.

And without the ordinances thereof, and the authority of the priesthood, the power of godliness is not manifest unto men in the flesh;

For without this no man can see the face of God, even the Father, and live.

Now this Moses plainly taught to the children of Israel in the wilderness, and sought diligently to sanctify his people that they might behold the face of God;

---

[1]Exodus 34:1-8, Inspired Version of the Bible.

But they hardened their hearts and could not endure his presence; therefore, the Lord in his wrath, for his anger was kindled against them, swore that they should not enter into his rest while in the wilderness, which rest is the fulness of his glory.

Therefore, he took Moses out of their midst, and the Holy Priesthood also;

And the lesser priesthood continued, which priesthood holdeth the keys of the ministering of angels and the preparatory gospel;

Which gospel is the gospel of repentance and of baptism, and the remission of sins, and the law of carnal commandments, which the Lord in his wrath caused to continue with the house of Aaron among the children of Israel until John, whom God raised up, being filled with the Holy Ghost from his mother's womb.[2]

Restrictions Were Necessary

It might seem to some that the Lord was rather harsh with Israel by making this decree, leaving them with the law of Moses but denying them the fulness of the gospel. However, a closer study of the situation will show that the Lord used wisdom in making these restrictions. Evidently the time had not come for the complete restoration, and it was divine wisdom to restrict the Israelites and give them a "schoolmaster" until the coming of our Redeemer, when the gospel's fulness was restored.—(The Improvement Era, January, 1967.)

---

[2]D&C 84:19-27.

The proper interpretation of this wonderful prophecy is that the Lord has set up his Church (or kingdom) for the last time; it is to grow and increase until it shall fill the earth, and, according to the prophetic interpretation of Daniel, this kingdom shall stand forever.

Nebuchadnezzar's Vision of the Kingdom

The great King Nebuchadnezzar had a wonderful dream in relation to a great image that was terrible.

This image's head was of fine gold, his breast and his arms of silver, his belly and his thighs of brass,
His legs of iron, his feet part of iron and part of clay.
Thou sawest till that a stone was cut out without hands, which smote the image upon his feet that were of iron and clay, and brake them to pieces.
Then was the iron, the clay, the brass, the silver, and the gold, broken to pieces together, and became like the chaff of the summer threshingfloors; and the wind carried them away, that no place was found for them: and the stone that smote the image became a great mountain, and filled the whole earth.[1]

Daniel's Interpretation

Daniel gave the interpretation of this vision in these words:

Thou, O king, art a king of kings: for the God of heaven hath given thee a kingdom, power, and strength, and glory.

_____
[1]Daniel 2:32-35.

And wheresoever the children of men dwell, the beasts of the field and the fowls of the heaven hath he given into thine hand, and hath made thee ruler over them all. Thou art this head of gold.

And after thee shall arise another kingdom inferior to thee, and another third kingdom of brass, which shall bear rule over all the earth.

And the fourth kingdom shall be strong as iron: forasmuch as iron breaketh in pieces and subdueth all things: and as iron that breaketh all these, shall it break in pieces and bruise.

And whereas thou sawest the feet and toes, part of potters' clay, and part of iron, the kingdom shall be divided; but there shall be in it of the strength of the iron, forasmuch as thou sawest the iron mixed with miry clay.

And as the toes of the feet were part of iron, and part of clay, so the kingdom shall be partly strong, and partly broken.

And whereas thou sawest iron mixed with miry clay, they shall mingle themselves with the seed of men; but they shall not cleave one to another, even as iron is not mixed with clay.

And in the days of these kings shall the God of heaven set up a kingdom, which shall never be destroyed: and the kingdom shall not be left to other people, but it shall break in pieces and consume all these kingdoms, and it shall stand for ever.

Forasmuch as thou sawest that the stone was cut out of the mountain without hands, and that it brake in pieces the iron, the brass, the clay, the silver, and the gold; the great God hath made known to the king what shall come to pass hereafter: and the dream is certain, and the interpretation thereof sure.[2]

A Wonderful Portrait

This vision of the kingdom is a wonderful portrait of historical events down through the ages of time, from the day of Daniel to our present dispensation. Let us not forget that the promise of the Lord in this vision was that in the latter days of these kingdoms the Lord was to set up a kingdom that was not to be left to any other people, "*which shall never be destroyed*," but which was to endure and consume all other kingdoms and stand forever.

---

[2]Daniel 2:37-45.

The proper interpretation of this wonderful prophecy is that the Lord has set up his Church (or kingdom) for the last time; it is to grow and increase until it shall fill the earth, and, according to the prophetic interpretation of Daniel, this kingdom shall stand forever.

Now, let us speak plainly and clearly in relation to this remarkable vision and Daniel's interpretation.

Great Kingdom Is the Church

This great kingdom is verily the Church of Jesus Christ, which has been established in the earth for the last time. It is not to be destroyed but is to continue to endure and increase until it shall fill the earth in the due time of the Lord.

From time to time there have been apostates withdraw from the Church. There have been attempts to set up opposition organizations, but they do not prosper, nor can they.

This remarkable prophetic vision that was interpreted by Daniel is bound to be fulfilled. The Lord set up his kingdom, or divine Church, through the ministry of the Prophet Joseph Smith. The stone cut out of the mountain is indeed The Church of Jesus Christ of Latter-day Saints, which is to endure through all time, or "stand for ever." —(*The Improvement Era,* February 1967, p. 4.)

The Lord himself, had called and ordained, beside the twelve, seventies, and sent them forth throughout Judea bearing the message of truth. . . . That the Twelve Apostles were empowered to set in order all things pertaining to the church, is, nevertheless, beyond dispute.

Dispensation of the Meridian of Time

In the dispensation of the meridian of time, when the Savior ministered among the Jews, he restored the gospel with the higher priesthood. He called and ordained Twelve Apostles and gave them power, before his ascension into heaven, to complete the church organization, and commissioned them to carry the message of divine salvation into all the world. In restoring that which had been taken away, he annulled the carnal law, which had been added in the place of the higher law, for it had filled the measure of its creation.

Commission of the Apostles

Under the commission Jesus gave the apostles to carry the gospel message into all the world and preach it to every creature, they commenced their active ministry on the day of Pentecost, preaching in power to the convincing of many souls. As the work of the ministry grew, and the assistance of other laborers was required to carry on the work, men were divinely called and ordained to specific offices in the Church. The Lord, himself, had called and ordained, besides the twelve, seventies, and sent them forth

throughout Judea bearing the message of truth. When
they returned from that missionary journey it was with
much rejoicing because even the devils were subject unto
them. What other officers the Lord ordained and set
apart, the scriptures do not reveal. That the Twelve Apostles were empowered to set in order all things pertaining
to the Church, is, nevertheless, beyond dispute. We learn
that under their direction and ministry, as branches were
formed and the work of the ministry required it, high
priests, evangelists (patriarchs), elders, bishops, deacons,
priests, pastors and teachers were called into the service of
the Church. The organization was in this manner ef-
fected during the days of the apostles. The Church was
also blessed with the divine gifts and blessings of the Spirit
of the Lord in those early days, just as it was during the
Savior's ministry. There were in the Church many prophets
who uttered, by the gift of the Holy Ghost, many remarkable predictions.

Essential Offices in the Church

All of these offices in the Church are essential to the
advancement of the members and cannot be discarded with
impunity. Paul said, the Lord "gave some apostles; and
some prophets; and some evangelists; and some pastors and
teachers; for the perfecting of the saints, for the work of
the ministry, for the edifying of the body of Christ." These
were not merely to remain in the Church during the forma-
tive period, or for a brief season in order to start the work,
and then to be replaced by other officers of another kind.
Men were ordained to these callings "for the edifying of
the body of Christ, till we all come to the unity of the faith,
and of the knowledge of the Son of God unto a perfect man,
unto the measure of the stature of the fulness of Christ."[1]
Evidently, then, as long as there is imperfection in the

---

[1]Ephesians 4:11-13.

Church among the members, in doctrine, knowledge, or love, they fall short of "the stature of the fulness of Christ."

These officers are all needed and cannot justly be removed, for the Lord never so intended. The writer of the epistle to the Ephesians also further compares all these officers to the various parts of the human body and says: "From whom the whole body fitly joined together and compacted by that which every joint supplieth, according to the effectual working in the measure of every part, maketh increase of the body unto the edifying of itself in love."[2] This same apostle also likens the spiritual gifts to the physical body, declaring each to be essential in the Church, just as the parts of the body are each necessary and one part cannot say to another, "I have no need of you," for all are necessary that all men may "profit withal."[3]

The Body of the Church Destroyed

Notwithstanding that the early officers of the Church were endowed with the Holy Priesthood and exercised the spiritual gifts, which were to remain until all came "unto a perfect man unto the stature of the fulness of Christ," there came a great and terrible change, absolutely destroying the perfect body of the Church. In its place arose a strange organization which eventually gained dominion over the earth and ruled the destinies of men, not in love unfeigned, but in blood and carnage most appalling, and with an iron hand.

The rise of this power had been predicted by many of the prophets of old and by the apostles of our Lord. Even the Savior, when instructing his disciples regarding the sign of the times, intimated that this would occur. Isaiah, seven centuries before the birth of Christ, predicted

[3]I Corinthians 12:21. Read the entire chapter 12.
[2]Ephesians 4:16.

that the time would come when the earth would be defiled under its inhabitants because of the transgression of the law, the changing of ordinances and the breaking of the new and everlasting covenant. It is evident that this was to occur in the latter days, and not in the days of Israel's subjection to the law, for the law of Moses was not an everlasting covenant. This prophecy was to receive its consummation in the day when the earth, defiled by the wickedness and corruption of its inhabitants, should be cleansed by fire and few men left.[4]

The Prophecies of Isaiah, Amos, and Daniel

Speaking of this event Isaiah says: "For the Lord hath poured out upon you the spirit of deep sleep, and hath closed your eyes: the prophets and your rulers, the seers hath he covered."[5] Shortly before this time, Amos also predicted that the time would come when the Lord would send a famine in the land, "not a famine of bread," said he, "nor a thirst for water, but of hearing the word of the Lord."[6]

Daniel saw in vision the overthrow of the Church established by the Savior in the meridian of time. In his vision of the four beasts, representing the kingdoms seen by Nebuchadnezzar in his dream, he saw one horn, or power, come up among the ten that succeeded the Roman Empire "more stout than his fellows." This horn had eyes and a mouth that spake very great words against the Most High, and three other kingdoms were subdued by this great horn. The same power "made war with the saints and prevailed against them," and through continued conflict and exercise of might was able to "wear out the saints of the Most High" and thought to "change times and laws." This blasphemous power was to rule until the coming of

---

[4]Isaiah 24:1-6.
[5]Isaiah 29:10.
[6]Amos 8:11.

the Ancient of Days, when the kingdom and dominion was to be "given to the people of the saints of the Most High whose kingdom is an everlasting kingdom."[7]

Apostasy Commenced in Days of Apostles

The falling away from the faith commenced before the close of the ministry of the apostles. Paul, when at Miletus taking his final departure from the elders of Ephesus who had come to meet him, earnestly entreated them to take heed to feed the Church of God, for, said he,

> For I know this, that after my departing shall grievous wolves enter in among you, not sparing the flock. Also of yourselves shall men arise, speaking perverse things to draw away disciples after them.[8]

He also took occasion to warn the Saints at Thessalonica not to be deceived regarding the ushering in of the second advent of the Son of God, "for that day," he wrote to them, "shall not come, except there come a falling away first, and that man of sin be revealed, the son of perdition; who opposeth and exalteth himself above all that is called God, or that is worshiped; so that he as God sitteth in the temple of God, showing himself that he is God."[9]

The Predictions of Paul

The Saints at Galatia commenced very early to depart from the faith. Timothy was warned by Paul, and instructed that in the last days perilous times would come and men would be "lovers of their ownselves, covetous, boasters, proud, blasphemers, disobedient to parents, unthankful, unholy, without natural affection, truce breakers, false accusers, incontinent, fierce, despisers of those that

---

[7]Daniel 7:21-25.
[8]Acts 20:29-30.
[9]II Thessalonians 2:3-4.

are good, traitors, heady, highminded, lovers of pleasures more than lovers of God; having a form of godliness but denying the power thereof." Moreover, he said the time would come, "when they will not endure sound doctrine; but after their own lusts shall they heap to themselves teachers, having itching ears; and they shall turn away their ears from the truth, and shall be turned unto fables."[10]

Prophecy of Peter

Peter, likewise, by the spirit of prophecy, bore record of the departure from the faith when he wrote to the Saints saying:

> But there were false prophets also among the people, even as there shall be false teachers among you, who privily shall bring in damnable heresies, even denying the Lord that bought them, and bring upon themselves swift destruction.
>
> And many shall follow their pernicious ways; by reason of whom the way of truth shall be evil spoken of.[11]

Then he sought to impress upon the minds of the Saints the fact that the prophets before him had also predicted these direful events, saying:

> That ye may be mindful of the words which were spoken before by the holy prophets, and of the commandment of us the apostles of the Lord and Savior:
>
> Knowing this first, that there shall come in the last days scoffers, walking after their own lusts,
>
> And saying: Where is the promise of his coming? for since the fathers fell asleep, all things continue as they were from the beginning of the creation.[12]

The Mystery of Iniquity

As already stated, Paul declared to the Thessalonians that the "mystery of iniquity" was already at work, and

---

[10]II Timothy 3:1-5; 4:3-4.
[11]II Peter 2:1-2.
[12]II Peter 3:2-4.

to Timothy he said: "All they which are in Asia be turned away from me."[13] He had, we are led to believe, had some dispute with Asiatic converts, for he wrote to Timothy in great sorrow because some of his companions had forsaken him and were advocating doctrines contrary to the gospel of Jesus Christ. In trying to correct these evils he was left to contend alone, for he adds: "At my first answer no man stood with me, but all men forsook me."[14]

It was not long after the departure of the apostles that spiritual gifts ceased to be manifest in the Church. The decline of these blessings, which are inseparably connected with the Church of Christ, led to the belief, so prevalent even in this day, that they were not to be continued, having been instituted in the incipiency of the Church, merely as a means of aiding in its establishment, after which they were no longer needed.

Revelation and heavenly communication also came to an end. There was no more vision, for the people had closed their eyes. This condition also led to the universal belief, which the world holds even now, that the canon of scripture is full, and there is to be no more scripture, notwithstanding the Lord has revealed through his servants that revelation is to continue.

Changes in Church Government

The offices in the priesthood were also changed because those unto whom the gospel was preached would not endure sound doctrine, but after their own lusts heaped to themselves teachers having itching ears, and were "men of corrupt minds, reprobate concerning the faith."

Instead of apostles and prophets there came, as time went on, a very different ecclesiastical order from that instituted by the Lord. The Church established by the Re-

---

[13]II Timothy 1:15.
[14]II Timothy 4:16.

deemer was taken from the earth because of continued persecution and apostasy, until there was but a dead form of the true Church left. The great ecclesiastical organization that arose and claimed to be the Church of Christ was of gradual growth. The change from truth to error was not made all in one day. It commenced in the first century and continued during the immediate centuries that followed, until the Church established in the days of the apostles was no more to be found among men. Without the direction of inspired men, who could communicate with God, the change was a natural one.

In the beginning of the fourth century this great religious power, under the Emperor Constantine became the state religion of the Roman Empire. From that time forth its dominion spread and before many years had passed away it became the ruling power in religion in the so-called civilized world. By it "times and laws" were changed. The simple principles of the Christian faith were embellished almost beyond recognition with pomp and mystic rites borrowed from pagan worship. The priests and potentates, who officiated in these ceremonies, no longer followed the simple customs of the humble fishermen of Galilee, but dressed in splendid and costly robes, with mitres on their heads, they performed their various parts in pride and with mystifying ceremonies that over-awed and bewildered the humble people.

Changes in the Doctrines of the Church

The correct doctrine regarding the Godhead taught by Jesus Christ, was changed into a mystery. The ordinance of baptism was changed from burial in the water for the remission of sins, to sprinkling of a little water on the head. Sprinkling of infants, miscalled baptism, a custom which "is mockery before God, denying the mercies of

Christ, and the power of the Holy Spirit,"[15] became a fixed and universal custom. Changes in the administration of the sacrament of the Lord's supper were also introduced, and the doctrine advanced that the bread and wine became the flesh and blood of our crucified Redeemer, by transubstantiation. Those who entered the ministry were forbidden to marry, and many other changes, which need not be mentioned here, were made in the principles of the gospel, in the functions of the priesthood and the worship of the Lord.

Temporal Power of the Pope

Rome became the capital of this ecclesiastical power and the bishop or pope, as he was called, its head. As its power grew it claimed dominion not only in matter religious, but in civil affairs as well. By it kings were made and by it they were dethroned. Unless they bowed before the papal power in abject submission they were made to feel the weight of its mighty hand.

Frederick Seebohm, in his *Era of the Protestant Revolution,* says:

> Kings were not secure on their thrones till they had the sanction of the Church. On the other hand the clergy claimed to be free from prosecution under the criminal laws of the land they lived in. They struggled to keep their own ecclesiastical laws and their own ecclesiastical courts, receiving authority direct from Rome, and with final appeal, not to the crown, but to the pope.[16]

"To establish an accusation against a bishop," writes Motley, in his *Rise of the Dutch Republic,* "seventy-two witnesses were necessary; against a deacon, twenty-seven; against an inferior dignitary, seven; while two were sufficient to convict a layman."[17]

—————
[15]Moroni 8:23.
[16]Seebohm, *Era of the Protestant Revolution,* p. 9.
[17]Motley, *Rise of the Dutch Republic,* Vol. I, p. 69.

Power of the Clergy

Few outside of the clergy were educated enough to read and write; therefore priests became the lawyers, diplomats, ambassadors, instructors and prime ministers in the nations. All learned men talked and wrote in Latin, which was the language of Rome. It is said that for centuries a man convicted of a crime in England, by showing that he could read or write, could claim the benefits of a trial in the ecclesiastical court, which, "by long abuse came to mean exemption from the punishment of the criminal law of the land."

Not only did the priests fill these important offices where they were enabled to wield great power and to control, very largely, the destinies of nations, but many of them became extremely avaricious and "divined for money." Jean de Valdez, brother of the secretary to King Charles V, wrote of the times as follows:

> I see that we can scarcely get anything from Christ's ministers but for money; at baptism money, at bishoping money, at marriage money, for confession money — no, not extreme unction without money! They will ring no bells without money, no burial in Church without money; so that it seemeth that Paradise is shut up from them that have no money. The rich is buried in the Church, the poor in the church-yard. The rich may marry with his nearest kin, but the poor not so, albeit he be ready to die for love of her. The rich may eat flesh in Lent, but the poor may not, albeit fish perhaps be much dearer. The rich man may readily get large indulgences, but the poor none, because he wanteth money to pay for them.[18]

In addition to all this they taxed the people in various ways, receiving a tithing from all produce of the farms, a tenth of the land and of the wages of the working man. Writes Motley:

> Not content, moreover, with their territories and their tithings, the churchman perpetually devised new burdens upon the peasantry.

---

[18]*Era of the Protestant Revolution*, p. 60.

Plows, sickles, horses, oxen, all implements of husbandry were taxed for the benefit of those who toiled not, but who gathered into barns.[19]

Sale of Indulgences

Some of these ecclesiastical rulers became so avaricious and filled with the spirit of greed that they advanced the blasphemous doctrine of forgiving sins by the sale of indulgences. It is claimed by the Church of Rome that these evils were the sins of individuals who perverted the doctrine of the church in relation to penance and forgiveness of sin. The indulgence was, according to their teaching, "a pardon usually granted by the pope, through which the contrite sinner escaped a part, or all, of the punishment which remained even after he had been absolved. The pardon did not therefore forgive the guilt of the sinner, for that had necessarily to be removed before the indulgence was granted; it only removed or mitigated the penalties which even the forgiven sinner would, without the indulgence, have expected to undergo in purgatory."

However, the sale of indulgences in various parts of Europe, was a means of creating large fortunes for those who sanctioned it. There was no crime in the category for which the power of forgiveness was not offered if the party seeking it could pay the price. The various countries were districted and farmed for the collection of these revenues, according to John Lathrop Motley, the historian, who writes:

. . . Throughout the Netherlands, the price current of the wares offered for sale was published in every town and village. God's pardon for crimes already committed, or about to be committed, was advertised according to a graded tariff. Thus poisoning, for example, was absolved for eleven ducats, six livres tournois. Absolution for incest was afforded at thirty-six livres, three ducats. Perjury came to seven livres and three carlines. Pardon for murder, if not by poison, was cheaper. Even a parricide could buy forgiveness at

---

[19]*Rise of the Dutch Republic*, Vol. I, p. 69.

God's tribunal at one ducat, four livres, eight carlines. Henry de
Mountfort, in the year 1448, purchased absolution for that crime at
that price. Was it strange that a century or so of this kind of work
should produce a Luther? Was it unnatural that plain people, who
loved the ancient Church, should rather desire to see her purged
of such blasphemous abuses than to hear of St. Peter's dome rising
a little nearer to the clouds on these proceeds of commuted crime?
. . . The Netherlands, like other countries, are districted and
farmed for the collection of this papal revenue. Much of the money
thus raised remains in the hands of the vile collectors. Sincere
Catholics, who love and honor the ancient religion, shrink with
horror at the spectacle offered on every side. Criminals buying
paradise for money, monks spending the money thus paid in gaming
houses, taverns, and brothels; this seems to those who have studied
their Testaments a different scheme of salvation from the one
promulgated by Christ. There has evidently been a departure from
the systems of earlier apostles. Innocent conservative souls are
much perplexed; but at last all these infamies arouse a giant to do
battle with the giant wrong.[20]

Thus were the prophecies of the scriptures fulfilled; the
laws transgressed by a power that exalted itself "above all
that is called God" and in his sacred name speaking "great
words against the Most High."

The Protestant Revolution

The *Dark Ages*. Not content with absolute dominion
over the spiritual and temporal affairs of the people, this
papal kingdom attempted the exercise of authority also over
the consciences of men. Especially was this so during the
dark ages, when this power was at the zenith of its glory.
This exercise of authority extended also far into the day
when the light of religious freedom commenced to break
forth, during the period known as the revival of learning.
Previous to this revival, as we have seen, the language of
learning was the Latin tongue. The people were help-
lessly dependent upon their priests for all instruction in

---

[20]*Ibid.*, pp. 71-72, 75.

scientific as well as religious thought. The few copies of the Bible extant were guarded by the clergy, and the scriptures were not accessible to the common people, and since they could neither read nor write, and in very few instances understood Latin, they would have been helpless even with the Bible in their hands. Under these conditions it is not to be wondered at that the poor people of those benighted countries of Europe, credulous and filled with superstitious fear, were ready to accept almost anything that was made known to them, in doctrine or deed, by unscrupulous priests.

The Revival of Learning

Neither is it to be wondered at that priests attempted to use force and coercion during the revival of learning to check the opportunities of the people in obtaining light and truth. It was due to the exercise of greater knowledge on the part of the priests and their performance of mystic ceremonies, that over-awed the people and enabled the clergy to keep them shackled by the chains of ignorance and superstition. Ignorance was a ready tool in the hands of the priests by which they shaped and moulded the masses into vessels to their liking. The increase of learning among the people, aided by the discoveries and inventions of the times, would change all this; for the people would not be so ready to accept every wind of doctrine without some mental cogitation and desire to have a reason given why things were thus and so. Moreover, the revival of learning meant the end of many practices and blasphemous doctrines advanced in the name of Jesus Christ, such as the exercise of force over the consciences of men and the sale of indulgences for the pardon of sin—if not the end, at least a wonderful modification of such an evil system.

Early Translations of the Bible

Evidently this ruling ecclesiastical power realized that

enlightened conditions would bring rebellion against its
authority. For that reason stringent laws were framed to
enforce the edicts and regulations of the church of Rome.
During the "Reformation" and before, there were several
translations of the Bible made in the languages which the
common people understood. Wycliffe's Bible appeared in
1380 and was followed by translations at a later date, both
in English and other tongues. At first there was an attempt to destroy these copies which were prepared without
authority or sanction from the Catholic Church. With the
invention of printing in the fifteenth century, however, the
cause of religious freedom received a wonderful impetus,
and Bibles were distributed all over Europe. Before the
time of printing, a Bible cost five hundred crowns, and such
copies as were in existence were in the keeping of the clergy,
who guarded them with the utmost zeal. Through the aid
of printing, the price of Bibles was reduced to five crowns,
which made it possible for the people not only to have the
privilege of hearing the scriptures read in their own tongue,
but also to acquire the understanding by which they could
read them for themselves.

Scripture Reading Forbidden

An English chronicler, Henry Kneighton, many years
before the "Reformation" expressed the prevailing notion
about the reading of the scriptures when he denounced the
general reading of the Bible, lamenting "lest the jewel of
the Church, hitherto the exclusive property of the clergy
and divines, should be made common to the laity." Arch-
bishop Arundel in England had issued an enactment that
"no part of the scriptures in English should be read, either
in public or in private, or be thereafter translated, under
pain of the greater excommunication." The New Testament translation of Erasmus was forbidden at Cambridge,
and the Vicar of Croyden said from his pulpit: "We must

root out printing, or printing will root us out." In the reign of Henry VIII, the reading of the Bible by the common people, or those who were not of the privileged class, had been prohibited by act of Parliament, and men were burned at the stake in England as well as in the Netherlands and other parts of Europe for having even fragments of the scriptures in their hands.

For those who were considered derelict in church duties or heretical in doctrine, edicts were declared, forbidding them to gather in private assemblies for devotion, in various parts of Europe. All reading of the scriptures; all discussion within one's own doors concerning faith, the sacraments, the papal authority, or other religious matter, was forbidden "under penalty of death. The edicts were no dead letter. The fires were kept constantly supplied with human fuel by monks who knew the act of burning reformers better than of arguing with them. The scaffold was the most conclusive of syllogisms, and used upon all occasions."[21]

The Inquisition

Continuing this woeful account of conditions in the rebellious Netherlands and other countries under Spanish rule, the author of *The Rise of the Dutch Republic* says: "Charles V introduced and organized a papal institution, side by side with those horrible 'Placards' of his invention, which constituted a masked inquisition even more cruel than that of Spain. The execution of the system was never permitted to languish. The number of Netherlanders who were burned, strangled, beheaded, or buried alive, in obedience to his edicts, and for the offense of reading the scriptures, of looking askance at a graven image, or of ridiculing the actual presence of the body and blood of Christ in a wafer, have been placed as high as one hundred thousand

---

[21]*Ibid.,* p. 78.

by distinguished authorities, and have never been put at a lower mark than fifty thousand.[22]

Conditions like these could not go on forever. The dawn of a better day began to break over the nations. The Spirit of the Lord was striving with men and preparations commenced for the introduction into the world of the re-established gospel at a later day. It was necessary that the shackles of superstitious fear and illiteracy, which bound the world so completely should be broken, that men might exercise their right of free agency before the fulness of gospel light should break forth. Not only was advancement made in the art of printing, but there came a revival of learning and research in all directions and in all parts of Europe. It was not confined to one land or to one people, but the whole of Europe took on a new life. The discovery of the telescope, the law of gravitation, the invention of gunpower and many other wonderful things were revolutionizing the thoughts of men.

The Mission of Columbus

With the discovery of the mariner's compass navigators became more bold and daring, and gradually extended their explorations until they discovered the ways to India around the Cape of Good Hope. Near the close of the fifteenth century the belief prevailed that the earth was flat and inhabited only on the upper side. Beyond the shores of lands then known it was thought there hung a pall of fog and darkness. The sea was referred to as the "Sea of Darkness" beyond the boundaries known to man. Far off in or beyond the ocean it was believed great dragons had their lair, and if any man should be so unfortunate as to drift among them he would return no more. Mariners had been afraid to traverse the seas far beyond the sight of land. Shortly before the end of this century there came

---

[22]*Ibid.*, p. 114.

one navigator more daring than his fellows, who proposed to cross the sea. After many pleadings and attempts to interest some one with means in the venture, he finally succeeded and the remarkable feat was done. In accomplishing this he made discoveries that the Lord, in his wisdom, had kept hid from the nations of the east all down through the ages, until in his own due time, he desired them to be revealed. Columbus was moved upon by the Spirit of the Lord and crossed the waters in fulfillment of predictions made by a prophet, who lived on this continent, five hundred years before the birth of Christ.

It is well known that the prophets predicted the scattering of Israel into all parts of the earth long before that dispersion commenced. The promise of the return of Israel was just as emphatically proclaimed and must be fulfilled just as surely as the dispersion. The purpose of Orson Hyde's mission to Palestine was to dedicate that land for the return of the Jews. The promises of the Lord to the house of Judah are being fulfilled.

Dedication of Holy Land and the Return of the Jews

At the general conference of the Church held April 6, 1840, Elder Orson Hyde was called to take a mission to Palestine. Two days later Elder John E. Page was called to accompany Elder Hyde on this mission, but unfortunately for him, he failed to go. The purpose of that mission was to dedicate that land for the return of the Jews according to the promises of the Lord to them.

This land was given to Abraham by the Lord as an everlasting inheritance for himself and his seed after him. Abraham was a resident of Ur of Chaldea, a land that was given over to idolatry and wickedness. Abraham's father had fallen under this spell, but notwithstanding this, Abraham prayed earnestly seeking to be a follower of righteousness and a possessor of great knowledge of the things of God all the days of his life.

Because Abraham refused to worship as his father did, his life was sought as a sacrifice to the false gods of that land; but the Lord preserved him. "Get thee out of thy country, and from thy kindred, and from thy father's house, unto a land that I will shew thee," was the word of the

Lord to him. Obedient to this commandment Abraham
gathered his substance and taking those of his kindred who
would accompany him, set out from Ur for the land of
Canaan. As he journeyed the Lord again instructed him,
saying:

> And I will make of thee a great nation, and I will bless thee,
> and make thy name great; and thou shalt be a blessing:
> And I will bless them that bless thee, and curse them that
> curseth thee: and in thee shall all families of the earth be blessed.[1]

Blessings Conferred Upon Abraham

When Abraham arrived in Canaan the Lord said:

> Lift up now thine eyes, and look from this place where thou
> art northward, and southward, and eastward, and westward:
> For all the land which thou seest to thee will I give it, and to
> thy seed forever.[2]

Not only was Abraham given all the land which he
could see with the natural eye, but all the land from "the
river of Egypt to the great river, the river Euphrates," was
included in the land grant deed to him by the Lord. These
blessings were re-conferred upon Jacob, or Israel, unto whom
the Lord said:

> And thy seed shall be as the dust of the earth, and thou shalt
> spread abroad to the west, and to the east, and to the north, and
> to the south; and in thee and in thy seed shall all the families of
> the earth be blessed.[3]

However, the seed of Jacob were not to possess this
land as an inheritance until "the iniquity of the Amorite"
is full, the Lord said to Abraham. When the time arrived
and the "iniquity of the Amorite" was full, the descendants

---

[1]Genesis 12:2-3.
[2]Genesis 13:14-15.
[3]Genesis 28:14.

of Jacob, known as the twelve tribes of Israel, came out of Egypt where they had grown into a powerful nation through Egyptian bondage. Under the leadership of Moses and later Joshua, and with the blessings of the Lord upon them, they took possession of the land. In course of time they established a kingdom but failed to keep the commandments of the Lord, although they had become by covenant the chosen people of the Lord.

Before the Israelites entered their possessions the Lord warned them through Moses that if they forsook his laws and failed to heed his sacred commandments he would punish them with bondage and affliction and if then they continued to ignore the words of their prophets, he would drive them out of the land and it should cease to be a residence for their children as they would be scattered in all parts of the world. Among these warnings the Lord declared in all kindness but emphatically the following:

I am the Lord your God, which brought you forth out of the land of Egypt, that ye should not be their bondmen; and I have broken the bands of your yoke, and made you go upright.

But if ye will not hearken unto me, and will not do all these commandments,

And if ye shall despise my statutes, or if your soul abhor my judgments, so that ye will not do all my commandments, but that ye break my covenant;

I also will do this unto you; I will even appoint over you terror, consumption, and the burning ague, that shall consume the eyes, and cause sorrow of heart: and ye shall sow your seed in vain, for your enemies shall eat it.

And I will set my face against you, and ye shall be slain before your enemies: they that hate you shall reign over you; and ye shall flee when none pursueth you.

And if ye will not yet for all this hearken unto me, then I will punish you seven times more for your sins. . . .

And I will make your cities waste, and bring your sanctuaries unto desolation, and I will not smell the savor of your sweet odours.

And I will bring the land into desolation; and your enemies which dwell therein shall be astonished at it.

And I will scatter you among the heathen, and will draw out a sword after you; and your land shall be desolate, and your cities waste.

Then shall the land enjoy her sabbaths, as long as it lieth desolate, and ye be in your enemies' land; even then shall the land rest, and enjoy her sabbaths.

As long as it lieth desolate it shall rest; because it did not rest in your sabbaths, when ye dwelt upon it.[4]

Importance of Keeping Commandments

In this manner the Lord endeavored to impress upon the children of Israel the need of keeping his commandments. However, he also promised that he would still remember his covenant made with their fathers. Said he:

Ye shall be left few in number among the heathen, whither the Lord shall lead you. And there ye shall serve gods, the work of men's hands, wood and stone, which neither see, nor hear, nor eat, nor smell. But if from thence thou shalt seek the Lord thy God, thou shalt find him, if thou seek him with all thy heart and with all thy soul. When thou art in tribulation, and all these things are come upon thee, even in the latter days, if thou turn to the Lord thy God, and shalt be obedient unto his voice (for the Lord thy God is a merciful God); he will not forsake thee, neither destroy thee, nor forget the covenant of thy fathers which he sware unto them.[5]

For a short time these commandments of the Lord impressed their minds; but soon the people began to forget the warnings. To remind them of the dire consequences of this rebellion, many prophets were sent among them, but the voice of the Lord went unheeded. At first the Lord permitted their neighboring tribes to oppress and punish them, but this was not severe enough, and so it became necessary to bring upon them the major calamities which had been predicted. At the beginning of the reign of Israel's fourth king, Rehoboam, the nation became divided

---

[4]Leviticus 26:13-18, 31-35.
[5]Deuteronomy 4:27-31.

forming two kingdoms; one known as Israel, or Ephraim, and the other as Judah. The kingdom of Israel rebelled and became extremely wicked, and therefore it was destroyed and its inhabitants carried captive into Assyria by Shalmaneser, about 730 B.C. From this captivity they never returned and are known as the lost Ten Tribes of Israel. The kingdom of Judah continued to exist until about 600 B.C., when it also was practically destroyed and its inhabitants carried captive into Babylon by Nebuchadnezzar. In Babylon they remained 70 years and were then restored by Cyrus, the Persian, to their former inheritance. From that time forth they have been known as Jews. Under the protection of the Medo-Persian kingdom they were privileged to rebuild Jerusalem and its temple, and again spread over much of the land which they formerly occupied. Again they were guided by divinely appointed prophets; however they never again exercised unrestricted freedom as they had done before, and most of the time were subject to foreign oppression.

Corruption among Jews

At the time of the birth of our Savior, the Jews had again become very corrupt, notwithstanding the fact that outwardly and apparently, they followed more strictly than ever before the laws given through Moses. This was outward service only, for spiritually as a people, they were dead. The mighty works performed by our Savior failed to penetrate their hardened hearts, and only made the leaders of the people more bitter towards him, resulting, finally, in his crucifixion for the sins of the world. Shortly before his death, Jesus severely rebuked the leaders of the Jews saying:

Woe unto you, scribes and Pharisees, hypocrites! because ye build the tombs of the prophets, and garnish the sepulchres of the righteous.

And say, If we had been in the days of our fathers, we would not have been partakers with them in the blood of the prophets.

Wherefore ye be witnesses unto yourselves, that ye are the children of them that killed the prophets.

Fill ye up then the measure of your fathers.

Ye serpents, ye generation of vipers, how can ye escape the damnation of hell?[6]

Jesus predicted the destruction of Jerusalem and the scattering of the Jews, saying:

And they shall fall by the edge of the sword, and shall be led away captive into all nations: and Jerusalem shall be trodden down of the Gentiles, until the times of the Gentiles be fulfilled.[7]

This destruction predicted by our Lord fell upon Jerusalem and the Jews in the year 70 A.D., and the Jews were scattered over all the face of the earth. They have been persecuted, murdered, driven, abused and hated by all peoples, and yet they have prospered in material things: and they have maintained their identity as a race, which is a marvelous miracle.

After the destruction of Jerusalem, and the scattering of the Jews from their possessions in Palestine, a curse was placed upon the land. Jerusalem was practically destroyed and has been trodden down of the Gentiles. The mountains of Canaan, once very beautiful, and covered with trees and vegetation became denuded, and the soil, having no protection from the rains, was washed down into the valleys making stagnant pools. The once thriving villages and pleasant farms and vineyards disappeared and the land became barren and unfruitful. The surface of the earth was so stricken until very recent times that it has been the general opinion that the land can support but a very meager population. Yet in the past, when the blessings of the Lord were upon it, it supported millions of

---

[6]Matthew 23:29-33.
[7]Luke 21:24.

people. Isaiah predicted that this condition would come to pass, but in the latter days the Lord would send swift messengers to gather these people who were "scattered and peeled," a nation meted out and trodden down, "whose land the rivers have spoiled," and again they would be gathered from the lands of their dispersion.

Conditions Are Changing

Today conditions in Palestine are changing. The curse has been removed from the land and the Jews are returning in fulfilment of the many promises of the Lord made through the prophets. There are some people among us today who feel that the prophetic declarations in relation to the return of the Jews, must fail because all physical conditions are against the fulfilment of the word of the Lord, and to restore the Jews is "an utter impossibility." Yet the Lord said it shall be done!

Fear not; for I am with thee: I will bring thy seed from the east, and gather thee from the west;

I will say to the north, give up; and to the south, keep not back; bring my sons from far, and my daughters from the ends of the earth.[8]

Go and proclaim these words towards the north, and say, Return, thou backsliding Israel, saith the Lord: and I will not cause mine anger to fall upon you; for I am merciful, saith the Lord, and I will not keep anger forever.[9]

Therefore say, Thus saith the Lord God; Although I have cast them far off among the heathen, and although I have scattered them among the countries, yet will I be to them as a little sanctuary in the countries where they shall come.

Therefore say, Thus saith the Lord God; I will even gather you from the people, and assemble you out of the countries where ye have been scattered, and I will give you the land of Israel.[10]

[8]Isaiah 43:5-6.
[9]Jeremiah 3:12.
[10]Ezekiel 11:16-17.

Numerous Predictions in Scriptures

There are numerous predictions of this kind in the scriptures. The Lord, because of his promises to Abraham, Isaac, and Jacob, and to Israel in later years, even in this present dispensation, is bound to restore the Jews and Israel to their "everlasting" possessions. And that day is now at hand.

As previously stated, Elder Orson Hyde was called to go to Palestine and dedicate the land for the return of Israel. Sunday, October 24, 1841, Elder Hyde ascended the Mount of Olives and dedicated the land of Palestine by prayer for the gathering of the Jews.

It is a curious fact that in the year 1841, there were in all of Palestine less than 12,000 Jews, and down through the ages since their dispersion the Jews had never ceased to mourn and wail for the loss of their heritage and to look forward to the day when they shall be delivered from bondage and be privileged to return. Under Gentile rule this return was denied them. Jerusalem, from the time of its destruction by Titus until the close of the World War, had ceased to be a Jewish city and Palestine a Jewish home. It is also a curious fact that following the dedication of this land there was a greater impetus given to the activities in relation to the return of the Jews. In the hearts of both Jews and Gentiles there seemed to be a feeling that something should be done to colonize these ancient people.

In 1844, Warden Creason, the United States consul in Palestine, lent encouragement to such a movement. Among English Jews, Disraeli and Sir Moses Montefiore became champions of such a movement, but the British Government could do little in the matter as Palestine was under the dominion of the Sultan. England did, however, send an expedition to explore the part of Sinai which lay within the Egyptian frontier, but nothing of importance came of this undertaking.

In 1903, through the efforts of Joseph Chamberlain, then colonial secretary for Great Britain, Lord Landsdowne was authorized to offer the Zionists a tract of land in the highlands of British East Africa for the creation of a Jewish home, with full powers of autonomy under the British Government's control. The Jews, however, had their eyes set on Palestine as their home, which is according to the revealed word of the Lord, and they vehemently opposed this offer to settle in Africa.

Lovers of Zion Societies

In the sixties David Gordon, Hirch Lalischer and Moses Hess, with others, aided in the creation of the foundation of the "Chovevei Zion (Lovers of Zion) societies, the chief object being the colonization of Palestine by the Jews. The Zionist Federation was commenced in 1896, and was supported by Theodore Hertzl and Baron Rothschild. The first congress of this federation was held in Basel, Switzerland, in 1897. Since that day the efforts on the part of leading and influential Jews has increased, to bring to pass a national home for the Jews.

The first modern settlement of Jews in Palestine was established in 1876, by the International Association of the Alliance Israelites. This organization established an agricultural school, Mikweh Israel (the Gathering of Israel) a few miles from Jaffa. All colonization in Palestine by Jews before the World War was undertaken in the midst of great difficulties. The Turks placed many restrictions upon those who endeavored to gather there, and about all the Jews could do was to look with longing eyes towards their ancient heritage with uncertain hopes.

It was not until the land had been freed from Turkish rule in 1917, that the return of the Jews appeared on the horizon as a coming reality. However the result of the earlier movements did bring an increase in Jewish population. In 1881, there were about 25,000 Jews in all of Palestine and by 1914, the number had grown to nearly 80,000. At the close of the war Great Britain was given the mandate over Palestine and France that over Syria. This was indeed a significant sign. Palestine was freed by General Allenby from the Turks in December 1917. In 1920 Sir Herbert Samuel, a Jew, was sent to Palestine by Great Britain, as its governor, or high commissioner, and a civil government was set up under his direction. It is very significant that from the days when Christ predicted the downfall of Jerusalem and Palestine, until the close of the World War, there never was a time when a Jew held authority as governor or commissioner, or any other authority in that land.

Rehabilitation of Jerusalem

Immediately following the war the rehabilitation of Palestine commenced. Following the freedom of Palestine from the Turkish yoke, Sir Arthur Balfour, in behalf of the British Foreign office, wrote to Lord James Rothschild the following memorable declaration:

His Majesty's Government views with favor the establishment in Palestine of a national home for the Jewish people, and will use their best endeavors to facilitate the achievement of that object, it being clearly understood that nothing shall be done which may prejudice the civil and religious rights of existing non-Jewish communities in Palestine or the rights and political status enjoyed by Jews in any other country.

As the United States had taken part in the war, that government claimed the right to be consulted in the terms of the mandates in relation to Palestine and Syria. To this request the British Government agreed. The draft of the Palestine mandate was submitted to the United States Government, and at its request certain minor changes were made in it. On June 30, 1922, the following joint resolution was adopted by Congress, favoring the establishment in Palestine of a national home for the Jewish people:

> Resolved by the Senate and House of Representatives of the United States of America in Congress assembled, That the United States of America favors the establishment in Palestine of a national home for the Jewish people, it being clearly understood that nothing shall be done which may prejudice the civil and religious rights of Christian and of all other non-Jewish communities in Palestine, and that the holy places and religious buildings and sights in Palestine shall be adequately protected.

The Balfour Proclamation

The Balfour proclamation thus endorsed by the United States Government, brought great joy to thousands of downtrodden and persecuted Jews throughout the world, and under the protectorate of Great Britain they commenced to gather there in great numbers. Before this time things in Palestine were most primitive. Wooden ploughs, water-wheel irrigation, the use of germ-infested wells and streams, the carrying of water in skins as anciently, and many other primitive customs prevailed. Sanitation was in a deplorable condition, but the British endeavored to change all of these conditions. Now the sacred Sea of Galilee forms a great reservoir, and flood waters from the various streams are being diverted into this beautiful body of water. Canals have been built in all parts of the land, and the Jordan has been turned from its natural channel into artificial concrete canals on each side of the original stream. These are being used to irrigate nearly 7,000,000 acres which would not be under cultivation otherwise. Hydroelectric stations have been erected on the streams. One power plant is located about eight miles below the lake of Galilee, where a dam, similar to the Hoover Dam in Arizona, has been built. This contains about ten billion cubic feet of water for irrigation and power purposes. After passing through the turbines most of this water is returned to the Jordan. The power plants are ample for a territory the size of Vermont. The Palestine Electric Corporation which supplies electric power and light for all of Palestine, except Jerusalem and its vicinity, in 1934 sold 34,348,515 KWH in electrical energy. The fall of the Jordan from the Sea of Galilee to the Dead Sea, is about 690 feet through a depression below sea level.

The mountains which lost their vegetation during the years of "Sabbath rest" which the Lord gave to them, are now becoming covered with trees and vegetation. Afforestation has been conducted by various interests. Great Britain has spent in this work upwards of $45,000,000 up to 1934. Many other millions have been spent by the Zionists and other organizations. Before the war there were in Palestine 1,235 industrial undertakings, most of them by Arabs. In 1933 there were 5,390 of which 3,900 were Jewish, with a capital of over $22,500,000 and employing 16,000 workers. The area of land possessed by Jews increased from 102,150 acres in 1920 to 251,970 in 1934, of which 28,374 are orange groves. Agriculture has increased with great rapidity. Flour mills flourish and many kinds of cereal products are manufactured. There are now established factories of many kinds. Salt, potash and nitrates are obtained in vast quantities from the Dead Sea.

The Zionist Movement

The Zionist movement from the beginning has been associated with the revival of the Hebrew language as a popular tongue among the Hebrews who are assembling there. Before the World War the Hilsfverein der Deutschen Juden pressed their claim for German as a language to be spoken in Palestine among the Jews, but the teachers in the schools "struck" and refused to teach German and many of the children withdrew from the schools until the Hebrew language was restored.

The Jewish National Home is created for a place of refuge for Jews who desire, under regulations, to go to Palestine. This does not include, however, all the Jews who have gone and are now going there. Fourteen years ago this National Home was considered as an experiment, but today it is a reality. During these years its numbers have increased fourfold. In 1925 the number of Jews was 121,000, but today there are about 500,000 [1940] who have gone into that land under this plan. During the long dispersion the Jews were forced into channels of trade and barter and away from the soil. Originally they were tillers of the soil. Strange as it may appear the amount of land now in Jewish ownership for agricultural purposes in 1936 was 1,333,000 dunums. A dunum is about one quarter of an acre. There are now 203 agricultural settlements containing some 100,000 people. The city of Tel Aviv, wholly Jewish, has a population of over 150,000, and covers more than 1,500 acres. The population of Jerusalem has grown to include 125,000 Jews. Other towns have also been settled by Jews for habitations. They have a national flag and a national anthem, a cultural system including schools, a university and other civic organizations. The internal affairs are managed by a National Assembly and Council and a Rabbinical Council.

In 1929-30 the value of the fruit exported from Jewish orange, grapefruit and lemon enterprises, was valued at $1,500,000. In 1937 it was estimated to have increased to $20,000,000. During the same period the productions of the industrial enterprises of the Jewish people rose from $11,000,000 to over $40,000,000. From 1898 to the present the sum of over $70,000,000 has been invested in Palestine through the "national funds" and roughly the sum of $315,000,000 by private investors, nearly half of this sum in the course of the past four or five years.

It is estimated by the Palestine Royal Commission (British) that if the present rate of immigration continues

until 1950, ten years, there will be in Palestine a population
of 1,280,000 Jews.[11] While there are many skeptical people who, when looking at the natural conditions which prevail today, declare that it is impossible for the Jews to ever
return to Palestine, we may be assured that the word of
the Lord will not fail. It is true that today the Arabs
and others occupy much of the land and that too most of
the choicest sections. It is true that they bitterly oppose
the return of the Jews, and this may lead to serious and
bloody strife. Whatever the outcome may be we may have
the perfect assurance that the Jews will return in sufficient
numbers to fulfill the word of the Lord. The day is near
at hand when Israel will again flourish in that land; when
the Lord will again build his temple there; when his sanctuary will be found among the people and when they shall
be cleansed from all their iniquity. The Lord has spoken
it! His word will not fail! "And the heathen shall know
that I the Lord do sanctify Israel, when my sanctuary shall
be in the midst of them forevermore," declared the Lord
through Ezekiel.[12]

In our own dispensation the Lord has commanded:

"And let them who be of Judah flee unto Jerusalem,
unto the mountain of the Lord's house."[13] When the rem-
nant which is designed to return is established in that land,
and the nations have gathered to battle against them and
they are in sore distress, then will Jesus of Nazareth appear
to them as their Deliverer for whom they have looked for
all these many years. Then will the prophecy of Zechariah,
be fulfilled as repeated to the Prophet Joseph Smith. The
Lord shall set his foot upon the Mount of Olives and it

---

[11]In 1970 the population of Palestine was listed as 2,745,000. The above
article was written in 1940 commemorating 100 years after dedication of the
Holy Land for the return of the Jews. Statistics quoted reflect situation as of
that date.
[12]Ezekiel 37:28.
[13]D&C 133:13.

shall cleave in twain, "and the earth shall tremble, and reel to and fro, and the heavens also shall shake. . . .

And then shall the Jews look upon me and say: What are these wounds in thine hands and in thy feet?

Then shall they know that I am the Lord; for I will say unto them: These wounds are the wounds with which I was wounded in the house of my friends. I am he who was lifted up. I am Jesus that was crucified. I am the Son of God.

And then shall they weep because of their iniquities; then shall they lament because they persecuted their king.[14]—(Church Section, *The Deseret News*, April 6, 1940.)

---

[14]D&C 45:51-53. Read verses 48-53. For further information on this subject see also *The Signs of the Times*, Lesson Three, pp. 50-71.

*The missionaries of The Church of Jesus Christ
of Latter-day Saints are modern miracles. . . .
They do have one thing that the world does
not have, and cannot have, and that is a
testimony and the determination to go out
into the field, as unprepared as they are,
and spend two or maybe more years bearing witness to the restoration of the gospel,
expounding the scriptures, as they learn them.*

Missionaries...Modern Miracles

The missionary of The Church of Jesus Christ of Latter-day Saints is a modern miracle. In the world the idea prevails that a man must go to school, college, get an education, be trained and get a degree to qualify him to preach and to teach the gospel of Jesus Christ, as he understands it. We call our young men and women at the beginning, really, of life, when they are just budding into manhood and womanhood. We send them out into the world untrained, with no degrees, with a common school education, in most cases, (maybe not even that) but depending upon the guidance of the Spirit of the Lord.

These missionaries come from all walks of life—from the farm, from the factory, mostly from the schoolroom. They are unprepared, insofar as education and knowledge are concerned. Most of them have never read the Book of Mormon, a great part of them, if not the greater part, have never read the New Testament. They are not familiar with the revelations in the Doctrine and Covenants. I find this out when I interview them. But they do have one thing that the world does not have, and cannot have, and that is a testimony and the determination to go out into the field, as unprepared as they are, and spend two

or maybe more years bearing witness to the restoration of
the gospel, expounding the scriptures, as they learn them.

Importance of Section Four

One thing that I have been impressing upon missionaries for a number of years is that they make themselves
familiar with section four of the Doctrine and Covenants
above everything else. That is a revelation that, I tell the
missionaries, is my revelation. The Lord gave it to me.
Originally, it was given to my great-grandfather before the
Church was organized, but it is a revelation that uses the
plural pronoun, and thus it applies to every soul that goes
into the mission field. I ask each group of missionaries
as I meet with them to read section four of the Doctrine and
Covenants about every two weeks. I suggest that they sit
down, each pair of missionaries, and just consider it very
carefully. The Lord here states what it is that is necessary to qualify a missionary. The Lord holds out to them
blessings through their faith and the punishment which
they bring upon themselves should they fail. I think we
ought to become very familiar with this section of the Doctrine and Covenants. There are only seven verses, and
they do not need to bother with the first because I think that
has very well been fulfilled, but I try to impress upon them
the need of remembering particularly what the Lord says
in the second and the fourth verses.

> Therefore, O ye that embark in the service of God, see that
> ye serve him with all your heart, might, mind, and strength, that
> ye may stand blameless before God at the last day. . . .
> For behold the field is white already to harvest; and lo, he
> that thrusteth in his sickle with his might, the same layeth up in
> store that he perisheth not, but bringeth salvation to his soul.

I think that ought to be impressed upon every missionary who goes into the field. They volunteer their time,
they are not forced, therefore, when they go out into the

field to preach the gospel they become the servants of our Lord and Savior Jesus Christ, voluntarily, and they should understand that they have made the promise or covenant with him to serve him with all they have— heart, might, mind and strength. If they fail, then there may be a penalty. If they do not put forth every effort to serve the Lord, the Spirit of the Lord will withdraw from them, and they may lose the faith.

I think that a missionary and his companion should sit down together frequently, read these verses, then consider the sixth verse, for there the Lord points out the qualifications of a successful missionary:

Remember faith, virtue, knowledge, temperance, patience, brotherly kindness, godliness, charity, humility, diligence.

Now these are the qualifications they should seek, and with the Spirit of the Lord they can obtain them. If they have no faith, then they are useless in the mission field. Missionaries should be instructed to pray—pray together, pray secretly, seek the guidance of the Spirit of the Lord on their knees quietly and alone, and together. Every week or two they should get their Doctrine and Covenants out and go over this revelation and ask themselves, "Have we increased in faith since we came into the mission field or in the last two weeks?" Virtue—that term means more than just keeping the body clean from evil. A man can be unvirtuous in his thinking. The Lord made that clear. Therefore, missionaries' thoughts should be pure. They should think virtuously as well as act that way.

What Have We Gained?

Knowledge? They can ask each other, "What have we gained the last week or two? Have we learned something that helps us, that makes us better missionaries than we were two weeks ago?"

Temperance — not just refraining from drinking liquor! I think this word has a different meaning as it is
used here. I think they should be temperate in their language and in their actions—not make extravagant statements in their proselyting and never quote anyone unless
they have absolute assurance of the source of the substance
of their quotation. Teach the elders to be temperate in
what they say, wise in their counsel, and patient.

When they get out in the world they associate with
people who have been trained in the traditions of the
so-called Christian world in doctrines that have come down
for hundreds of years. But the missionaries go out fresh
with the understanding and the testimony of the restoration of the gospel. They may be a little impatient with
these poor people when they are not ready to accept our
views or doctrines readily, even though they are earnest and
sincere, just as earnest and sincere as we are. Let missionaries learn patience, brotherly kindness—I heard a missionary in a foreign country express himself in regard to
the people to whom he was carrying the message in an un-
complimentary manner. Well, they were different from
us in many of their habits, in their looks, and in the teachings that they had received. We must know, that as missionaries, we have to learn to love the people whether in
Japan or China, the South Seas, South America, no matter
where it is on the face of the earth. The Lord scattered
Irsael to every part of the earth according to his predictions, and we are sending our missionaries out to preach the
gospel and gather them in, so we should have a brotherly
feeling. If we have the right spirit, we will.

Try To Be Like God

Godliness — means that we should try to be as nearly
like God as we can. If we keep that in mind, that will help
to keep us humble.

Charity—we should have charity for these poor people. It was my privilege to go down through Central and South America a few months ago. I saw the conditions there. Brother Tuttle and I went into some of the great churches. We saw those poor people in the midst of their poverty coming in, putting their coins into receptacles, kneeling down, and praying. They were sincere in all their ignorance. I could not go out of one of those buildings and say something mean or unkind about those poor people. I felt sorry for them. My heart went out to them because they did not know any better, and in the humility of their souls they were doing those things faithfully and ignorantly. I felt more like weeping than making unkind remarks. I could make the unkind remarks about the people who led them to do it.

Humility—we need to keep ourselves humble, and then last of all—*diligence*. Our missionaries should prepare themselves by study and by faith.

In Section 88, verse 79, the Lord gives some instructions intended for missionaries as well as others on which we should be prepared "Of things both in heaven and in the earth, and under the earth; things which have been, things which are, things which must shortly come to pass; things which are at home, things which are abroad; the wars and the perplexities of the nations, and the judgments which are on the land; and a knowledge also of countries and of kingdoms—."

More particularly I want to call attention to the next verses—

That ye may be prepared in all things when I shall send you again to magnify the calling whereunto I have called you, and the mission with which I have commissioned you.

Behold, I sent you out to testify and warn the people, and it becometh every man who hath been warned to warn his neighbor.

Therefore, they are left without excuse, and their sins are upon their own heads.[1]

Our mission is not just one of gathering out the honest, bringing into the Church the repentant, but we have the duty and responsibility of warning the world and leaving them without excuse.

Bear Your Testimony

When they are warned, if that is all you can do with them, bear your testimony of the restoration of the gospel, and when they are in the hands of the Lord, you are clear. "Therefore, they are left without excuse, and their sins are upon their own heads."

Now, you good mission presidents, be kind to these young, inexperienced missionaries. A young man can be ruined in the first month or six weeks of his mission. He can become discouraged, disappointed. He needs your sympathy; he needs your guidance; he needs your help and encouragement to lead him along, because of the opportunities he is to receive as he goes forth to teach the gospel. He will meet with people who apparently know more than he does, and sometimes the first few months are months of discouragement. Help him, buoy him up, and strengthen him that he may, through the help of the Lord, have humility to perform the labor that he is sent there to perform.

Encourage these young men; help them. If they are a little weak in the beginning, help them to become strong. Do not force them too greatly. Every missionary does not have the same ability, the same personality. Some of them are more or less plodders, but their hearts are right. We cannot place them on the same level. Some are quicker to learn. We must take all of these things into consideration. Be kind and considerate and encouraging. Because some other missionary makes a far greater success, let noth-

---

[1]D&C 88:80-82.

ing happen, as far as we are concerned, by way of discouragement to the young missionary who does not have quite the same ability.

I am going to read to you the covenant of baptism that the Lord has given us. I don't think people should be brought into this Church before they know something about it. It is in Verse 37 of Section 20 in the Doctrine and Covenants:

And again, by way of commandment to the church concerning the manner of baptism—All those who humble themselves before God, and desire to be baptized, and come forth with broken hearts and contrite spirits, and witness before the church that they have truly repented of all their sins, and are willing to take upon them the name of Jesus Christ, having a determination to serve him to the end, and truly manifest by their works that they have received of the Spirit of Christ unto the remission of their sins, shall be received by baptism into his church.

That is the covenant of baptism.

Then this other verse which does apply to every missionary and every member of the Church.

He that seeketh me early shall find me, and shall not be forsaken.[2]—(*The Improvement Era*, October 1961.)

---

[2]D&C 88:83.

The reason for the Bible's great influence for good is because it is inspired, containing the word of the Lord delivered to his prophets who wrote and spoke as they were moved upon by the Holy Ghost. . . .

Authority of the Bible
Supported by Archaeology

The Holy Bible has had a greater influence on the world for good than any other book ever published. It has been printed in more editions and translated into more languages and read by more people than any other book. No other publication has been more severely and critically examined. The reason for the Bible's great influence for good is because it is inspired, containing the word of the Lord delivered to his prophets who wrote and spoke as they were moved upon by the Holy Ghost since the world began. It has drawn the fire of adverse criticism for the self-same reason. Had it not been an inspired record less attention would have been paid to it by the opposing critics, who have drawn their inspiration from the author of evil, who in the very beginning swore in his wrath that he would endeavor to destroy the work of God.

Nearly six hundred years before the birth of Christ, a prophet on this western hemisphere predicted that in the last days criticism of the sacred record of the Jews would arise. The Lord revealed to this prophet that the record of his people, the Nephites, would be brought to light from

the dust to speak as a witness for the record of the Jews,
and by the means of this second witness the truth of the
first would be established.   Another prophet among the
Nephites, writing some four hundred years after the coming of Christ, when about to hide up the record of his
people in the earth also declared that it would again come
forth in the last days to the convincing of both "Jew and
Gentile that *Jesus* is the *Christ, the Eternal God,* manifest-
ing himself unto all nations."

Criticisms against the Bible have been going on for
centuries, but in a sporadic fashion.   There was no concerted effort until about the middle of the nineteenth century.   The man who is considered to be the founder of
modern criticism was a French physician, Jean Astruc,
who was born in 1684, and died in 1766.   Others at different
times followed in his wake, but it was not until after the
restoration of the gospel that the attacks upon the Holy
Scriptures took definite form.

Criticism Rages

It remained for the second half of the nineteenth century and the first quarter of the twentieth, for this concerted
effort to reach its full force in the endeavor to destroy the
word of God.   During these years this criticism raged with
great intensity, and it continues on even to the present
day, notwithstanding these theories are now as dead as
the extinct dodo.

The work of Charles Darwin and his followers gave
impetus to this work of higher and lower criticism of the
Bible, for the same methods have been employed as were
employed by Darwin in his researches.   Unfortunately these
theories, like that of organic evolution, have found their
way into the curriculum of the universities and colleges of
America and Europe, and through them the minds of the
youth have been and are being poisoned.

This modern criticism, of which Julius Wellhausen, (born in 1844, died in 1918) was the great high priest, is known as the *Later Documentary Hypothesis* or the *Development Hypothesis*. Among the varied criticisms loudly proclaimed by these men who pose as great scholars, we find the following:

1. The question of authorship of the books of the Bible.

2. The question of the antiquity of the writings in the Bible.

3. The question of accuracy in the Bible.

4. The question of the development of the idea of God.

While these do not cover all the criticisms, they are, nevertheless, the outstanding ones indulged in by those who have taken it upon themselves to enlighten the benighted people in the world who have for so long accepted the Holy Scriptures as the inspired word of God, but which criticisms are nothing better than a compilation of fable and myth.

During the closing years of the nineteenth century and in recent years of the present century, there have arisen a great many scholars who have taken these matters in hand with the idea of discovering the truth rather than the establishing of a pet or malicious theory. These impartial researchers number among them some of the world's greatest scholars. They have not made their discoveries, as Sir Charles Marston has said, sitting in "armchairs," but out making the actual research. Among these scientists may be mentioned the following: B. P. Grenfell, Arthur S. Hunt, Edouard Naville, Adolph Deissmann, W. F. Albright, Dr. Gerstang, Dr. Langdon, Leonard Woolley, Camden M. Coburn and A. S. Yahuda.

Reference to Deity

One of the puzzling problems in the Bible which had

given a large handle to this criticism, is the fact that in
the early part of the Book of Genesis God is spoken of in
the Hebrew as Elohim and also as Jehovah. Therefore the
critics have hit upon the unique thought that this record
is the composite writing of two different authors who wrote
at widely different times, and in the joined account we have
a composite record of the creation.

Moreover, they declare that this record in Genesis was
composed long after the days of Moses, and is not his account at all. The claim is made that these writings belong
to a time as late as the ninth or eighth centuries before
Christ, while much of the Pentateuch could not have been
prepared before the time of Ezekiel, at the time of the Babylonian exile which commenced in the sixth century, B.C.

The Prophet Joseph Smith has pointed out the fact
that the name Elohim is the plural form of the name of
Deity, which all scholars admit. It is, they say, however,
used in the singular although being the plural form. We
have also learned from modern revelation that Jehovah is
not the Father, but the Son Jesus Christ, and we are taught
that the Father and the Son, were both concerned in the
creation of the earth.

The meaning, therefore, of the expression, "And God
said, Let us make man in our image," becomes perfectly
clear. The Book of Genesis was written by Moses. This
we know from modern revelation, and Christ when in his
ministry confirmed that fact. He also declared that the
Pentateuch was the work of Moses; such is the testimony of
the Son of God.

These supposed mixed accounts are known by the
critics as the *Elohistic* and the *Jehovistic*. The books of
Moses are further divided, and we are given the *Priestly*
and the *Deuteronomistic*, as being the main sources of the
Pentateuch. These are usually referred to as the "E" and
"J" or "JE," the "P" and the "D" sources from which this

record is obtained which we have cherished, and which was accepted by our Lord when he was in his ministry.

Denies Authorship

This criticism declaring that the entire Pentateuch was written long after the time of Moses, denies to him, of course, the authorship of these books. The "Law of Moses," as mentioned so frequently in the Bible, and by the Savior himself, as being the word of God given to Moses, under such a criticism if it were true, would lose its significance. This criticism is largely philological and based upon the study of ancient languages and the endeavor to show from the use of words the time and place when they were in current usage. It has been truly said that it would be just as consistent for a critic to rise up—and who can tell when he *will*—*who* will contend that the Gospels of Matthew, Mark, Luke, and John, each is the composite work of several authors, one writing of our Lord as Jesus, another of him as Christ, another as Master, another as Messiah, and so on, since these several titles are given to him in these accounts.

Dr. Yahuda says of these destructive methods of Bible criticism:

No one, and the present writer least of all, would make the slightest attempt to belittle the great merits and achievements of Biblical criticism. But it must be said that, so long as modern views prevailed, there was a sane and sound method of Biblical research. Unfortunately this method has since deteriorated through the more radical views adopted by the modern school of Higher Criticism, especially under Wellhausen and his followers.

The whole system has degenerated into a mass of far-fetched hypotheses and haphazard theories, which only fitted within a frame of preconceived ideas about the history, the development and the composition of the scriptures. In the long run it became customary to consider it as highly scientific to challenge everything biblical and to alter the text at one's heart's desire.

The whole Pentateuch is represented as a conglomeration of various sources. In many cases one chapter is attributed to two, three, or more sources. Even in each one of these sources two or more underlayers are discerned. Thus, taking the whole Pentateuch as it is made to appear, the impression is left of a patch-work stuck together by stupid authors and ignorant scribes, the result being a most disproportionate and inharmonious composition.

Indeed, the mania of seeing everywhere a wrong text and detecting all kinds of interpolations, glosses and anachronisms, and likewise the zeal to heap emendations upon corrections resulted in creating a new specialty for speculative 'experts' to exert themselves in the art of text alterations and source-hunting.[1]

Dr. Campbell Quoted

That the reader may have a clear idea of the nature of this Bible dissecting the following is taken from *The Bible Under Fire*, by Dr. John L. Campbell. This is a representation taken from the Polychrome Bible, in which the different writings of the supposed authors are printed in different colors. The difference is here given in different kinds of type:

THEN HE DIVIDED HIS THREE HUNDRED MEN INTO THREE COMPANIES AND FURNISHED THEM ALL WITH HORNS, *and empty jars, and said to them: Ye must watch me, and do as I do;* when I come to the edge of the camp, ye must do just what I do; and when I and all those who are with me give a blast on the horn, then ye also must blow your horns all about the camp, AND SAY: FOR JHVA AND GIDEON! Now Gideon and the hundred men who were with him reached the edge of the camp at the beginning of the middle watch (the guards had just been posted), and they blew their horns, AND BROKE THE JARS THEY HELD IN THEIR HANDS. Then the three companies blew their horns, *and shattered the jars, grasping with their left hands the torches.*

---

[1] *The Accuracy of the Bible*, pp. xx-xxi of the introduction.

These super-critics can tell to the very letter where to draw the line between the writings of these ancient scribes, but they are absolutely unable to segregate in like manner any modern writing, such as the writings of Alexander Hamilton and James Madison, who wrote in the *Federalist,* or even a composite editorial in a modern newspaper. This Dr. Campbell has pointed out. This criticism of segregation has been thoroughly examined by Dr. A. S. Yahuda, and its ashes thrown to the four winds. Some of these critics have declared that the Israelites were never in Egypt, that the story of Joseph is a myth. Dr. Yahuda, who has devoted a careful study to these charges, is most emphatic in his statement, giving the direct evidence, that these stories are all true. The language of the Old Testament and the history of the times, both prove beyond any doubt that the accounts in the Bible are accurate in the very details. This eminent scholar has written two wonderful books within the last three years. The first, *The Language of the Pentateuch in Its Relation to Egyptian,* is a technical work dealing with this subject; the other is for the lay-reader, and is, *The Accuracy of the Bible.* This book should be read by every Bible student.

Dr. Yahuda also declares:

Now, Assyriologists long ago discovered Assyro-Babylonian elements in the Bible, and established more especially the relation between the Babylonian myths of primeval times and the Genesis stories. Egyptologists have also found a certain number of words of Egyptian origin in the Joseph and Exodus narratives. But my investigations have led me to establish that, on one side, the influence of Assyro-Babylonia was much less than has been assumed, and that, on the other side, the influence of the Egyptian language is far more discernible in the Pentateuch than Egyptologists have ever admitted.

Influence Shown

That influence is, indeed, very palpable, not only in the Joseph and Exodus narratives, but even in those portions of the Pentateuch,

which most strongly disclose Assyro-Babylonian influence, such as
the Flood story; and this is so to such an extent that the language of
the Pentateuch cannot be explained except as a new creation of a
common Hebrew-Egyptian environment, when the Hebrews lived
for a long period in a constant and most intimate contact with the
Egyptians.

As there is no other period in which this could have happened
than the time assigned by the Pentateuch to the sojourn of Israel
in Egypt, this process can only have been the result of a long stay
in Egypt itself. . . .

All this will contribute to demonstrate that the presence of
Egyptian elements in the Pentateuch is the best indication that the
Books of Moses have actually been composed in the epoch, in which
the Hebrews were still under the immediate influence of their connections with the Egyptians, just as it is stated in the Pentateuch
itself.[2]

In March, 1935, Dr. E. L. Sukenik, professor of
archaeology at the Hebrew University of Jerusalem, translated the writings on some recently unearthed pottery,
which he declared to be the most valuable find since the
Siloam inscriptions in 1890. This writing is in the Ma-
soretic text, the form used by the Jews today throughout the
world. This inscription dates back 2,500 years and records historical events of that day corresponding accurately
with the Bible. Dr. Torcznyer, another Hebrew scholar,
who examined these writings, declared that they of themselves were sufficient to "destroy the theory of Higher
Criticism."

Answers Exodus Stand

Another charge of the Higher Critics has been that
the Exodus from Egypt could not possibly have taken place
at the time indicated in the Bible record. The history of
this event informs us that the Israelites wandered in the
wilderness for forty years before they were permitted to

---

[2]*The Accuracy of the Bible,* pp. 24-32.

cross the Jordan under Joshua, after Moses had been taken away.

One of the first cities to fall after the crossing of the Jordan was that of Jericho. The skeptics have laughed at and ridiculed the story of the fall of Jericho. The idea of the walls falling down at the blast of the trumpets of the army of Israel! It was made to appear absurd. Moreover the time of the destruction of that city, it was said, did not correspond with this account. This story of Jericho illustrates the many other charges and their thorough refutation which have come about through modern research.

Sir Charles Marston, who financed and accompanied the expedition to some of these old ruins in Palestine, has written a book giving some account of the excavations of this expedition in 1932 and 1933. The title of the book is *New Bible Evidence*. In this book Sir Charles Marston tells of the excavation at the city of Jericho. This was done under the direction of Dr. Garstang.

According to this story, the archaeologists discovered in their research that the walls of Jericho had the appearance of having suddenly fallen on three sides of the city, as if they had been thrown down by an earthquake. This confirmed the story in the Book of Joshua. A careful examination of the ruins revealed to the workmen the very date when this happened.

To illustrate how this was done I give the following example. Suppose that the city of New York should suddenly be destroyed and that a thousand years later the ruins were discovered and a scientific investigation by archaeologists of that day should be made. They would no doubt discover books written at various times as well as magazines and other periodicals. Coins would likely also be found. These might date back to very early times, but they would all come to a sudden end at the time of the destruction of the city. There would not be found any newspapers, magazines, or books, bearing dates later than the time of the destruction; but they would be found down to the very year.

So it was in Jericho. The excavations found scarabs in the ruins, and writings on the pottery, which declared that the destruction corresponded accurately with what is written in the book of Joshua. Of this find, Sir Charles Marston writes:

Evidence Cited

As the series of dated scarabs all came to an end with the two royal seals of Amenhetep III, there is evidence, quite independent of the pottery, that the city also ceased to exist during that period. For the two centuries that followed there were no interments, the very distinctive pottery and decorations of the time of Akhenaten and Tutonkhamen was not represented at all. Thus everything pointed to the reign of Amenhetep III (1413-1377 B.C.) as marking the period when Jericho fell.[3]

Another serious doctrine of the modernistic critic is the teaching that the idea of God is of gradual development. They have emphatically declared that the earliest men were polytheistic. That their gods in the beginning were very cruel and had all the characteristics of human beings, some of them even being subject to death. They tell us that even among the Hebrews the idea of God was progressive, that the God of the early Hebrews was a very different personage from the God of the later years.

Sir James George Frazer, a leading advocate of this school of critics, has in a most blasphemous manner depicted the Hebrew God in his books entitled *Folk-Lore in the Old Testament*. He has ridiculed the story of creation and practically all else in the Pentateuch, in his endeavor to show that the development of worship was gradual and came out of the folk-lore and mythology of the distant past.

---

[3]*New Bible Evidence*, p. 137.

Similar writers could be named by the legion; but what of the facts?

Unchangeable God

The scriptures teach us that the God of Abraham, Isaac and Jacob, who was also the God of Adam, Enoch and Noah, is from everlasting, "the same unchangeable God, the framer of heaven and earth, and all things which are in them." He taught the gospel first to Adam and it was through transgression that it was lost among men.

Recent explorations among peoples of the earth and the history of tribes and nations of antiquity, have revealed the fact that in the very earliest times men worshiped, but their worship was their worship of one Supreme God. They were not polytheistic.

Dr. W. Schmidt has said that the earliest tribes of which we have any knowledge had the worship of The Supreme Being, or one Supreme God. — *The Origin and Growth of Religion.* This doctrine is confirmed by Dr. Langdon, Sir Charles Marston, on this point has this to say:

But the outstanding feature of all this remote civilization in its relation to the Bible is the evidence it affords that monotheism (the belief in one supreme God) preceded polytheism, or the belief in many gods. This is the very careful and deliberate conclusion of Dr. Langdon, Professor of Assyriology at Oxford, probably the greatest living authority on cuneiform literature, and this very remote period of civilization.[4]

The New Testament has undergone similar attacks, but space will not permit a proper presentation of this matter, although it is a very interesting story. It is sufficient for this writing to say that the discoveries which have been made under the close of the nineteenth century

---

[4]*Ibid.,* p. 52.

thoroughly and emphatically refute all the claims of the
Higher Criticism. Tons of records have been collected
dating from the first century which prove the authenticity
of the Gospels and the Epistles of the New Testament. Dr.
Edouard Naville, professor of archaeology in the Univer-
sity of Geneva, in the introduction to Dr. Camden M.
Coburn's work *The New Archeological Discoveries, and
Their Bearing Upon the New Testament,* has said:

> Truth will best be reached by the concurrence and the mutual
> help both of literary and archeological evidence. Considering only
> what is within the limits of this book—the New Testament—the
> recent discoveries compel us, as we said, to replace the authors of
> its different parts in the time when they are said to have lived, and
> among their readers or the hearers to whom they spoke. This
> seems to the present writer the best answer to the radical criticism
> and the most telling way of showing how insufficient and often
> misleading are its results, which are generally brought forward as
> being above discussion.
>
> If we put side by side the Gospels, the epistles of Paul, and
> the writings which have been discovered of the first century, we
> shall find in those 'as it were a new autobiographic commentary,'
> the explanation of many expressions showing that 'the New Testa-
> ment writings were not theological treatises, but were mostly com-
> posed in the non-technical and rather careless language of the street
> and home.' This comparative study has led Dr. Milligan to de-
> clare that 'in view of all the new light coming upon the question
> from recent discovery, it is safe to conclude that 'with the probable
> exception of 2 Peter, all our New Testament writings may now be
> placed within the first century,' though the collection called the
> New Testament may be of much later date.
>
> This goes a long way to disprove many of the critical theories,
> attributing parts of a book like the gospel of John to a later epoch,
> and cutting it up between various authors, some of them quite un-
> known and mere literary creations.—(Church News, January 2,
> 1937.)

I started to read the Book of Mormon before I was old enough to be a deacon, and I have been reading it ever since. I know that it is true. Every member of the Church ought to be prepared with an answer to all of these critics who condemn it.

The Book of Mormon, a Divine Record

I consider this a great honor and a privilege to stand before this vast body, mostly of men holding the priesthood, to bear testimony unto them of my faith. I seek the guidance of the Spirit of the Lord in what I have to say.

During the past week or two I have received a number of letters from different parts of the United States written by people, some of whom at least are a little concerned because they have been approached by enemies of the Church and enemies of the Book of Mormon, who had made the statement that there have been one or two or more thousand changes in the Book of Mormon since the first edition was published. Well, of course, there is no truth in that statement.

It is true that when the Book of Mormon was printed the printer was a man who was unfriendly. The publication of the book was done under adverse circumstances, and there were a few errors, mostly typographical—conditions that arise in most any book that is being published—but there was not one thing in the Book of Mormon or in the second edition or any other edition since that in any way contradicts the first edition, and such changes as were made, were made by the Prophet Joseph Smith because under those adverse conditions the Book of Mormon was published. But there was no change of doctrine.

Every Member Should Know Truth of Book of Mormon

Now, these sons of Belial who circulate these reports evidently know better. I will not use the word that is in my mind. I started to read the Book of Mormon before I was old enough to be a deacon, and I have been reading it ever since. I know that it is true. Every member of the Church ought to know that it is true, and we ought to be prepared with an answer to all of these critics who condemn it. They are laying themselves open to punishment when they come to the judgment, and the Lord has said that such characters would arise. Moroni wrote about them, and the Lord answered him in regard to the critics that "fools mock, but they shall mourn."[1]

We have been trying this year to get every man holding the priesthood, and our sisters, too, to read the Book of Mormon—no matter how many times they may have read it before. It seems to me that any member of this Church would never be satisfied until he or she had read the Book of Mormon time and time again, and thoroughly considered it so that he or she could bear witness that it is in very deed a record with the inspiration of the Almighty upon it, and that its history is true.

I can testify of that, for I know the Book of Mormon is true just as well as I know I am standing here in this building facing you.

So much for that. I want to address myself to the men holding the priesthood, particularly, and to their wives and to all other members of the Church. No member of this Church can stand approved in the presence of God who has not seriously and carefully read the Book of Mor-

---

[1]Ether 12:26.

mon, and I think I could add to that also, as far as our brethren are concerned, the Doctrine and Covenants.

Another Book That Is Priceless

We have besides the Book of Mormon and Doctrine and Covenants, another record which is priceless, as these records are, that every member of this Church ought to have read, and which I fear many have not read. I have reference to the Pearl of Great Price. It seems to me that a member of this Church would not be able to rest in peace and comfort and have a clear conscience without having knowledge by study and by faith of the standard works of the Church. These records are priceless. The world mocks at them, but through their teachings we are permitted to come nearer unto God, get a better understanding of our Heavenly Father and his Son Jesus Christ, become closer acquainted with them and to know more in regard to the wonderful plan of salvation which they have given unto us and unto the world if it will receive the plan that will exalt us in the kingdom of God to become his sons and his daughters, receiving the fulness of that kingdom.

In closing this record, Moroni wrote these words:

And I exhort you to remember these things; for the time speedily cometh that ye shall know that I lie not, for ye shall see me at the bar of God; and the Lord God will say unto you: Did I not declare my words unto you, which were written by this man, like as one crying from the dead, yea, even as one speaking out of the dust?

I declare these things unto the fulfilling of the prophecies. And behold, they shall proceed forth out of the mouth of the everlasting God; and his word shall hiss forth from generation to generation.

And God shall show unto you, that that which I have written is true.

And again I would exhort you that ye would come unto Christ, and lay hold upon every good gift, and touch not the evil gift, nor the unclean thing.[2]

---

[2]Moroni 10:27-30.

Moroni's Counsel to the Members of the Church

That is the counsel of Moroni as he closed his record, not only to the members of the Church, but to every soul unto whom this record comes. I want to bear testimony to you, my good brethren here, and to our sisters and to the members of the Church who listen in and to everyone else, that I know that the Book of Mormon is true; that Joseph Smith received it from the hand of God through an angel that was sent to reveal it, the same angel who, while living in this world, finished the record and sealed it up to come forth in this dispensation of the fulness of times.

I would like to call your attention to one thing in the Book of Mormon. The Lord has promised us greater knowledge, greater understanding than we find in the Book of Mormon, when we are prepared to receive it. When the brother of Jared went upon the mount to have the Lord touch stones to give them light to light their way across the great ocean, the Lord revealed to him the history of this world from the beginning of it to the end. We do not have it.

I am going to read one or two passages of scripture from the Book of Mormon in relation to that matter.

> And he (that is, Christ) did expound all things, even from the beginning until the time that he should come in his glory—yea, even all things which should come upon the face of the earth, even until the elements should melt with fervent heat, and the earth should be wrapt together as a scroll, and the heavens and the earth should pass away. . . .[3]

All of that was written and given to the Nephites. We do not have that record, and the Lord said this—which is concerning us particularly—and Mormon wrote it:

> And these things have I written, which are a lesser part of the things which he taught the people; and I have written them

---

[3] 3 Nephi 26:3.

to the intent that they may be brought again unto this people, from the Gentiles, according to the words which Jesus hath spoken.

And when they shall have received this, which is expedient that they should have first, to try their faith, and if it shall so be that they shall believe these things then shall the greater things be made manifest unto them.

And if it so be that they will not believe these things, then shall the greater things be withheld from them, unto their condemnation.[4]

History of Earth Revealed to Brother of Jared

I say that when the brother of Jared went on the mount, the Lord revealed the history of this earth to him from the beginning to the end thereof, but we do not have it. But when the Nephites became righteous, after the visit of the Son of God, the Lord revealed that record to them, and then when they began to fall away, he took the record away again and hid it up. Here is what the Lord says about it:

And after Christ truly had showed himself unto his people, he commanded that they should be made manifest. (That is, the full record.)

And now, after that, they have all dwindled in unbelief; and there is none save it be the Lamanites, and they have rejected the gospel of Christ; therefore I am commanded that I should hide them up again in the earth.[5]

For the sake of time I will skip a little and say that the Lord has promised that we can have that hidden record when we are prepared to receive it. I will read it.

For the Lord said unto me: They shall not go forth unto the Gentiles until the day that they shall repent of their iniquity, and become clean before the Lord.

And in that day that they shall exercise faith in me, saith the Lord, even as the brother of Jared did, that they may become sancti-

---

[4] 3 Nephi 26:8-10.
[5] Ether 4:2-3.

fied in me, then will I manifest unto them the things which the brother of Jared saw, even to the unfolding unto them all my revelations, saith Jesus Christ, the Son of God, the Father of the heavens and of the earth, and all things that in them are.[6]

Placed on Probation

Now the Lord has placed us on probation as members of the Church. He has given us the Book of Mormon, which is the lesser part, to build up our faith through our obedience to the counsels which it contains, and when we ourselves, members of the Church, are willing to keep the commandments as they have been given to us and show our faith as the Nephites did for a short period of time, then the Lord is ready to bring forth the other record and give it to us, but we are not ready now to receive it. Why? Because we have not lived up to the requirements in this probationary state in the reading of the record which had been given to us and in following its counsels.

Brethren, teach the men who hold the priesthood in their quorums. Teach the members of the Church in their meetings, and also when you visit them in their homes as home teachers. Whenever the opportunity presents itself, teach them to read and study in faith and prayer the revelations the Lord has given us that we may not be deceived and led astray by false teachers.

We have false teachers among us. We have apostates among us who are endeavoring to tear down and destroy the kingdom of God, and they are disturbing a great many members of the Church. Why? Because they haven't the faith nor the background in knowledge to resist these false teachers and their false doctrines.

Let me plead with the membership of this Church for humility, for faith, for more prayer, more study, more love in their hearts for God their Eternal Father and his Son Jesus Christ.—(*Conference Report*, Sept. 29, 1961.)

---

[6]Ether 4:6-7.

*If the three witnesses had by any means en-
tered into a fraud or had concocted a story
in relation to the Book of Mormon, the fact
appears perfectly clear that when they were
at cross purposes with the Church they would
have been the first to reveal the fraud. The
fact that each of them remained true to his
testimony to the time of his death is one of
the strongest evidences that we have that the
witnesses spoke the truth. . . .*

The Three Witnesses

In considering the attitude of the three witnesses to the Book of Mormon, we have to take a number of circumstances into account. The great fact is that notwithstanding the loss of membership, each of them remained true to the death to that sacred testimony. There was no shadow of turning. That testimony was just as true to them in their later years as it was the day they signed their names to the document that is found in each copy of the Book of Mormon.

Oliver Cowdery and Martin Harris found their way back again in the depth of humility and died faithful to the Church. David Whitmer, while he never returned to the Church, was true to that testimony and endeavored to build up a church of his own. Martin Harris in later years became a pioneer in the valleys of the mountains and died there among the Latter-day Saints. Oliver Cowdery died a faithful member of the Church and David Whitmer, while he drew away feeling that the Church had gone astray, gathered around him an organization that he maintained was composed of the true followers of the Prophet Joseph Smith.

Sympathy for David Whitmer

Personally, I have had a great deal of sympathy for David Whitmer. I believe him to be an honest man but one who had become overcome by the persuasion of others. To his honor be it said that to his dying day he bore testimony to the coming forth of the Book of Mormon and that he with Oliver Cowdery and Martin Harris had voluntarily given his testimony. There were occasions when plotting individuals attempted to trip him on his testimony, but they failed entirely.

On one occasion Elders Orson Pratt and Joseph F. Smith, while visiting in Missouri, called to see him, and they had a long interview with him. He was glad to see them, and part of their conversation had to do with incidents of early church history. On this occasion David Whitmer bore his testimony as pertaining to the coming forth of the Book of Mormon, which testimony never varied from the first and with which his signature appeared together with the signatures of Oliver Cowdery and Martin Harris. In fact, while he never sought to be reinstated in the Church, he erroneously felt that he had a perfect right to form an organization of his own, which he did. It is unfortunate that he did not follow Oliver Cowdery and Martin Harris, each of them dying as faithful members of the Church.

Permit me to call attention to these facts as I view them. If the story of the coming of the Book of Mormon had been a falsehood, that Moroni never existed and that Joseph Smith the Prophet had by trickery and fraud brought forth the Book of Mormon, then that production would have been so completely filled with errors, doctrinally and historically, that the fraud would have been apparent to every intelligent person who obtained a copy of it. I can challenge and even defy any man, no matter how greatly informed, to produce a work of fiction that could be com-

pared with the Book of Mormon. I have read the Book
of Mormon through many times, and each time I gain
something to my advantage. Where can you go and find
a more intelligent, far-reaching, and comforting doctrine
than the words of Mormon? Moreover, when you read
them, you cannot resist the feeling that they were declared
by the Spirit of Christ:

> For behold, the Spirit of Christ is given to every man, that he
> may know good from evil . . . [and] the way to judge; for every
> thing which inviteth to do good, and to persuade to believe in
> Christ, is sent forth by the power and gift of Christ; wherefore ye
> may know with a perfect knowledge it is of God.
>
> But whatsoever thing persuadeth men to do evil, and believe
> not in Christ, and deny him, and serve not God, then ye may
> know with a perfect knowledge it is of the devil; for after this man-
> ner doth the devil work, for he persuadeth no man to do good, no,
> not one; neither do his angels; neither do they who subject them-
> selves unto him.[1]

Guidance through the Holy Ghost

Such a sentiment as this could come only by and
through the guidance of the Holy Ghost. There is also
another fact that must be considered in relation to the
testimonies of these three witnesses. If they had by any
means entered into a fraud or had concocted a story in
relation to the coming forth of the Book of Mormon, the
fact appears perfectly clear that when they were at cross
purposes with the Church, they would have been the first
to reveal the fraud. Moreover, the fact that each of them
remained true to his testimony to the time of his death, notwithstanding he had problems to overcome that appeared
to him as being difficult, is one of the strongest evidences
that we have that the witnesses spoke the truth and their
testimony is true.—(*The Improvement Era*, July 1966.)

---

[1]Moroni 7:16-17.

If Oliver Cowdery had remained faithful and true, he would have died with the Prophet Joseph Smith; but the Lord transferred the keys and authorities that had been given to Oliver Cowdery to the head of Hyrum Smith to make him the second President of the Church and the second witness of the restoration of the gospel of Jesus Christ.

The Forgotten Witness

This is the anniversary of the birth of the forgotten man—the man who held the keys of the dispensation of the fulness of times jointly with the Prophet Joseph Smith. I do not suppose there is a ward in the Church holding a meeting today where he has been remembered—the man who stood second in the dispensation of the fulness of times; who took the place of Oliver Cowdery because Oliver lost it, and who held the keys of the gospel in this dispensation jointly with the Prophet Joseph Smith. I just thought I would like to call attention to that, and repeat that he is the forgotten man—seldom thought of—who had to die by the shedding of his blood.

I said "had"—had to die by the shedding of his blood, as well as the Prophet Joseph Smith, because he was the second witness, taking the place of Oliver Cowdery, who could have had that honor.

I had placed myself on record, at the April Conference, 1930, that if Oliver Cowdery had remained true and faithful to his end, he would have died a martyr with the Prophet Joseph Smith and would have stood as the second elder of the Church—a man holding the keys jointly with the Prophet for the dispensation of the fulness of times. But

Oliver Cowdery lost that place. Hyrum Smith received
it. And it was just as necessary that Hyrum Smith die a
martyr, as a witness, as it was for the Prophet to so die.
That is in fulfilment of a law which the Savior stressed
in speaking to the wicked Pharisees in Jerusalem. There
had to be two witnesses, divinely appointed, to testify.
Oliver Cowdery lost his place. It was taken by Hyrum
Smith.

"I Do Not Stand Alone"

One day the Savior stood before the Jews. If I remember correctly it was in the temple. They said this to
him after he had been speaking to them, "We do not have
to believe you because you stand alone. Nobody will speak
for you." The Savior's answer to them was, "I do not
stand alone. There is another witness — my Father in
Heaven."[1] No one else could be a witness for the Son of
God but his own Father.

Was his Father ever a witness to the Jews? Yes. He
served as a witness for his Son Jesus Christ at the birth of
the Savior; at the time of his baptism, when his Father
spoke and the Jews heard him bearing witness that Jesus
Christ was his only begotten Son. One day in the company
of the Jews—they were accusing the Savior, "We do not
have to believe you because you stand alone." And the
Savior said, "I do not stand alone. There is another witness—my Father testifies for me." And the Father did
testify for him on a number of occasions. The Father
testified at the time of the birth of the Son of God; he testified at the baptism; he testified in the company, that is,
in the group—and spoke out of the heavens to them and
bore witness that the Savior was his Son; and they said it
thundered. And there were a number of occasions when
the Father spoke to the assembled people and bore witness

---
[1]John 8:12-18.

that Jesus Christ was his Son and he was the only witness the Son could have. But there is that divine law that there must be at least two witnesses.

If Joseph Smith had come out of the woods and said, "I went in to pray and I saw the Father and the Son," and he was the only one who could bear witness to that and if he had come out and said that, they would have said, "We do not have to believe you." If he had said, "The angel came to me and gave me commandments," and at no time had anybody else been called to witness, being a divine manifestation, the Jews could have said with good cause, "We do not have to believe you because you have no witness and nobody could be a witness for Christ except his own Father.

A Witness on Several Occasions

Therefore, at the baptism the Father spoke and called attention to the fact that the young Man being baptized was his beloved Son. There were a number of such occasions that took place, and so when the Jews said to the Savior, "We do not have to believe you because you are alone. Nobody testifies for you," they failed to recognize the truth and there were a number of occasions when his Father's voice was heard. And he spoke from the heavens declaring that Jesus Christ was his beloved Son.

So the Savior fulfilled the law of witnesses. If Joseph Smith had been the only one to testify of the opening of the heavens and the coming of holy messengers, then everybody could have said, "We do not believe you because your testimony is not true." He would have had no defense. But he had witnesses. Oliver Cowdery was called to be a witness who stood with the Prophet in the presence of Jesus Christ. He was with the Prophet when there was a restoration of the keys. He was with the Prophet on a number of occasions. And when Sidney Rigdon became a counselor in the Presidency of the Church the heavens were opened to him, and he testified with the Prophet Joseph Smith of the presence to them, of the coming of the Son of God, and they bore witness together of the restoration of this gospel. So brethren and sisters, nothing was overlooked. This Church was established in accordance with divine law—commandments.

Now today is the birthday anniversary of Hyrum Smith. I repeat, if Oliver Cowdery had remained faithful and true, he would have died with the Prophet Joseph Smith; but the Lord transferred the keys and authorities that had been given to Oliver Cowdery to the head of Hyrum Smith to make him the second President of the Church and the second witness of the restoration of the gospel of Jesus Christ.

Two Presidents

I think there are a few members of the Church who know that we had to have two Presidents in the beginning. Oliver Cowdery was chosen to be one of them and he lost his place, could not take it, and turned away. Fortunately, in his defense, I am glad to say he came back again. He humbly repented and died faithful to the Church, but he lost his place as the second witness. Hyrum Smith was called to take it, as you find recorded in the Doctrine and Covenants, and there had to be two witnesses of the restoration of the gospel. And I am mentioning this because this is the ninth day of February, the birthday of Hyrum Smith. Hyrum Smith had to die by the shedding of his blood with the Prophet, and thus they sealed their testimony against the world for all mankind and made that testimony binding upon this world.—(Remarks in Salt Lake Eighteenth Ward, February 9, 1964.)

I understand that many of you plan to return to your homes after graduating. By partaking of the activities here you will be able to serve your own people. Then the promises of the Lord to your forefathers "that he would preserve their seed "and in the future generations" make them "a righteous branch unto the house of Israel" will be fulfilled.

The Prophesied Future
of the Indian People

My dear brethren and sisters, I am very happy to be here with you this evening. I was asked to come and speak to you tonight, and I hope and pray that the Lord will bless me with his Spirit, that I might give you something, that will build your spirits.

I understand you have a wonderful organization down here at this school in the student ward, and I am very happy to learn of this, because you young men and women have a great work to perform for your people. If you seek out the love for the gospel, the Lord will reward you. I understand that many of you plan to return to your homes after graduating. By partaking of the activities here you will be able to serve your own people. Then the promises of the Lord to your forefathers "that he would perserve" their seed "and in future generations" make them "a righteous branch unto the house of Israel will be fulfilled."[1]

I understand that during the school year 1966, that ninety percent attended sacrament meeting, 75 percent of the elders attended priesthood meeting and that 75 percent

[1] 2 Nephi 9:53.

of the ward attended MIA and 70 percent regularly attended Sunday School. This record and training, along with the
experiences you get, and the testimonies that come by doing
these things, will enable you to assume responsible positions
of leadership, and help bring about the temporal and spiritual redemption of your own people. Read Helaman 15:
12-13. This shows the love that the Redeemer has for them,
and again the promises of the Lord are being fulfilled, as in
the days of Samuel the Lamanite, the Indian people are
being "brought to a knowledge of the truth" and are becoming "firm and steadfast in the faith. . . ."[2] When you
return to your people go to them with this new home teaching program so they will be able to study in their own
homes, but do not neglect your duty. These young women
can also teach them about Relief Society work and its benefits.

Colonization by Chosen People

From time to time the Lord has colonized various parts
of the earth with remnants of the chosen people. The scattering of Israel commenced before the captivity of the Ten
Tribes, and continued after the captivity of Judah by the
Babylonians, at the time when Lehi was called from Jerusalem.

The promise had been made from the beginning of the
Nephite nation that when Christ should rise from the dead
he would pay a visit to the people on this hemisphere.
After his resurrection the Lord fulfilled this promise. Immediately before the crucifixion the people had destroyed
the unity of their government and had broken up into tribes
and petty kingdoms. Wickedness ruled supreme in most of
the land, and the corruption and violence was appalling.
When Christ was crucified there were three days of darkness upon the American continent. This was preceded by

---

[2]Helaman 15:7-8.

a severe tempest such as had never been known, and the whole face of the land, we are informed, was changed. Many cities were buried in the depths of the sea, others were burned with fire, and still others carried up, upon the tops of new mountains which were formed by the sudden convulsions of the earth. In this manner the more wicked part of the people, and that was the greater part of them, were all destroyed. All who survived were granted the privilege of a visitation from Jesus Christ. The account of his visitation and his teachings to the survivors among the people is a very interesting and profitable story. He established his Church among them and for two hundred years there were neither Nephites or Lamanites, or any manner of "ites" in the land. All of the people became united in one kingdom and one church. Their kingdom was the kingdom of God, a theocracy, and they were ruled by twelve disciples comparable to the twelve apostles of the Savior who were ordained in the Church in the land of Palestine. Following the appearance of the Savior, for a period of two hundred years the Church of Jesus Christ ruled, and the people lived, as did the people in the city of Enoch, the law of consecration.

Historian's Account

The historian says of these people during this time:

And it came to pass that there was no contention among all the people, in all the land; but there were mighty miracles wrought among the disciples of Jesus. . . .

And it came to pass that there was no contention in the land, because of the love of God which did dwell in the hearts of the people.

And there were no envyings, no strifes, nor tumults, nor whoredoms, nor lyings, nor murders, nor any manner of lasciviousness; and surely there could not be a happier people among all the people who had been created by the hand of God.

There were no robbers, nor murderers, neither were there Lamanites, nor any manner of -ites; but they were in one, the children of Christ, and heirs to the kingdom of God.

And how blessed were they! For the Lord did bless them in all their doings; yea, even they were blessed and prospered until an hundred and ten years had passed away; and the first generation from Christ had passed away, and there was no contention in all the land.[3]

From that time forth the Lamanites divided into bands and tribes and fought among themselves. Their greatest civilizations, at the time of the discovery of America, were in Mexico and Peru.

Promises Yet To Be Fulfilled

However the Lord has not altogether cast them off. There are promises made to them which are yet to be fulfilled. The day will come when they shall again rise up and be a blessed people, white and favored of the Lord. That day will come when they in all sincerity accept the fulness of the gospel.

Moroni hid his records in the hill known as the Hill Cumorah, which is located in western New York. It was here where Joseph Smith, in our present dispensation, was led by this same Moroni—who had by then received his resurrection—to obtain and translate the abridgment of this ancient history made by Moroni's father Mormon, and by himself. Today that record speaks as from the dust from those who are dead, with a warning voice to all who are living, that they may, upon this land, avoid the pitfalls and the rebellions which brought destructions upon the peoples who formerly dwelt here, and thus escape a similar destruction. The decree has gone forth that no people may possess this land indefinitely in rebellion against God, for when their cup of iniquity is full they shall be swept off the face of the land, for the Lord has decreed that "wickedness shall

---

[3]4 Nephi 13:15-18.

not stand." The Lord said, my kingdom pertains to the life to come. I am here to teach people the way which will lead them back to God, where they will attain to everlasting life, and where they may be crowned as kings and priests of the Most High. Latter-day Saints are perhaps more directly interested in this than any other people in the world. Some of these countries have the majority of their citizens, whom the world call Indians, but to whom the Latter-day Saints refer to as Lamanites, people whom we believe to be of the chosen and promised seed of Abraham, brought to this continent and established here under the direction of God our Father, under the leadership of their inspired prophets.

Words of President Anthony W. Ivins

In October conference of 1926, President Anthony W. Ivins said, "Let the young men of Israel, the descendants of this Joseph, look upon their ancestor and be inspired to die rather than to be defiled that they may be worthy to come into the great heritage that God has for his faithful sons and daughters. For if this generation shall keep themselves clean and undefiled they shall reap honors and distinction like unto which their fathers who subdued the deserts and made it blossom never attained." About 1960, when Sister Smith and I went into South America, we stood on the ground that was dedicated by Brother Melvin J. Ballard, Brother Rey L. Pratt and Brother Rulon Wells, and it was a glorious experience. That date of dedication was December 25, 1925, and then to see how the Lamanite people were responding to the gospel was delightful. We are thankful to the Lord for this. We feel a desire to continue our labors and to work zealously for the redemption of that particular branch of the house of Israel with which we are laboring, namely the Lamanite people, who are descendants of Joseph and who have resided upon this land

of America. While in Lima, Peru, Brother Vernon Sharp
took Sister Smith and me to visit a nonmember of the
Church. He had in his possession gold in different sizes.
We had the privilege of going into his home, and in the
glass cases there were many wonderful pieces made into
different items like vases and candle holders. We noticed
sheets of gold and the pile was about as high as half a
dozen *Juvenile Instructors*. They were a pure gold leaf, and
all that would need to be done would be to insert a ring
through the edges of this set of plates, and they would be
like the plates that the Prophet Joseph handled. It really
was a glorious sight and made it more convincing that the
Book of Mormon is true.

I spoke to Brother Sharp just a few days ago. He told
me that the man had passed away but that his wife had
possession of the gold display. She invited Brother Sharp to
visit again, and this time she opened the glass case and
took out piece by piece. Brother Sharp took pictures of all
in the case and he has them—about 70 colored slides—so
we can see just what can be done in teaching the gospel.
So young men and young women, teach your people the
principles of the gospel, and the Lord will bless you and
magnify you in this work. Remember what the Lord has
said, "I, the Lord, am bound when ye do what I say; but
when ye do not what I say, ye have no promise."[4] I want
to tell you that the Lord will fulfill his promise if we fulfill
our promise. These prophecies and promises are valid. Elder
Rey L. Pratt said, "The Lord intends to redeem that people.
He intends to redeem them through those of us who are
brought out from among the Gentile nations and who in
very deed believe the words of the book that has come to
us. It has been revealed through the instrumentality of the
greatest prophet that has resided in this world, save it be
the Son of God himself; and it will stand the test of time.

---

[4]D&C 82:10.

It will stand the test of any investigation that can be brought to bear, and in the end it will triumph."

The Lord bless us and help us in carrying out the duty assigned to us in this great work of the Lord. —Address at Indian Students Ward, BYU, April 28, 1967.)

---

*What is the doctrine of the kingdom of God?
It is that every soul through the mercy of
God should have an opportunity to hear, repent, and receive the gospel. . . . It is the
word to all who have sojourned upon this
earth. . . . If it is applied universally, it must
reach out to those who have died without the
opportunities of repentance, to every soul who
never heard of Jesus Christ. . . . Anything
short of this would be an injustice.*

The True Meaning of Salvation

I want to preface what I say by making a few remarks in regard to salvation as it is generally applied. The Church of Jesus Christ of Latter-day Saints is a peculiar Church. It has to be, because it is the only church on the face of the earth that does not belong to this world. We have people in it who do belong to the world, but the Church does not belong to this world, and it has been recognized by our Lord and Savior, Jesus Christ, as his Church. Of course, in a church organization, and especially the Church of Jesus Christ, there must be laws and ordinances that are fixed and unchangeable because God is unchangeable, and the plan of salvation is the same today as it was in the days of Adam. It is the same plan that has been adopted in other worlds, because this plan is eternal, therefore, members of the Church are subject to eternal regulations, laws, rules, and decrees that were instituted before the foundation of the world for the government of the Church and for the salvation of men.

Same Plan Since the Beginning

I think the idea prevails throughout the so-called "Christian" world that the plan that was given from the days of Adam until the days of Jesus Christ was a different plan—something other than what our Savior gave—and that the gospel of Jesus Christ as introduced by him is another system entirely from that which was in force or required of mankind before the coming of our Lord in his ministry. But that is not true. The decrees of the Almighty are unchangeable so far as the laws pertaining to the kingdom of God are concerned. They always were what they are today. We have not changed them. They are not different from what the people had to subscribe to from the days of Adam on down.

I am presenting that to you without presenting any arguments. I do not intend to argue for them, and I ask you to accept it by the statement I have made. I could turn to the scriptures and prove it.

Every man lives for himself. Adam was able to open the way of the world and dress the Garden. Noah was born to save seeds of every kind when the world was washed of wickedness by the flood, and the Son of God came into this world to redeem it from the fall. But, except a man be born again he cannot see the kingdom of God. This eternal truth settles the question of "every man's religion." Now listen to this. A man may be saved after the judgment in the terrestrial kingdom and in the telestial kingdom, but he can never see the celestial kingdom of God without being born of the water and of the spirit. He may receive a glory like the moon—that is, that which the moon is typical of; or a star, that is, of which the light of a star is typical. But he can never come unto Mount Zion and the City of the Living God, the Heavenly Jerusalem.

Man Must Be Saved with Ordinances

"Verily, verily, I say unto thee, Except a man be born again, he cannot see the kingdom of God." And then when he (Nicodemus) did not understand, "Jesus answered,

Verily, Verily, I say unto thee Except a man be born of water and of the spirit, he cannot enter into the kingdom of God."[1]

That brings us to the point. If a man cannot be saved without the ordinances of baptism by water and the baptism of the Holy Ghost by the laying on of hands, what is going to become of all the dead who have died or who may yet die without a knowledge of the gospel? The Lord has given the only correct answer, and The Church of Jesus Christ of Latter-day Saints is the only Church upon the face of the earth that has accepted it. I am not going to take the time to read the statements of the Catholic Church and the Protestant churches, so-called, covering that point. They have no salvation for the dead who died without a knowledge of the gospel, without having heard the name of Jesus Christ. The Catholic Church and some of the Protestant churches even declare that infants dying without having been christened—sprinkled with water—are forever damned.

This is the doctrine of the Catholic Church. The absolute necessity of this sacrament, or this baptism, is necessary for infants. St. Irenius says Christ came to save all who are reborn through him to God. St. Augustine says, "If you wish to be a Catholic, do not believe, nor say, nor teach, that infants who die before baptism can obtain the remission of original sin." A still stronger passage from the same doctor reads: "Whoever says that even infants are vivified in Christ when they depart this life without participation of his Sacrament (Baptism) both opposes the Apostolic preaching and condemns the whole church which hastens to baptize infants, because it unhesitatingly believes that otherwise they cannot possibly be vivified in Christ."[2]

---

[1]John 3:3, 5.
[2]*Catholic Encyclopedia*, Vol. 2, p. 265. See also p. 267.

Catholic theologians are unanimous in declaring infants are excluded from the beatific vision of Christ unless baptized. As to the exact state of souls in the next world they are not agreed.

If a little infant who could not help itself is to be damned and denied vision of the Son of God, then what about grown people who are unbaptized? They, too, are forever damned. That is the doctrine of the world. Without going into all the arguments to the contrary, the Savior declares—you read it in the eighteenth and nineteenth chapters of Matthew—that little children are alive in Christ, that is, they belong to the kingdom of heaven. It is not necessary for me to continue the argument any further. We have plenty of evidence.

So, throughout the world, the idea prevails that they who have died without a knowledge of the gospel of Christ, or lived when they could not hear of him, that they are consigned to some degree of punishment and cast out of his presence.

The Doctrine of the Kingdom

What is the doctrine of the kingdom of God? It is that every soul through the mercy of God should have an opportunity to hear, repent, and receive the gospel. That is very emphatically referred to in the First Section of the Doctrine and Covenants, which is the Preface to the Doctrine and Covenants, and in the words of our Savior, Jesus Christ. Of course the doctrine of salvation for the dead was not a doctrine understood even in the Church when this revelation was given. I will begin with Verse 2.

For verily the voice of the Lord is unto all men, and there is none to escape; and there is no eye that shall not see, neither ear that shall not hear, neither heart that shall not be penetrated.

And the rebellious shall be pierced with much sorrow; for their iniquities shall be spoken upon the housetops, and their secret acts shall be revealed.

If this is the word of the Lord to all men, it is the word to all who have sojourned upon this earth. And how are they going to hear? How are their eyes to see and ears to hear and their hearts to be penetrated, when billions of people upon this earth have died in places and under conditions where it was not possible for them to hear the message of the gospel of Jesus Christ? They have died without hearing his name. They never had the opportunity to be baptized, because there was no one with authority to officiate in that ordinance. There was no one to teach them. There are millions upon millions of people upon the face of the earth today who have never heard, and they are dying every day.

Now I want to ask this question. Is it fair, is it just, is it according to divine mercy to declare that all these people who have so died, at times and in places where the gospel did not penetrate and where they have never had the opportunity to repent of their sins, that they should be forever damned and denied the blessings, the opportunities for the blessings of the gospel of Jesus Christ? And the answer to that—there is only one answer, is NO! It would not be just, it would not be merciful, it would not be in accordance with the divine law, and so the Latter-day Saints stand in a peculiar position, peculiar to the world.

The thing that makes us peculiar is the fact that we do not belong to the world, that we do not believe in the doctrines of the world, but we accept and believe in the doctrines of the Lord and Savior, Jesus Christ.

Father in Heaven Is Merciful

I believe that our Father in heaven is merciful, and I believe he is just. I believe with all my soul that he has revealed to the Prophet Joseph Smith, and he revealed it to the apostles of old, the doctrine of universal salvation— that is, salvation applied universally. If it is applied universally, it must reach out to those who have died without the opportunities of repentance, to every soul who never heard of Jesus Christ. Therefore, they who are dead must have the opportunity of having their ears hear, their eyes see and the privilege of repenting of their sins. Anything short of that would be an injustice.

To condemn the poor innocent little child who is helpless because its parents or some other individual had not sprinkled it with water before it died is the most damnable of all doctrines upon the face of the earth. I have good backing for that. It is not original with me, but I believe it. If you read the eighth chapter of Moroni, it says it as definitely as I would be able to do it. He said that those who teach that kind of doctrine will be damned unless they repent.

When I was in the mission field, I had a poor mother appeal to me for a little sympathy and a little help and comfort, for the doctrine she had received was gnawing at her soul. She had a child die in infancy. It had not been sprinkled, and when she asked the priest to give this child a burial, he refused, saying since it had not received baptism it could not have a Christian burial. He told her her child was forever lost. That thought had been preying at her heart, and she had been weeping and mourning and was in the depths of anguish of soul because of what this priest had told her. He refused to have anything to do with the funeral. She had to get somebody else to hold the funeral and the burial. I was in her home. She asked me if she could put a question to me that had been troubling her, and I said, "certainly."

She told me the circumstances of her child's death and how she had been treated and asked, "Is my baby forever lost?" That gave me the best opportunity in the world to preach the gospel to her. I turned to Moroni and read Mormon's instructions.

I turned to the Doctrine and Covenants and read what the Lord has said regarding infant death and told her her infant was not lost. I turned to the New Testament and read what the Lord set forth in it regarding little children, and I said, "Just forget the advice that the priest told you, for it is of the devil." I read her this,

I say unto you, that little children are redeemed from the foundation of the world through mine Only Begotten;

Wherefore, they cannot sin, for power is not given unto Satan to tempt little children, until they begin to become accountable before me.[3]

The idea of a little child being tied with Adam's sins of 6,000 years ago! Adam transgressed the law of God, and these people say this little infant born in the year 1951 must pay the price? Don't you believe it.

Every Man to Be Given a Chance

And so the Lord has made salvation a universal salvation, and he gives to every man a chance. The fact a man dies without having been baptized, without having heard the name of Jesus Christ does not condemn him. His actions will condemn him. If he has lived a faithless life and guilty of all manner of evils—murder in his heart—he will have the same kind of feeling over there. They are not all going to receive the gospel, but they have the right to hear it.

We are only a little handful considering the people upon the face of the earth, yet the Lord has placed upon us the burden of looking after our dead and preparing the records, going to the temples, being baptized, being confirmed, being endowed, performing the sealing for husbands and wives and children as far back as we can go. Does that mean every person for whom we have been baptized

[3]D&C 29:46-47.

and every person who is confirmed and endowed and sealed is going to receive salvation in the kingdom of God? No! Not any more than if we would force people to be baptized here. We could not force them. If we do the work and they accept it with all their hearts, the Lord will count it the same as if they did it for themselves.

They cannot be baptized over there because water is an element pertaining to the mortal existence. You cannot take spirits and baptize them and you cannot ordain them, you cannot confirm them and you cannot present them to the altar in the temple of the Lord and seal husband and wife, because they belong to a different world. They have left this sphere of action. But the Lord has given unto us the privilege of acting for them vicariously. He has commanded us to go into the temples of the Lord and perform the labor for them that they cannot do for themselves.

We cannot figure out all our progenitors who have gone before and have a clear understanding of who will or will not receive the gospel. We do the work for everyone, and the Lord will do the segregating. But it is our duty to go back and do the work for all we can search out.

Not Much Time to Redeem Dead

I have a statement here from Joseph Smith which says, "If we do it with all our might we would hardly get through." The Saints have not too much time to save and redeem their dead.

Now think of these things. I think from what I have read and said perhaps I have said enough to point out to you the responsibility that rests upon us. There is no greater responsibility (and the Prophet has said it) resting upon us as individuals and families than to seek after our dead. The man who will not seek after his dead and go to the temple and try to perform the labor to the best of his ability as far as he can do it will find himself barred. He will have to stay on the sideline of eternity—at least until somebody does the work for his kin. For we cannot be saved without our dead who are likewise worthy of salvation, and if we fail to do the work we will stand condemned.

The time is drawing to a close. We are getting pretty close to the coming of our Savior. All the signs point there, and we are supposed to do all we can to show the Lord by our works and faith that we are interested in our dead. If our hearts are not turned to our fathers, then we are not living the gospel of Jesus Christ. Their hearts have turned. The righteous who are dead, their hearts have turned to us. They are seeking our help, and if we do not help them we will be condemned.

Now somebody will raise the question—"But what about all the people who lived beyond the time we can find the records?" There is not anything to prevent us from searching the records we can find. I want to tell you what is going to happen. When we have exhausted every source and every facility, and have done all in our power to perform the work for our dead relatives and cannot go any further and no records are obtainable, the Lord will come to our rescue. The great work of the millennium will be the performing of work in the temples of the Lord for the dead who are entitled to salvation.

How is that going to come about? They who have passed to the other side and received their resurrection or will have received their resurrection after Christ comes will come to people who dwell in mortality and bring the names, bring records and say, "Now go in the temples and do this work, perform these labors for these people. These are of your lineage. Now do the work, and when you have done all of this we will bring you more." So the work will be done for every soul worthy to receive salvation.

Righteous Will Not Be Overlooked

The Lord is not going to overlook a single soul or anyone who is entitled to receive it. We do not need to worry for fear the Lord is going to forget somebody. The Lord will furnish the record when we cannot do it until every soul is ferreted out and every worthy soul has the privilege of the ordinances of the house of the Lord. Now that is the gospel of Jesus Christ.

So, let us get a proper understanding of salvation and what it means. Let us seek for exaltation in that celestial kingdom.—(Excerpts from an address in the Ogden Tabernacle, September 2, 1951.)

The Lord has never withdrawn or permitted his authority to be withdrawn absolutely from this earth, and so down through the years and through the great apostasy, which developed until the so-called Christian era, there have been individuals on the face of the earth holding divine authority.

This World Has Never Been Surrendered to Satan

The Lord has never surrendered this world to Satan. He tells us that. And there has never been a time when he did not have somebody on the earth to contend for righteousness. You do not know what I am referring to, but I am going to tell you. John the Revelator was given the promise that he should remain until the second coming of Christ. He is here on the face of the earth. There were a number of men among the Nephites, whom he chose to be among his Twelve for those people, who also wished to have the privilege given to them to remain here until the second coming of Christ. They have been here on the face of the earth from that day until now and will be until Christ comes. I am not acquainted with them. Neither are you. Maybe there will never be an occasion when any of them will come to me and tell me who they are—or you—but they are here, nevertheless, and will be until the time of Christ.

The Lord has never withdrawn or permitted his authority to be withdrawn absolutely from this earth; and so down through the years and through the great apostasy, which developed until the so-called Christian era, there have

been individuals on the face of the earth holding divine
authority. But it has not been their privilege to go forth
among the people proselyting or baptizing. They have been
here on the face of the earth to contend against Satan and his
followers, adversaries of righteousness, and to hold them
in check.

We understand that John the Revelator asked for the
privilege of remaining on earth until the coming of Christ,
and that was granted to him. Three Nephites asked for the
same privilege and it was granted. They have been here on
the face of the earth—advocates of righteousness and contending against Satan and his adversaries.

I think we have largely—that is, members of the Church
—almost universally believed the Lord fully surrendered this
world to Satan, and there were hundreds of years when there
was no representative on the face of the earth with authority
to contend against Satan and his adversaries. The Lord has
never permitted Satan to have absolute control, so there
were individuals who were granted the privilege of continued
life or the privilege of living until Christ should come the
second time. They might come to your door and you would
not know them. But they have been here through all these
years. They were not authorized to organize the Church.
They were authorized to contend against Satan and hold
him in check; but they do not have the privilege to organize
wards and stakes and set up upon the face of the earth these
organizations.—(Remarks at Ensign Stake Conference, January 30, 1966.)

The world does not comprehend the revelations of God. It did not in the days of the Jews; yet all that the prophets had spoken concerning them came to pass. So in our day these things will come to pass. We cannot draw a veil over the events that await this generation.

Judgments of the Lord to Pour Forth

According to the dictionary, chastity means "the quality or state of being chaste, free from sexual impurity—free in thought; modest, virtuous and free from vulgarity."

When the Savior was with the Nephites he emphasized this principle and said to them:

And no unclean thing can enter into his kingdom; therefore nothing entereth into his rest save it be those who have washed their garments in my blood, because of their faith, and the repentance of all their sins, and their faithfulness unto the end.

Now this is the commandment: Repent, all ye ends of the earth, and come unto me and be baptized in my name, that ye may be sanctified by the reception of the Holy Ghost, that ye may stand spotless before me at the last day.

Verily, verily, I say unto you, this is my gospel; and ye know the things that ye must do in my church; for the works which ye have seen me do that shall ye also do; for that which ye have seen me do even that shall ye do;

Therefore, if ye do these things blessed are ye, for ye shall be lifted up at the last day.[1]

Repentance Is Essential

From the observation that we make as we travel from

---
[1] 3 Nephi 27:19-22.

one place to another and from what we read in the public
press, we are of necessity forced to the conclusion that repentance from sin is extremely essential throughout the
world today. There has seldom been a time in the history
of mankind when sin was not prevalent and the violation
of the divine commandment was almost, if not entirely, universal. We read in the sacred writings that it was not long
after the children of Adam and Eve were grown that these
children began to pair off and establish families in the earth,
and the influence of Satan was felt among them, and they
began to forget the teachings their parents had given them.
Thus do the scriptures read:

> And Adam and Eve blessed the name of God, and they made
> all things known unto their sons and daughters.
> And Satan came among them, saying: I am also a son of God;
> and he commanded them saying: Believe it not; and they believed
> it not, and they loved Satan more than God. And men began from
> that time forth to be carnal, sensual, and devilish.[2]

Very frequently I have this question asked of me:
"When Lucifer, or the devil, was cast out of heaven, why
did the Lord permit him to come to this earth to tempt and
torment mankind? Why did he not punish him by sending
him to some other, but isolated, place with his angels?"

My answer has been that the Father permitted Lucifer
to come here so that he could tempt us and test our faith.
It is a divine decree, and one that is evidently essential, that
we have this mortal probation; we are in it to be tested and
proved to see if we can keep the commandments in the face
of temptation or trial.

Our Eternal Father did not place us here without some
protection against sin and the temptations of Satan. In the
very beginning Adam and Eve were definitely instructed
in the way of salvation and were given strict commandments to serve the Lord and bring their children up in the

---

[2]Moses 5:12-13.

light and truth of the gospel, the principles of which are essential to man's salvation. Evidently angels from heaven were their instructors, and while the record does not reveal the event, Eve was baptized as well as Adam. Let it be remembered that the Fall was not the terrible thing which so many good people believe it to have been and which is proclaimed quite generally in the so-called Christian world. It is customary for many religious teachers in the world to refer to the Fall as "man's shameful fall," and it is so recorded in the King James translation of the Bible. However, the Fall was an essential part of man's mortal probation. It is a mistaken notion that prevails quite generally in the world that Adam and Eve would have lived in a world of ease, with their posterity, free from temptation and sin, if that fruit had not been taken. The fact is very clear, nevertheless, that had Adam and Eve not partaken, the great gift of mortality would not have come to them. Moreover, they would have had no posterity, and the great commandment given to them by the Lord would not have been fulfilled.

The divine truth is that Adam and Eve were expected to do the very thing that they did. All of this was part of the divine plan.

Mortal Existence Is Part of Eternal Life

This mortal life is a part of our eternal life. Adam's "transgression," and I place the word in quotation marks, was an essential act which opened the doors for the millions of spirits to come to this earth and receive bodies of flesh and bones preparatory to their eternal salvation and exaltation.

Mortality, therefore, is a part of the eternal plan in relation to the salvation and exaltation of the human family. Here we are tried, tempted, and proved to be either worthy of exaltation to thrones and kingdoms or partakers of his displeasure and thus assigned to some lesser kingdom.

Lehi, when giving counsel to his son Jacob, spoke by prophecy of the coming of the Son of God in the meridian of time and had this counsel for him:

Wherefore, redemption cometh in and through the Holy Messiah; for he is full of grace and truth.

Behold he offereth himself a sacrifice for sin, to answer the ends of the law, unto all those who have a broken heart and a contrite spirit; and unto none else can the ends of the law be answered.

Wherefore how great the importance to make these things known unto the inhabitants of the earth, that they may know that there is no flesh that can dwell in the presence of God, save it be through the merits and mercy, and grace of the Holy Messiah, who layeth down his life according to the flesh, and taketh it again by the power of the Spirit, that he may bring to pass the resurrection of the dead, being the first that should rise.

Wherefore, he is the first-fruits unto God, inasmuch as he shall make intercession for all the children of men; and they that believe in him shall be saved.

And because of the intercession for all, all men come unto God; wherefore, they stand in the presence of him to be judged of him according to the truth and holiness which is in him. Wherefore, the ends of the law which the Holy One hath given, unto the inflicting of the punishment which is affixed, which punishment that is affixed is in opposition to that of the happiness which is affixed, to answer the ends of the atonement—

For it must needs be, that there is an opposition in all things. If not so, my first-born in the wilderness, righteousness could not be brought to pass, neither wickedness, neither holiness nor misery, neither good nor bad. Wherefore, all things must needs be a compound in one; wherefore, if it should be one body it must needs remain as dead, having no life neither death, nor corruption nor incorruption, happiness nor misery, neither sense nor insensibility.

Wherefore, it must needs have been created for a thing of naught; wherefore there would have been no purpose in the end of its creation. Wherefore, this thing must needs destroy the wisdom of God and his eternal purposes, and also the power, and the mercy, and the justice of God.[3]

---

[3]2 Nephi 2:6-12.

In course of time, so the scriptures say, "God saw that the wickedness of man was great in the earth, and that every imagination of the thoughts of his heart was only evil continually."[4]

Punishments To Be Meted Out

And thus, down through the ages, we discover, if we are willing to believe what is written in the scriptures, that judgments and destructions had to be poured out upon the wicked because they would not repent.

Not only were these punishments meted out to the inhabitants of the so-called Old World, but destructions awaited the inhabitants of this western world for the same cause. Through their prophets (I am speaking of the Nephites and Lamanites), they were constantly reminded that this land is "choice above all other lands, which the Lord God had preserved for a righteous people."[5]

We who live in the present day should take heed and profit by the experiences of those who have gone before and not fall into their grievous errors. We should remember that the same warnings have been given to us and "to all the inhabitants of the earth," that destruction awaits this age unless men refrain from wickedness and abominations. Let us not forget that the Lord said it should be in this day as it was in the days of Noah. We should remember also that he is still a "God of wrath" as well as a "God of love," and that he has promised to pour out his wrath upon the ungodly and to "take vengeance upon the wicked" who will not repent.

Not only did the ancient prophets predict that such should be the case in these latter days; the Lord has also spoken it in our own dispensation.

I want to bear testimony to this congregation, and to the heavens and the earth, that the day is come when those

---

[4]Genesis 6:5.
[5]Ether 2:7.

angels are privileged to go forth and commence their work.
They are laboring in the United States of America; they
are laboring among the nations of the earth; and they will
continue. We need not marvel or wonder at anything that
is transpiring in the earth. The world does not comprehend
the revelations of God. It did not in the days of the Jews;
yet all that the prophets had spoken concerning them came
to pass. So in our day these things will come to pass. We
cannot draw a veil over the events that await this generation. No man who is inspired by the Spirit and power of
God can close his ears, his eyes, or his lips to these things.

And thus we might quote indefinitely from the ancient
prophets as well as from the prophets of this dispensation
and even from the Lord himself, in relation to the troubles,
destructions, wars, and plagues which are to come upon
the inhabitants of the earth—yes, even Zion also—unless
the people repent. "The Lord's scourge," so he says, "shall
pass over by night and by day, and the report thereof shall
vex all people: yea it shall not be stayed until the Lord
come;

"For the indignation of the Lord is kindled against
their abominations and all their wicked works."

But the promise has been made to Zion and the pure
in heart, that they shall escape if they "observe to do all
things whatsoever I [the Lord] have commanded. . . ."[6]

What is here given will suffice as a warning to a "per-
verse generation" and to remind the members of the Church
that the Lord has said:

> Even so it shall be in that day when they shall see all these
> things, then shall they know that the hour is nigh.
> And it shall come to pass that he that feareth me shall be look-
> ing forth for the great day of the Lord to come, even for the signs
> of the coming of the Son of Man.
> And they shall see signs and wonders, for they shall be shown
> forth in the heavens above, and in the earth beneath.

---

[6] D&C 97:23-25.

And they shall behold blood, and fire, and vapors of smoke.[7]

And take heed to yourselves, lest at any time your hearts be overcharged with surfeiting, and drunkenness, and cares of this life, and so that day come upon you unawares.

For as a snare shall it come on all them that dwell on the face of the whole earth.

Watch ye therefore, and pray always, that ye may be accounted worthy to escape all these things that shall come to pass, and to stand before the Son of Man.[8]—(Conference Report, October, 1966.)

[7]D&C 45:38-41.
[8]Luke 21:34-36.

In his great mercy, love and justice, we see our Father in heaven has provided that all his children who have gained mortality shall live again. The soul cannot be destroyed. The spirits of all men are eternal. They lived before this mortal life came, and through the atonement of Jesus Christ, they shall live after this mortal life is ended.

The Resurrection

The doctrines of the fall of man and the atonement of Jesus Christ are two fundamental principles of the gospel which are greatly misunderstood. The erroneous idea prevails throughout the Christian world, that Adam was placed on this earth with a definite mission in which he shamefully and sinfully failed.

Bible commentators have spoken of Adam's act as "Man's shameful fall." They decry it as a deplorable wicked rebellion which brought upon Adam, Eve and all their posterity, a condition of sin and evil that could have been kept from the world perpetually so that all mankind could have lived in love, peace and happiness, without sin or death, in a lovely world free from pain and sorrow. Those who hold this view fail to grasp the significance that such a condition, if it were possible, would have precluded the necessity for the coming of Jesus Christ as the world would have been without a reason for a Redeemer.

In the scriptures we are instructed that the plans of the Almighty were not destroyed or changed. Jesus Christ was appointed as "the Lamb slain from the foundation of the world,"[1] and we were redeemed "with the precious

---

[1] Revelation 13:8.

blood of Christ, as of a lamb without blemish and without spot; who verily was foreordained before the foundation of the world but was manifest in these last times. . . ."[2]

Fortunately the correct doctrine in relation to Adam's transgression, or the fall, was restored to the Prophet Joseph Smith. Information beyond what is found in the Bible states that after the fall, an angel made known to Adam and to Eve the true nature of their transgression. Adam rejoiced and said: "Blessed be the name of God, for because of my transgression my eyes are opened, and in this life I shall have joy, and again in the flesh I shall see God." Eve, also received the true vision of the consequences of that transgression, and exclaimed: "Were it not for our transgression we never should have had seed, and never should have known good and evil, and the joy of our redemption, and the eternal life which God giveth unto all the obedient." With this knowledge "Adam and Eve blessed the name of God, and they made all things known unto their sons and their daughters."[3]

Of Greatest Value

Surely this was information of the greatest value, and a condition greatly to be desired, notwithstanding all the vicissitudes of mortality and the evils that have come into the world. The Lord has made it clear that in order for mankind to obtain salvation and exaltation it is necessary for them to obtain bodies in this world and pass through the experiences and schooling that are found only in mortality. The Lord has said that his great work and glory is, "to bring to pass the immortality and eternal life of man."[4] Without mortality this great blessing could not be accomplished. Therefore worlds are created and peopled with the children of God and they are granted the privilege to pass

---

[2]I Peter 1:19-20.
[3]Moses 6:6-12.
[4]Moses 1:39.

through the mortal existence, with the great gift of agency in their possession. Through this gift they choose good or choose evil, and thus receive a reward of merit in the eternities to come. Because of Adam's transgression we are here in mortal life. It is written:

> And now, behold, if Adam had not transgressed he would not have fallen, but he would have remained in the Garden of Eden. And all things which were created must have remained in the same state in which they were after they were created; and they must have remained forever, and had no end.
>
> And they would have had no children; wherefore they would have remained in a state of innocence having no joy, for they knew no misery; doing no good, for they knew no sin.
>
> But behold, all things have been done in the wisdom of him who knoweth all things.
>
> Adam fell that men might be; and men are, that they might have joy.[5]

Blessing in Disguise

We learn from the scriptures, then, that the fall of man came as a blessing in disguise and was the means of furthering the purposes of the Lord in the progress of man, rather than a means of hindering them. Adam's transgression did, however, place him and all things upon the earth, under the curse of death, the separation of the spirit and the body. Without the means of escape from this condition all mankind would have been lost forever and the purposes of the Lord would have been destroyed.

To obviate this threatened disaster our Savior was chosen and fore-ordained to mend the broken law caused by Adam's fall. In other words, Christ came to restore mankind and all creatures to life through the resurrection of the dead. Paul made it very plain that ". . . since by man came death, by him came also the resurrection of the dead. For as in Adam all die, even as in Christ shall all be

---

[5] 2 Nephi 2:22-25.

made alive."[6] With the true understanding of this mortal
existence and the need of death in order that through the
atonement of our Lord there will come a re-uniting of spirit
and body, never again to be divided, the sting of death is
removed. Jacob, the brother of Nephi, made this clear in
the following words:

> For as death hath passed upon all men, to fulfil the merciful
> plan of the Great Creator, there must needs be a power of resur-
> rection, and the resurrection must needs come unto man by reason
> of the fall; and the fall came by reason of transgression; and be-
> cause man became fallen they were cut off from the presence of
> the Lord.

Flesh Would Rot

> Wherefore, it must needs be an infinite atonement—save it
> should be an infinite atonement this corruption could not put on
> incorruption.   Wherefore, the first judgment which came upon man
> must needs have remained to an endless duration.   And if so, this
> flesh must have laid down to rot and to crumble to its mother earth,
> to rise no more.
>
> O the wisdom of God, his mercy and grace!   For behold, if the
> flesh should rise no more our spirits must become subject to that
> angel who fell from before the presence of the Eternal God, and be-
> came the devil, to rise no more.
>
> And our spirits must have become like unto him, and we be-
> come devils, angels to a devil, to be shut out from the presence of
> our God, and to remain with the father of lies, in misery, like unto
> himself; yea, to that being who beguiled our first parents, who
> transformeth himself nigh unto an angel of light, and stirreth up the
> children of men unto secret combinations of murder and all manner
> of secret works of darkness.
>
> O how great the goodness of our God, who prepareth a way
> for our escape from the grasp of this awful monster; yea, that mon-
> ster, death and hell, which I call the death of the body, and also
> the death of the spirit.
>
> And because of the way of deliverance of our God, the Holy
> One of Israel, this death, of which I have spoken, which is the
> temporal, shall deliver up its dead; which death is the grave.

---

[6]I Corinthians 15:22.

Deliver Up Dead

And this death of which I have spoken, which is the spiritual, shall deliver up its dead; which spiritual death is hell; wherefore, death and hell must deliver up their dead, and hell must deliver up its captive spirits, and the grave must deliver up its captive bodies, and the bodies and the spirits of men will be restored one to the other; and it is by the power of the resurrection of the Holy One of Israel.[7]

It is refreshing to learn, as we do in the teachings of Jacob, that death has been decreed upon all men "to fulfil the merciful plan of the great Creator." This is a better thought than to look upon death as the overthrowing of the plan of the great Creator, making it necessary for him to change his plan because he failed to foresee the disaster of the fall. Moreover, we are informed that through the atonement of Jesus Christ, is made possible for every creature the restoration of spirit and body, which were disturbed by the fall. Again we read:

And he cometh into the world that he may save all men if they will hearken unto his voice; for behold, he suffereth the pains of all men, yea, the pains of every living creature, both men, women, and children, who belongeth to the family of Adam.

And he suffereth this that the resurrection might pass upon all men, that all might stand before him at the great and judgment day.[8]

Resurrection Universal

From these and other scriptures we learn these two great and important truths, that there shall be a universal resurrection of every creature that has ever lived upon the earth, and that mankind will receive the remission of their sins only through the atoning blood of Jesus Christ and faithful obedience to his laws. The resurrection of the dead

---

[7] 2 Nephi 9:6-12.
[8] 2 Nephi 9:21-22.

is a gift of God that is given to every creature through the atonement of Jesus Christ, just as death is a condition which came to every creature through Adam's transgression. We are taught that every thing that has life has received it as a gift from God.

Every creature had a spiritual existence. The spirits of men, beasts, and all animal life, existed before the foundation of the earth was laid, and are living entities.[9] As death, through the fall, has passed upon all, so the resurrection through the mission of Jesus Christ, comes to all. Alma said to his son Corianton:

> I say unto thee, my son, that the plan of resurrection is requisite with the justice of God; for it is requisite that all things should be restored to their proper order. Behold, it is requisite and just, according to the power and resurrection of Christ, that the soul (spirit) of man should be restored to its body, and that every part of the body should be restored to itself.
>
> And it is requisite with the justice of God that men should be judged according to their works; and if their works were good in this life, and the desires of their hearts were good, that they should also, at the last day, be restored unto that which is good.
>
> And if their works are evil they shall be restored unto them for evil. Therefore, all things shall be restored to their proper order, every thing to its natural frame—mortality raised to immortality, corruption to incorruption—raised to endless happiness to inherit the kingdom of God, or to endless misery to inherit the kingdom of the devil, the one on one hand, the other on the other—

One to Happiness

> The one raised to happiness according to his desires of happiness, or good according to his desires of good; and the other to evil according to his desires of evil; for as he has desired to do evil all the day long even so shall he have his reward of evil when the night cometh.
>
> And so it is on the other hand. If he hath repented of his sins, and desired righteousness until the end of his days, even so he shall be rewarded unto righteousness. . . .

---

[9]D&C 29:22-25; Moses 3:4-9.

Now, the decrees of God are unalterable; therefore, the way is prepared that whosoever will may walk therein and be saved.[10]

While *unconditional* salvation will be given to every creature, which is the redemption from the grave, *conditional* salvation will come only to those sons and daughters of Adam who fully repent of their sins and accept the gospel of Jesus Christ. It is written:

Must Be Baptized

And he commandeth all men that they must repent, and be baptized in his name, having perfect faith in the Holy One of Israel, or they cannot be saved in the kingdom of God.

And if they will not repent and believe in his name, and be baptized in his name, and endure to the end, they must be damned; for the Lord God, the Holy One of Israel, has spoken it.[11]

Wherefore redemption cometh in and through the Holy Messiah; for he is full of grace and truth.

Behold he offereth himself a sacrifice for sin, to answer the ends of the law, unto all those who have a broken heart and contrite spirit; and unto none else can the ends of the law be answered.[12]

But behold, and fear, and tremble before God, for ye ought to tremble; for the Lord redeemeth none such that rebel against him and die in their sins; yea, even all those that have perished in their sins ever since the world began, that have wilfully rebelled against God, that have known the commandments of God, and would not keep them; these are they that have no part in the first resurrection.

Ought to Tremble

Therefore ought ye not to tremble? For salvation cometh to none such; for the Lord hath redeemed none such, yea, neither can the Lord redeem such; for he cannot deny himself; for he cannot deny justice when it has its claim.[13]

For behold, I, God, have suffered these things for all, that they might not suffer if they would repent;

But if they would not repent they must suffer even as I.

---

[10]Alma 41:2-6, 8.
[11]2 Nephi 9:22-23.
[12]2 Nephi 2:7.
[13]Mosiah 15:26-27.

Which suffering caused myself, even God, the greatest of all, to tremble because of pain, and to bleed at every pore, and to suffer both body and spirit—and would that I might not drink the bitter cup, and shrink—

Nevertheless, glory be to the Father, and I partook and finished my preparations unto the children of men.[14]

In his great mercy, love and justice, we see our Father in heaven has provided that all his children who have gained mortality shall live again. The soul cannot be destroyed. The spirits of all men are eternal. They lived before this mortal life came, and through the atonement of Jesus Christ, they shall live after this mortal life is ended. Our Redeemer told Martha,

I am the resurrection and the life; he that believeth in me, though he were dead, yet shall he live:

And whosoever liveth and believeth in me shall never die. Believest thou this?[15]

Dead Shall Hear

The Savior's teachings and mission went still further than this. On one other occasion he said to the Jews:

Verily, verily, I say unto you, the hour is coming, and now is, when the dead shall hear the voice of the Son of God: and they that hear shall live. . . .

Marvel not at this: for the hour is coming, in the which all that are in their graves shall hear his voice,

And shall come forth; they that have done good, unto the resurrection of life; and they that have done evil unto the resurrection of damnation.[16]

The soul (spirit) shall be restored to the body, and the body to the soul (spirit); yea, every limb and joint shall be restored to its body; yea, even a hair of the head shall not be lost; but all things shall be restored to their proper and perfect frame. . . . And then shall the righteous shine forth in the kingdom of God.

---

[14]D&C 19:16-19.
[15]John 11:25-26.
[16]John 5:25, 28-29.

But behold, an awful death cometh upon the wicked; for they die as to things pertaining to things of righteousness; for they are unclean, and no unclean thing can inherit the kingdom of God; but they are cast out, and consigned to partake of the fruits of their labors or their works, which have been evil; and they drink the dregs of a bitter cup.[17]

Earn Redemption

It has been taught by some that the resurrection would not be universal among those who have received mortal bodies; that some known as sons of perdition would be denied the privilege of the resurrection. It is very strange that such a doctrine could be entertained in the face of the many instructions and revelations coming from the Lord and his holy prophets. They universally testify, that ALL shall come forth from the dead. Justice demands this because men are not responsible for death and hence are entitled to redemption from its grasp. Alma has clearly stated this:

. . . we must come forth and stand before him (the Lord) in his glory, and in his power, and in his might, majesty, and dominion, and acknowledge to our everlasting shame that all his judgments are just; that he is just in all his works, and that he is merciful unto the children of men, and that he has all power to save every man that believeth on his name and bringeth forth fruit meet for repentance.

And now behold, I say unto you then cometh a death, even a second death which is a spiritual death; then is a time that whosoever dieth in his sins, as to a temporal death, shall also die a spiritual death; yea, he shall die as to things pertaining unto righteousness.

Then is the time when their torments shall be as a lake of fire and brimstone, whose flame ascendeth up forever and ever; and then is the time that they shall be chained down to an everlasting destruction, according to the power and captivity of Satan, he having subjected them according to his will.

Doctrine Confirmed

Then, I say unto you, they shall be as though there had been

----

[17]Alma 40:23-26. Compare Alma 11:40-45.

no redemption made; for they cannot be redeemed according to God's justice; and they cannot die, seeing there is no more corruption.[18]

From this we learn that those who are to be cast out into outer darkness with the devil and his angels, will remain in their resurrected bodies, which can die no more, "seeing there is no more corruption," as though there had been no redemption made for them: that is redemption from their fallen, or banished, state.

This doctrine is confirmed by the leaders of the Church. I quote a few of these teachings:

What will every body be resurrected? Yes, every living being; but every man in his own order, Christ the first fruits; afterwards they that are Christ's at his coming. Then cometh the end. That is, the Saints shall live and reign with Christ a thousand years: One of the apostles says, "But the rest of the dead live not again until the thousand years are expired." But all must come forth from their graves, some time or other, in the self-same tabernacles that they possessed while living on the earth. It will be just as Ezekiel has described it.[19]

With regard to redemption, Paul said all the children of Adam are redeemed from the fall by the atoning blood of Jesus.[20]

All Made Alive

Then all the bodies that lie in the grave are called forth; not all at the first resurrection, nor in the morning of the first resurrection, but some perhaps in the last resurrection, and every soul will be required to go before the bar of God and be judged according to the deeds done in the body. If his works have been good, then he receives the reward of well doing. Nevertheless, he is an immortal being, because he possesses his resurrected body. Every creature that is born in the image of God will be resurrected from the dead, just as sure as he dies, you can write that down if you please, and never forget it, or ever allow yourself to have any un-

---

[18]Alma 12:15-18.
[19]President John Taylor, *Journal of Discourses,* 18:333. Ezekiel 37:1-14.
[20]President Wilford Woodruff.

belief on that account. "As in Adam all die, even so in Christ shall all be made alive."[21]

Those who commit the unpardonable sin are doomed to Gnolom, to dwell in hell, worlds without end. As they concocted scenes of bloodshed in this world, so they shall rise to the resurrection which is as the lake of fire and brimstone. Some shall rise to the everlasting burnings of God; for God dwells in everlasting burnings; and some shall rise to the damnation of their own filthiness, which is as exquisite a torment as the lake of fire and brimstone.[22]

The second, or spiritual, death is not as some suppose, the annihilation of spirit and body, for neither spirit or body can be annihilated. After they are united in the resurrection they become inseparable and eternal. The spiritual death is banishment of the individual who partakes of it from the presence of the Lord into "outer darkness" with the devil and his angels. How terrible this punishment is, only those know who receive it, but we are informed that it is most severe.

Banish Only a Few

There is some happiness in knowing that only a few out of the many are to receive this punishment, and then because they have sinned against the light of truth and crucified Christ again in their acts and desires. The Lord loves all of his children. He has said that "the worth of souls is great in the sight of God." He weeps over their transgressions and wickedness and has said: "How often would I have gathered thy children together even as a hen gathereth her chickens under her wings, but ye would not!"[23]

Of necessity there are eternal laws by which mankind are governed. These laws cannot be changed or abrogated; but through the mercy and justice of the Lord sinful men

---

[21]President Joseph F. Smith, *The Improvement Era*, Vol. 19, p. 386.
[22]*Teachings of the Prophet Joseph Smith*, p. 361.
[23]Matthew 23:37.

may repent, and through the atoning blood of Jesus Christ obtain a remission of their sins. For all such he, our Redeemer, paid the price on condition of true repentance and faithfulness to gospel laws, but for no others is the remission of sins granted through the blood of Jesus Christ. It is only just that men should receive according to their works the rewards decreed in the heavens.

The Lord has provided different kingdoms, or glories, to fit the capacity and merits of every soul. In the great day of judgment, when these rewards and punishments are meted out, every knee shall bend and give reverence to God the father and his Son Jesus Christ, and every soul will acknowledge and "confess before God that his judgments are just," even though many will be deprived of the exaltations and the joy of the eternal presence of the Father and the Son.—(Church Section, *The Deseret News*, Feb. 15, 1941.)

A Personal Testimony

Brethren:

I have a perfect knowledge of the divine mission of the Prophet Joseph Smith. There is no doubt in my mind that the Lord raised him up and gave him revelation, commandment, opened the heavens to him, and called upon him to stand at the head of this glorious dispensation. I am perfectly satisfied in my mind that in his youth, when he went out to pray, he beheld the actual presence, stood in the actual presence of God the Father and his Son, Jesus Christ; in my mind there is no doubt; I know this to be true. I know that he received later the visitations from Moroni, the Aaronic Priesthood under the hands of John the Baptist, the Melchizedek Priesthood under the hands of Peter, James, and John, and that The Church of Jesus Christ of Latter-day Saints was organized on the sixth day of April, 1830, by divine command.

These things I know. The Lord has revealed them to me, and this knowledge I have had since the day I was baptized. I know that the power of the Almighty is guiding this people, that we are under covenant to keep his commandments, to walk in light and truth. It is my firm conviction that every member of this Church should be able to bear witness and declare by words of soberness that these things are true, that the Book of Mormon is true, that the destiny of this latter-day work is true, and, according to the revelations, must and will be fulfilled.—(Seminar, Regional Representatives of the Twelve, April 3, 1969.)

Index

Declaration of Independence, reference to, 157
Decree, 400
Deissmann, Adolph, 365
Deity, Elohim is plural form of, 366
Deliverer, 348
Despotism, 165
Destruction, wickedness brings, 27
Deuteronomistic, 366
Development Hypothesis, 365
Devil, 424
Devil's angels, 442
Diligence, 357
Discernment, lack of, 95
Discourses of Brigham Young, quoted on slothful servants, 69; on honesty, 138
Disease, control of, 164
Dispensation of fulness of times, 253
Disraeli, 342
Divine authority, Adam held, 9; priesthood is, 233
Divorce, 163; violations result in, 289
Doctrine and Covenants, reference to, 13; quotes from, on binding of Satan 16; on Adam's authority, 17-18; on laws and government, 29; on laws and kingdoms, 35, 37; on man's dominion, 39; on obeying God's commandments, 39; on restoration of all things, 41; on light of Christ, 42-43; on sanctification through grace, 54; on walking uprightly, 57; on being deceived, 57; reference to Section 79, on servants of the Most High, 91; on days of probation, 100; on Christ's suffering, 120, 152; on love for God, 131; on sanctification through law, 145; on teaching one another, 148; on forgetting God, 163; originally Lectures on Faith in, 194; on schools for prophets, 197-198; on teaching one another, 199; on falling from grace, 212; on two divisions of priesthood, 240; on lineage of priesthood, 252; on rebellion of Israel, 252; on conditions of the law, 255; on new heaven and new earth, 261; on four beasts, 261; on creation of world, 276; on priests and kings, 299; on importance for work in temples, 300; on Christ's appearance to Jews, 349; on importance of Section 4, 354; on testifying to world, 357; on covenant of baptism, 359; on seeking early, 359; a priceless book, 379; on secret acts, 410; on redemption of little

children, 413; on great day of Lord's coming, 428; on watch and pray, 429
Doctrine of the kingdom, 410
Duty, to teach mission of Jesus Christ, 118; of man, 226; priesthood holders, 229
Duty, Mary, 175

—E—

Earth, is the Lord's, 22; Christ to reign on, 91; redemption of, 102; before foundation of, 169; created by Son, 270; condition of, 271; destiny of, 274; cursing of, 280; transgression caused defilement of, 317-318
Eber, 220
Ecclesiastes, quote from, on keeping commandments, 68
Eden, Adam driven from, 13
Egypt, patriarchal government of, 24; reference to, 25; gods of, 248
Egyptian bondage, 337
Elder, authority of, 255
Elders, teach temperance to, 356
Elections, reference to, 35
Elias, appearance to, 185
Elijah, appearance of, 186; sons of prophets taught by, 195; held keys of sealing power, 226
Elisha, sons of prophets taught by, 195
Elohim, 366
Elohistic, 366
Enoch, Adam's baptism recorded by, 10; keys held by, 205; record of, 281
Enos, 205
Ephesian Saints, reference to, 68
Ephraim, 220
Epistles, reference to, 74
Era of the Protestant Revolution, quote from, on power of Rome, 323
Erasmus, New Testament, translation of, 328
Erroneous doctrines, 11
Essentials in Church History, quote from, on prophecy concerning Joseph Smith, 177
Eternal deaths, 63
Eternal Father, forgetting of, 21; power to become like, 69; gift of, 127; knows end from beginning, 169; gratitude for, 262; immortal, exalted man, 270
Eternal increase, 63
Eternal life, Christ's mission for, 126-127; unclean do not inherit, 260; mortal existence is part of, 425
Eternal lives, 63

Government, laws of, should be recognized, 23
Grand council in heaven, 169-170
Greece, reference to, 25
Grenfell, B. P., 365
"Guy in the Mirror," poem, 265

—H—

Hamilton, Alexander, 369
Hand of the Lord, nations controlled by, 28
Happiness, righteous resurrected to, 438
Harris, Martin, as witness, 385
Harris, Sydney J., quote from, 82-83
Hate, existence in world of, 136
Heathen, bought with a price, 77
Heavenly Jerusalem, 408
Hebrew, teaching of, 192
Hebrew University, 370
Hebrews, reference to, 68
Henry VIII, reference to, 329
Hermes, quote from, 90
Herod, temple repaired by, 300
Hertzel, Theodore, 343
Hess, Moses, 343
High priest, temple work required of, 228; authority of, 255
Higher Criticism, 370
Hill Cumorah, records hidden in, 400
Hilsfverein der Deutschen Juden, claims of, 346
Historian's office, records preserved in, 12
History, priesthood in relation to, 203-216
Holy City, 87
Holy Ghost, bestowal of, 54-55; non-members do not receive, 76; inspiration and guidance of, 108; to teach us, 117; gift of, 206; testimony of, 213; utterances by, 316; influence of, on Bible writers, 363; guidance through, 387; baptism of, 409
Holy Land, dedication of, 335-349
Holy priesthood, sacrifice offered through authority of, 13; early Church endowed with, 317
Holy Scriptures, divine truths in, 158; attacks on, 364-365
Holy Spirit, be worthy of, 95
Home, reverence begins in, 116
Home teaching, reference to, 97
Honesty, 135-139
Hoover Dam, reference to, 344
Hosannah Shout, 297
House of Israel, righteous branch of, 397

Human body, Church compared to, 317
Human family, 170
Humility, 212, 357
Hunt, Arthur S., 365
Hunter, Bishop Edward, 296
Hyde, Orson, communication written by order of, 193; cornerstone dedication by, 296; mission of, 335

—I—

Ignorance, 327
Immortality, 152
India, reference to, 330
Indian people, 397-403
Indians, seed of Abraham, 401
Indulgences, 325
Infinite atonement, 82, 127
Ingratitude, 108; 125-131
Inspired Version, quote from, on priesthood, 250
Inquisition, 329
International Association of the Alliance Israelites, 343
Inventions, 164
Isaac, maintained patriarchal order, 25
Isaiah, quote from, on hypocrites, 135; on prayer, 162; prophecy of, concerning words of a book, 172-173
Israel, rebellion against God's authority by, 25; commandments forgotten by, 158; Moses chosen to lead, 170; testimony of elders of, 235; to again flourish, 348
Israelites, warning to, 337
Irenius, reference to, 409
Ivins, President Anthony W., quote from, 401

—J—

Jacob, maintained patriarchal order, 25; seed of, 336
Jaffa, reference to, 343
James, quote from, on enduring temptation, 139; reference to, 184; apostleship of, 208
Japan, reference to people of, 356
Jared, 17, 285
Jared, brother of, see brother of Jared
Jealousy, 160
Jeans, Sir James, 277
Jehovah, 366; see also Christ, Jesus Christ, Lord, Redeemer, Son of God
Jehovistic, 366
Jeremiah, reference to foreordination of, 169-170
Jericho, fall of, 371

Jerusalem, destruction of, 340; rehabilitation of, 344; population of, 347

Jesus Christ, joint heirs with, 5; to worship in name of, 10; erroneous ideas concerning gospel of, 11; see also Christ, Jehovah, Lord, Redeemer, Son of God

Jew, meaning of term, 192

Jewish National Home, 347

Jews, captivity of, 28; bought with a price, 77; mission to, 335; corruption of, 339; return of, 341; record of, 363-364; accusations of, 392

Job, quote from, on wickedness and deceit, 137

John, quoted, on war in heaven, 16; on Christ's power, 81; on creations by the Word, 42; on everlasting life, 126; on resurrection of dead, 127; reference to, 184; translation granted to, 419

John the Baptist, 270

Jordan River, 345

Joseph of Egypt, reference to, 74; prophecy of, 171; descendants of, 401

Joseph Smith, see Smith, Joseph

Joshua, leadership of, 337

Journal of Discourses, quote from, on Joseph Smith's foreordination, 170; on universal resurrection, 442

Joy, 103

Judah, captivity of, 398

Judas, fall of, 208

Jude, references to Enoch by, 11; calling of, 208

Judea, 316

Judgments, to pour forth, 423

Justice, demands of, 151; Father's, 440

Juvenile Instructor, quote from, on honesty, 139; reference to, 402

—K—

Keys, President holds all, 242

Keys of priesthood, authorities have, 254

Kimball, Heber C., 17, 212, 296

Kimball, J. Golden, reference to, 278

King, Israel's demand for, 25

King Charles V, reference to, 324

King of kings, coming of, 177

Kingdom, doctrine of, 310, 410

Kingdom of God, perfect order in, 235

Kingdoms, preparation of, 145; different, for all souls, 444

Kirtland, reference to, 177; organization of Twelve in, 219

Kneighton, Henry, reference to, 328

Knowledge, reception of, 55; gaining of, 355

Kolob, authority on, 33; governing star, 233

—L—

Labor, problems of, 136

Lalischer, Hirch, 343

Lamanites, 399; seed of Abraham, 401

Lamb, reference to Christ, 433

Lamech, 205

Landsdowne, Lord, 343

Langdon, Dr., 365

Language, temperance in, 356

Language of the Pentateuch in its Relation to Egyptian, The, 369

Last days, we are living in, 143

Later Documentary Hypothesis, 365

Latin, language of Rome, 324

Latter-day Saints, attitude towards government of, 29; see also Church

Law, certain bounds to every, 37; given to all things, 204; written on tables of stone, 248; all things governed by, 233

Law of marriage, 290

Law of Moses, written on tables, 249; restrictions of, 305; word of God, 367

Law, William, 221

Laws, necessity of, 407

Lazarus, 61

Leadership Week, 199

Learning, revival of, 327, 329

Lectures on Faith, 194

Lehi, reference to, 74; counsel of, to Jacob, 426

Levi, tribe of, 196

Levites, lesser priesthood through, 254

Levitical Priesthood, 239

Leviticus, quote from, on unrighteous judgment, 137

Liberty, demand for, 26

Life of Joseph F. Smith, quote from, 176

Light, reception of, 55

Light of Christ, 43

Lima, experience in, 402

Little Cottonwood Canyon, 297

Lodge, Sir Oliver, quote from, 35

Lord, all things pronounced good by, 21; on eternal deaths, 63; never too early to serve, 146; word of, will never fail, 348; see also Christ, Jehovah, Jesus Christ, Lord, Redeemer, Son of God

Lord's scourge, 428

Nauvoo Temple, reference to, 300

Naville, Dr. Edouard, 365; statement of, 374

Nebuchadnezzar, appointed to punish Judah, 28; destruction of temple by, 300; vision of, 309-311; captivity by, 339

Nephi, quote from, on procrastination, 143

Nephite apostles, 399

Nephite prophets, writings of, 363-364

Nephites, rebellious history of, 22; reference to righteous, 111; record revealed to, 381; reference to, 399; principle of chastity emphasized to, 423

Netherlanders, execution of, 329

Netherlands, problems in, 325-326

New Archeological Discoveries and Their Bearing upon the New Testament, The, quote from, 374

New Bible Evidence, reference to quote from, 371-372

New Testament, had records in times of, 11; reference to writers of, 100; attacks on, 373-374

New York, reference to, 371

Nicodemus, reference to, 126

Noah, patriarchal reign of, 24; authority of, 25; Elias was, 186; keys held by, 205; to save seeds of every kind, 408

—O—

Obedience, necessity of, 70; through spirit of love, 120

Old Testament, elimination of plain doctrines in, 11; reference to, 252; language of, 369

Old World, 427

Olive Leaf, mention of, 192

Only Begotten, 213

Opposition, essential to progress, 47-49

Ordinance of sacrifice, 13

Ordinance work, commencement of, 298

Ordinances, necessity of, 407

Organic evolution, theory of, 364

Origin and Growth of Religion, The, 373

Orson Pratt, see Pratt, Orson

Ox teams, day of, 297

—P—

Page, John E., failure of, 335

Pain, become subject to, 4

Palestine, days of rebellion in, 22; changes in, 341; growth of, 342: population of, 347

Palestine Electric Corporation, 346

Palestine Royal Commission, 347-348

Parables, reference to, 99

Parliament, Bible reading prohibited by, 329

Patriarchal, first government was, 23

Patriarchal Priesthood, 219-222

Patriarchs, authority of, 221-222

Patriarchs to the Church, 222

Patten, David W., 212

Paul, speaks of Melchizedek, 11; words of, to Ephesian Saints, 68; words of, to Corinthian Saints, 74; on temple of God, 76; quoted on God's building, 88; on sacrament, 107-108; on perilous times, 159; on apostles and prophets, 208; on sinning against Holy Ghost, 214; on errors of Israel, 250

Peace, taken from earth, 136

Pearl of Great Price, 12; books published in, 13; on creation of worlds, 42; a priceless book, 379

Peleg, 220

Pentateuch, 336

People, patience with, 356

Perfect plan, Lord gave us, 97

Persia, reference to, 25

Personages, separateness of, 183

Personal purity, demand for, 87-92

Peru, Lamanite civilizations in, 400

Peter, quoted, on submission to authority, 29; reference to, 184; on royal priesthood, 247; on day of the Lord, 262; prophecy of, concerning false prophets, 320

Pharaoh, a righteous man, 24

Pharisees, Christ's answer to, 288; reference to, 290

Phelps, William W., 12; letter to, 192

Picnics, reference to, 102

Plagues, 428

Plan of salvation, nothing complicated in, 112

Polychrome Bible, 368

Polytheistic, 372

Pope, temporal power of, 323

Power, priesthood from God is, 234

Power of darkness, 161

Pratt, Orson, quoted, on kingdom and government of God, 22-23; visit of, to David Whitmer, 386

Pratt, Parley P., oration delivered by, 296

Pratt, Rey L., reference to, 401